Cambridge Elements

Elements in Quantitative Finance
edited by
Riccardo Rebonato
EDHEC Business School

DEEP LEARNING IN QUANTITATIVE TRADING

Zihao Zhang
University of Oxford

Stefan Zohren
University of Oxford

Shaftesbury Road, Cambridge CB2 8EA, United Kingdom

One Liberty Plaza, 20th Floor, New York, NY 10006, USA

477 Williamstown Road, Port Melbourne, VIC 3207, Australia

314–321, 3rd Floor, Plot 3, Splendor Forum, Jasola District Centre, New Delhi – 110025, India

103 Penang Road, #05–06/07, Visioncrest Commercial, Singapore 238467

Cambridge University Press is part of Cambridge University Press & Assessment, a department of the University of Cambridge.

We share the University's mission to contribute to society through the pursuit of education, learning and research at the highest international levels of excellence.

www.cambridge.org
Information on this title: www.cambridge.org/9781009707121
DOI: 10.1017/9781009707091

© Zihao Zhang and Stefan Zohren 2025

This publication is in copyright. Subject to statutory exception and to the provisions of relevant collective licensing agreements, no reproduction of any part may take place without the written permission of Cambridge University Press & Assessment.

When citing this work, please include a reference to the DOI 10.1017/9781009707091

First published 2025

A catalogue record for this publication is available from the British Library

ISBN 978-1-009-70712-1 Hardback
ISBN 978-1-009-70711-4 Paperback
ISSN 2631-8571 (online)
ISSN 2631-8563 (print)

Additional resources for this publication at www.cambridge.org/deeplearningquant

Cambridge University Press & Assessment has no responsibility for the persistence or accuracy of URLs for external or third-party internet websites referred to in this publication and does not guarantee that any content on such websites is, or will remain, accurate or appropriate.

For EU product safety concerns, contact us at Calle de José Abascal, 56, 1°, 28003 Madrid, Spain, or email eugpsr@cambridge.org

Deep Learning in Quantitative Trading

Elements in Quantitative Finance

DOI: 10.1017/9781009707091
First published online: September 2025

Zihao Zhang
University of Oxford

Stefan Zohren
University of Oxford

Author for correspondence: Zihao Zhang, zhangzihao@hotmail.co.uk

Abstract: This Element provides a comprehensive guide to deep learning in quantitative trading, merging foundational theory with hands-on applications. It is organized into two parts. The first part introduces the fundamentals of financial time-series and supervised learning, exploring various network architectures, from feedforward to state-of-the-art. To ensure robustness and mitigate overfitting on complex real-world data, a complete workflow is presented, from initial data analysis to cross-validation techniques tailored to financial data. Building on this, the second part applies deep learning methods to a range of financial tasks. The authors demonstrate how deep learning models can enhance both time-series and cross-sectional momentum trading strategies, generate predictive signals, and be formulated as an end-to-end framework for portfolio optimization. Applications include a mixture of data from daily data to high-frequency microstructure data for a variety of asset classes. Throughout, they include illustrative code examples and provide a dedicated GitHub repository with detailed implementations.

Keywords: deep learning, machine learning, reinforcement learning, time-series, neural networks, quantitative trading, portfolio optimization, market microstructure, momentum trading, volatility scalings

JEL classifications: A12, B34, C56, D78, E90

© Zihao Zhang and Stefan Zohren 2025

ISBNs: 9781009707121 (HB), 9781009707114 (PB), 9781009707091 (OC)
ISSNs: 2631-8571 (online), 2631-8563 (print)

Contents

Preface 1

1 Introduction 2

PART I: FOUNDATIONS 6

2 Fundamentals of Financial Time-Series 6

3 Supervised Learning and Canonical Networks 21

4 The Model Training Workflow 65

PART II: APPLICATIONS 75

5 Enhancing Classical Quantitative Trading Strategies with Deep Learning 75

6 Deep Learning for Risk Management and Portfolio Optimization 101

7 Applications to Market Microstructure and High-Frequency Data 123

8 Conclusions 143

Acronyms 147

Appendix A: Different Asset Classes 149

Appendix B: Access to Market Data 159

Appendix C: Investment Performance Metrics 162

Appendix D: Code Scripts 164

References 167

Additional resources for this publication at www.cambridge.org/deeplearningquant

Preface

Over the past decade, deep learning has attracted considerable interest, primarily due to its exceptional performance across a range of application domains, with image recognition and natural language processing standing out as two of the most notable examples. Deep learning algorithms possess the ability to learn complex, nonlinear relationships from large volumes of data. Unlike traditional mathematical or statistical models, which often struggle in such environments, deep learning models excel at uncovering complex patterns and making predictions. The capacity to manage and learn from large volumes of data has made deep learning models a transformative technology across industries like healthcare, finance, entertainment, and many others.

Given its successful applications in other fields, deep learning has also become a natural candidate for applications to quantitative trading, as trading firms and investment managers continuously seek innovative ways to uncover "alpha," or excess returns. With the rise of electronic trading, exchanges now process billions of messages daily, generating vast amounts of data well suited for deep learning algorithms. Additionally, investors also have access to a growing range of alternative data sources, such as mobile app downloads, social media trends, and search engine activity (e.g., Google Trends), which can be used to further improve decision-making. As a result, deep learning techniques are increasingly becoming powerful tools for quantitative researchers and traders, enabling more sophisticated strategies and potentially higher returns.

A significant body of research has explored the diverse financial applications of deep learning, including areas such as alpha generation, time-series forecasting and portfolio optimization. The goal of this Element is to weave these disparate threads together, placing a particular emphasis on how deep learning algorithms can be leveraged to develop quantitative trading strategies and systems. Whether an experienced quantitative trader aiming to enhance strategies, a data scientist exploring opportunities within the financial sector, or a student eager to delve into cutting-edge financial technology, the reader of this Element should come away with a comprehensive understanding of how deep learning is transforming the landscape of quantitative trading. By combining theoretical foundations with practical applications, we seek to equip readers with the insights and tools necessary to excel in this rapidly evolving domain. Our objective is to navigate the complexities of the field while inspiring innovation in the integration of deep learning within quantitative finance.

To promote reproducibility and enhance readers' understanding of the algorithms discussed in this Element, we have created a dedicated GitHub repository.[1] This repository contains many of the experiments presented in the book, and it includes everything from fundamental data processing pipelines to implementations of cutting-edge deep neural networks. By providing these resources, we aim to empower readers to apply the concepts and techniques in practical, real-world settings. This repository is designed to be user-friendly and accessible, and it includes step-by-step examples and demonstrations. All deep learning models are built using PyTorch, a widely used and flexible deep learning framework. Accordingly, readers can easily experiment with and extend these implementations. Whether readers are looking to replicate the included experiments, refine the models, or use the provided pipelines as foundations for their own projects, the repository offers a hands-on platform to bridge theory and practice. Our commitment to transparency and accessibility ensures that readers can not only learn but also actively engage with and contribute to the evolving field of quantitative finance powered by deep learning.

1 Introduction

Quantitative trading boasts a rich and fascinating history, with its origins dating back to the groundbreaking work of Louis Bachelier in 1900. In his seminal thesis, Bachelier introduced the concept of Brownian motion as a framework for modeling the stochastic behavior of financial price series. This pioneering work established the basis for the mathematical modeling of financial markets and set the stage for modern quantitative finance (Bachelier, 1900). Over the years, the field has undergone remarkable evolution, propelled by progress in mathematics, statistics, and computational advancements. From the introduction of fundamental theories like the Black-Scholes model in the 1970s to the emergence of algorithmic trading in the late twentieth century, quantitative trading has consistently been at the forefront of financial innovation. Key developments have been documented in works such as Cesa (2017), which offers a detailed exploration of quantitative finance's historical trajectory and major milestones.

As computational power and data availability have both increased, the field has expanded further, incorporating machine learning and deep learning techniques into its toolkit. Today, quantitative trading represents a dynamic intersection of finance, mathematics, and computer science, continuing to evolve as new methods and technologies emerge. Experts from diverse fields

---

[1] See DeepLearningQuant.com or https://github.com/zcakhaa/Deep-Learning-in-Quantitative-Trading.

have collaborated with a common goal: to optimize financial returns while minimizing the inherent risks of trading. This shared ambition has fueled the evolution of quantitative trading strategies, which harness the power of mathematical and computational models to analyze and interpret financial data.

Traditionally, statistical time-series models have served as the cornerstone of predictive signal generation in quantitative trading. These models, such as ARIMA and GARCH, have proven effective in capturing trends and volatility in financial time-series data. However, such models are often constrained by their linear nature and the stringent assumptions, such as stationarity and normality, that they impose upon the data. Given the inherently complex and nonlinear behavior of financial markets, these limitations can lead to suboptimal performance, particularly in dynamic and unpredictable market conditions. To address these challenges, practitioners have historically relied upon manually crafted features to enhance the predictive power of their models. By engineering features that capture specific market dynamics, such as momentum, mean reversion, and volatility clusters, researchers aim to approximate the underlying complexity of financial systems. However, this process is labor-intensive, requiring significant domain expertise and time. Moreover, manual feature engineering is susceptible to human bias, potentially introducing or overlooking critical patterns or relationships in the data.

The increasing demand for more robust and scalable solutions has underscored the need for advanced methodologies capable of identifying and leveraging nonlinear relationships within financial data. Deep learning, a specialized branch of machine learning, utilizes multi-layered neural networks to autonomously learn and uncover meaningful patterns within large and complex datasets. The core advantage of deep learning is its capacity to learn hierarchical representations of data. By progressively extracting features from raw inputs, deep learning models are capable of capturing complex relationships and subtle patterns that traditional statistical methods often fail to detect. These capabilities make them especially well suited for addressing the complexities of financial markets, which are characterized by high volatility, intricate interdependencies, and noisy data. Specifically, deep learning offers several distinct advantages: It can handle both structured and unstructured data, such as news articles and social media sentiment; it can adapt to changing market conditions and regimes; it can uncover complex patterns as more complex data increasingly requires more complex modeling techniques; it can be used for a range of strategy types, from high-frequency execution problems to long-term portfolios optimization.

This Element delves deeply into the transformative role of deep learning in modern quantitative trading, offering a thorough examination of how this advanced technology is transforming the landscape of financial markets. Through this exploration, we aim to showcase how deep learning models excel at automating complex feature extraction processes and uncovering patterns within vast volumes of financial data. Through their ability to do so, deep learning models drive more informed, precise, and effective trading strategies. Our objective is to guide readers, whether researchers, data scientists, or traders, through the practical applications and theoretical underpinnings of deep learning in quantitative trading. This Element seeks to demonstrate how the unmatched computational power and adaptability of deep learning can be leveraged to develop applications for real-world, high-stakes financial trading environments. Readers will obtain a meaningful understanding of how these models can be applied to automate decision-making, enhance predictive accuracy, and optimize trading performance in the ever-evolving financial markets.

The Element is split into two parts: **Foundations** and **Applications**. In the first part, we cover the fundamentals of financial time-series including statistics and hypothesis testing. Financial data, like any other type of data, has its own characteristics. Accordingly, a good understanding of a financial dataset's underlying statistics is the basis for any financial analysis. We then introduce the concept of supervised learning and deep learning models. These concepts range from basic fully connected layers to the attention mechanism and transformer architectures, which excel at capturing long-range dependencies in structured datasets. Despite the significant advancements in deep learning, deep networks frequently encounter challenges like overfitting, when models excel on training data but struggle to generalize to new, unseen data. To address this, we present a complete workflow for developing deep learning algorithms for quantitative trading. This process includes essential steps like data collection, exploratory data analysis (evaluating characteristics of the data, such as distribution and stationarity), and cross-validation techniques tailored specifically for financial data. These steps are critical for building models that are robust and reliable.

In the second part of this Element, we focus on applying deep learning algorithms to various financial problems. One of the most fundamental tasks in quantitative trading is generating predictive signals. We explore various deep learning architectures for this purpose, showcasing how these networks can be leveraged to predict market movements. Building on this foundation, we delve into more advanced frameworks where deep networks are adopted to enhance time-series momentum and cross-sectional momentum trading strategies. Further, we discuss portfolio optimization and present methods to optimize portfolio weights from market inputs that form an end-to-end framework. This bypasses the intermediate requirements of estimating returns and constructing a covariance matrix of returns, processes that are often difficult to implement in practice.

Alongside our exploration of deep learning techniques, this Element discusses the nature and intricacies of financial data itself. To provide a detailed perspective, we introduce the operational mechanisms of modern securities exchanges, illustrating how financial transactions occur and the ways in which high-frequency microstructure data, such as order book updates and trade executions, are generated. Additionally, we analyze the unique characteristics of several main asset classes, including equities, bonds, commodities, and cryptocurrencies, shedding light on the distinct challenges and opportunities they each present for deep learning applications. Throughout this Element, we include code scripts to highlight important concepts, and we provide a dedicated GitHub repository[2] to further demonstrate these ideas.

An Outline of the Element This Element contains two parts: **Foundations** and **Applications**. The Foundations part contains Sections 2, 3 and 4, in which we introduce the fundamentals of financial time-series and deep learning algorithms. The Applications contains Sections 5, 6, and 7, in which we discuss prediction, portfolio optimization, trade execution and real-world applications.

- **Section 2** discusses the statistics frequently used in the analysis of financial time-series, including returns, data distributions, hypothesis testing, statistical moments, serial covariance, correlation, and statistical time-series models such as AR and ARMA. This section also introduces the notions of "alpha" and "beta" and examines the phenomenon of volatility clustering.
- **Section 3** introduces supervised learning and its primary components, including loss functions and evaluation metrics. We then introduce neural networks, starting with the canonical fully connected layers, convolutional and recurrent layers. Finally, we explore some state-of-the-art networks, including WaveNet, encoder-decoders, and transformers.
- **Section 4** presents a complete training workflow from the very first step of data collection through the final model deployment. We discuss the problem of overfitting and introduce cross-validation for hyperparameter tuning. We also include a discussion of various popular model pipelines so that readers can choose the most appropriate platform for their respective applications.
- **Section 5** introduces classical quantitative strategies such as time-series momentum and cross-sectional momentum strategies, and shows how they

---

[2] See DeepLearningQuant.com or https://github.com/zcakhaa/Deep-Learning-in-Quantitative-Trading.

can be enhanced with deep learning methods. In particular, we explore networks that directly output trade positions and are end-to-end optimized for Sharpe ratio or other performance metrics.
- **Section 6** focuses on risk management and portfolio optimization. We demonstrate how deep learning models can help better forecast risk measures such as volatility. We also look into end-to-end deep learning frameworks for portfolio optimization, bypassing the need to estimate returns or construct a covariance matrix for classical mean-variance problems.
- **Section 7** introduces high-frequency microstructure data. We demonstrate how bespoke hybrid-networks can serve to forecast future price trends and exploit additional structure in limit order books. Additionally, we discuss various promising applications including the adoption of reinforcement learning for trade execution and generative modeling for financial data.
- **Section 8** brings together the insights and knowledge presented throughout this Element, summarizing the key takeaways from our exploration of deep learning and quantitative trading. Looking ahead, we discuss emerging trends and explore future possibilities where deep learning might bring innovative transformations to financial markets.

PART I: FOUNDATIONS

2 Fundamentals of Financial Time-Series

Financial time-series analysis is an indispensable tool in understanding the ever-changing nature of financial markets. It involves the study of certain data points collected or recorded at specific time intervals, such as daily stock prices. This analysis is crucial for identifying trends, modeling market behaviors, and making informed decisions in trading, risk management, and investment. This section explores the fundamental concepts of statistics used in such analyses, including returns, distributions, moments, hypothesis testing, serial covariance, various time-series models, and more. These concepts form the basis of financial time-series modeling and provide the foundation to move to more complex models later in the Element.

2.1 Returns

Returns are a key metric in the field of finance, playing an important role in evaluating investment performance over time. They reflect the profit or loss achieved relative to the initial value of an investment, demonstrating insights into the potential profitability and risks associated with different traded financial assets, including stocks, bonds, mutual funds, and other instruments.

By calculating and analyzing returns, investors, analysts, and portfolio managers can assess the effectiveness of their strategies, compare diverse investment options, and make data-driven decisions to enhance trading performance.

There are several different ways to calculate financial returns, with simple returns and logarithmic (log) returns being the most common. Simple returns calculate the percentage change in an asset's price between two consecutive periods. They are straightforward to calculate and understand, which makes them a widely used tool for routine financial analysis. In addition, simple returns are often used to calculate portfolio returns (which will be defined in later sections). However, simple returns have limitations, particularly when dealing with long-term investments or compounding returns.

Logarithmic returns, on the other hand, calculate the natural logarithm of the ratio of consecutive prices. This method provides a time-additive measure, meaning that the returns over multiple periods can be summed up to obtain the total return, which is particularly useful for continuous compounding contexts. Logarithmic returns are often more statistically desirable due to their properties, such as normality and symmetry, which make them more suitable for sophisticated financial models and risk assessments. The motivation for using those two forms becomes apparent when calculating the cumulative return of a security. For a single time step, we can define both returns as follows:

$$\text{Simple return: } r_{sim,t} = \frac{p_t - p_{t-1}}{p_{t-1}},$$
$$\text{Log return: } r_{log,t} = \log\left(\frac{p_t}{p_{t-1}}\right), \quad (1)$$

where p_t denotes the price of a security at time t. The aforementioned can easily be generalized for returns over multiple time steps from $t - L$ to t.

Understanding and analyzing financial returns is crucial for several reasons. First, returns directly impact an investor's wealth and financial planning, as they determine the growth of investments over time. Second, returns are used when assessing investment risks, and effective risk control is the key to ensuring long-term investment success. Third, analyzing historical returns helps investors identify trends and patterns, informing future investment decisions and strategy development. Finally, financial institutions and fund managers rely heavily upon return analysis to manage large portfolios and ensure they meet their performance benchmarks. By examining returns, they can allocate assets more effectively, diversify their portfolios, and carry out risk management strategies that can protect profits against adverse market movements.

In summary, financial returns are a cornerstone of investment analysis and decision-making. They provide a complete view of the performance and risk of financial assets, guiding investors and financial professionals in their pursuit of optimal investment strategies and wealth maximization. Understanding the different methods of calculating returns is important for anyone involved in the financial world. In many of the data-driven examples that we cover in this Element, a future return over a specific horizon serves as the target of a predictive supervised learning model. It reflects the direction and extent of the expected future price movement and plays a major role in portfolio optimization, which will be discussed more in later sections.

2.2 Distributions of Financial Returns

Loosely speaking, a distribution describes the way in which values of a random variable are spread or dispersed. Distributions are the foundation for the domains of probability and statistics, and distributions can be either discrete, where data points can take on values from a finite or a countable set, or continuous, where data points can take on any value within a given range. Understanding distributions is useful for making inferences about populations based on samples, assessing probabilities, and conducting various statistical tests.

Mathematically, we represent the distribution of a discrete variable by a probability mass function (PMF) and that of a continuous variable by a probability density function (PDF). The PMF simply indicates the probabilities of different finite or countable outcomes, and the PDF presents how the probability of a random variable taking values in a specific range is distributed. The key properties of PMFs or PDFs are that they are nonnegative and sum to one over the entire space of possible values. Taking a continuous variable X with the PDF $f(x)$ as an example, the probability that X lies within the interval $[a, b]$ is determined by the integral of $f(x)$ over that range:

$$P(a \leq X \leq b) = \int_a^b f(x)dx. \tag{2}$$

It is important to understand the concept of the distribution of financial returns as it gauges the quality and risk of investment performance. In practice, financial returns do not typically follow a normal distribution, which would suggest they tend not to be well behaved. Instead, they exhibit characteristics, such as heavy tails which indicate that extreme values (large gains or losses) are more frequent than would be predicted by a normal distribution.

There are several ways to understand a distribution. The most straightforward way is to use histograms to visually inspect the data distribution. For example, the left plot of Figure 1 depicts the histogram for the simple daily returns of Standard & Poor's 500 (S&P500) since its creation. The distribution

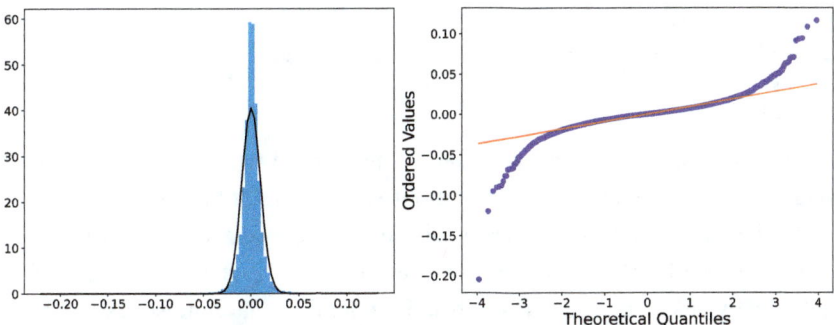

Figure 1 **Left:** histogram for the return distribution; **Right:** QQ-plot.

is bell-shaped and appears similar to a normal (Gaussian) distribution. However, upon inspection, this distribution exhibits fatter tails and a sharper peak compared to a normal distribution with the same mean and standard deviation (plotted in black).[3]

QQ-plot (quantile-to-quantile plot) is another popular tool to check if a data distribution is normal. A QQ-plot is made by plotting one set of quantiles against another set of quantiles. A quantile denotes an input value, in this case a return, such that a certain fraction (say 90%) of the data are less than or equal to this value (in which case we call it the 90% quantile). A straight line would be expected if two sets of quantiles are from the same distribution. The right of Figure 1 is the QQ-plot for the return distribution of the S&P 500 versus the assumed normal distribution. We can observe that the points align along a straight line in the central portion of the figure, but curve off at the two ends. In general, a QQ-plot like this indicates that extreme values are more likely to occur than the assumed normal distribution. Code to create a histogram and a QQ-plot in Python is shown next:

```
# ret is the return series of interest
import scipy.stats as stats
import matplotlib.pyplot as plt
import numpy as np

plt.figure(figsize=(12,4))
plt.subplot(121)
s = plt.hist(ret, bins=100, density=True)
xmin, xmax = plt.xlim()
x = np.linspace(xmin, xmax, 100)
p = stats.norm.pdf(x, np.mean(ret), np.std(ret))
plt.plot(x, p, "k", linewidth=2)

```

---

[3] We formally define mean and standard deviation in the next section.

```
14  plt.subplot(122)
15  a = stats.probplot(ret, dist="norm", plot=plt)
16  plt.xlabel("Theoretical Quantiles")
17  plt.ylabel("Ordered Values")
```

Empirical studies of financial markets have shown that the distribution of returns is often better fit by distributions such as the Student's t-distribution, which better accounts for the heavy tails, or the Generalized Error Distribution (GED). These distributions offer a more accurate depiction of the probability of extreme events, and consequently better model financial time-series. We need to be aware of such properties because a higher likelihood of extreme events means that financial models have a higher potential for significant losses.

Overall, a good understanding of return distributions helps with financial modeling, risk assessment, and strategic decision-making. By recognizing that returns are not normally distributed and accounting for the actual distributional characteristics, investors and analysts can develop more robust models that better capture the risks and potential rewards of their investments. This knowledge allows for more effective portfolio diversification, hedging strategies, and overall risk management practices, ultimately leading to more informed and potentially profitable investment decisions.

2.3 Statistical Moments

Statistical moments are sets of parameters used to describe a distribution. In general, we can define the k-th central moment of a random variable X as:

$$\mu_k = E[(X - \mu)^k], \quad \mu = E(X), \tag{3}$$

for $k \geq 2$ and $\mu_1 = \mu$. Typically, attention is given to the first four moments – mean (or expected value), variance, skewness, and kurtosis – as they capture a distribution's central tendency, spread, asymmetry, and peakedness, respectively. Statistical moments help us understand the behavior of a distribution and make predictions. For example, a normal distribution can be specified by giving a mean and standard deviation. However, these two moments alone might not be enough to fully describe a return distribution. As an example, the return distribution in Figure 1 exhibits heavier tails and a more pronounced peak than a normal distribution. In this case, we need to check higher moments of the distribution to better understand the data.

In statistics, skewness and kurtosis are the normalized third and fourth central moments. Skewness measures the asymmetry of data about its mean. There are two types of skewness: positive skew and negative skew. A symmetrical distribution, such as a normal distribution, has no skewness. However, a distribution that has larger values on the right tail is positively skewed. On the contrary, a negatively skewed distribution has larger values in the left tail that are further from the mean than those of the left tail.

In finance, skewness may stem from diverse market forces. Investor sentiment can lead to asymmetrical buying or selling pressures as market participants overreact to news or trends. Economic news can also introduce sudden, unidirectional shocks to asset prices as markets rapidly adjust to new information. Market microstructure might also contribute to skewness when imbalances in order flow, liquidity constraints, or trading mechanisms create price distortions. There are many other possible causes for deviations from a normal distribution in the returns.

The skewness of a return distribution can typically inform the reward profile of a security or strategy. A canonical example of a strategy that is negatively skewed is a reversion strategy. We can expect many small positive rewards when assets revert as expected, but we can also suffer large losses if reversion does not occur say due to an unexpected news event. Selling options and VIX futures are other examples of strategies with negatively skewed return distributions. Vice versa, a positively skewed return distribution typically corresponds to many small losses with a few large gains – a canonical example being momentum strategies. The most favorable type of skewness depends upon the risk preferences of investors.

Kurtosis is the fourth normalized statistical moment, describing the tail and peak of a distribution. In particular, kurtosis informs us whether a distribution includes more extreme values than a normal distribution. All normal distributions, regardless of mean and variance, have a kurtosis of 3. If a distribution is highly peaked and has fat tails, its kurtosis is greater than 3, and, vice versa, a flatter distribution has a kurtosis lesser than 3. Excess kurtosis can be attributed to market shocks, economic crises, and other rare but impactful events that significantly affect asset prices.

2.4 Statistical Hypothesis Testing

Hypothesis testing is another important concept in statistics, as it offers a systematic framework for making decisions and drawing conclusions about a population using sample data. It is widely adopted in several fields, including natural science, economics, psychology, and finance, where it is used to evaluate hypotheses and determine the validity of claims or theories. For example, we have already mentioned the fact that financial returns can have fat tails compared to a normal distribution. To objectively assess this, we resort to hypothesis testing which provides a formal framework for making inferences and offers a structured method for evaluating claims. Consequently, this allows researchers and analysts to draw conclusions with a quantifiable level of confidence. By using statistical techniques and predefined criteria, it also eliminates subjective biases and ensures that decisions are conditioned on empirical evidence rather than intuition or guesswork.

The fundamental concept of hypothesis testing involves using sample data to evaluate the evidence against a null hypothesis (H_0), which functions as the default or baseline assumption. The objective is to prove the alternative hypothesis (H_1), which constitutes the presence of a difference from the default assumption. The process of hypothesis testing involves several key steps. First, we need to define the null hypothesis and the alternative hypothesis. For instance, in a test to determine whether the distribution of returns is normal, the null hypothesis might state that the return distribution follows a normal distribution, while the alternative hypothesis might posit that the return distribution violates the assumption of normality.

We then need to select a significance level (α), typically 0.05, which delineates the probability of erroneously rejecting the null hypothesis when it is in fact true. The value of α reflects the strength of the evidence for rejection, and thus a small α imposes a requirement of strong evidence for the null hypothesis to be rejected. In addition, it is necessary to select an appropriate test statistic in accordance with the nature of the data and the hypothesis under examination. Popular test statistics include the z-score, t-score, F-statistic, and chi-square statistic.[4] Following is a complete example of one-sample hypothesis testing to determine whether the mean of a population is zero. Suppose we have a random sample $X_1, X_2, \cdots, X_n$ from some unknown distribution. We assume that the sample mean is approximately normally distributed for large n, and we want to test the null and alternative hypotheses:

$$H_0 : \mu = 0,$$
$$H_1 : \mu \neq 0, \tag{4}$$

where μ is the true mean of the population. To calculate the test statistic, we use a t-statistic with $n - 1$ degrees of freedom:

$$T = \frac{\overline{X} - \mu}{s/\sqrt{n}} = \frac{\overline{X}}{s/\sqrt{n}}, \tag{5}$$

---

[4] The Z-score quantifies the number of standard deviations by which a data point deviates from the mean and is typically employed for large samples or when the population variance is known. The t-score is used for small samples or unknown variances to compare means, while the chi-square statistic tests categorical data for goodness-of-fit or independence. The F-statistic, used in regression, evaluates variance ratios to assess group mean differences or model fit.

where $\overline{X}$ and s are the sample mean and standard deviation. Under H_0, this statistic approximately follows a t-distribution with $n-1$ degrees of freedom.

After computing the test statistic using sample data, we derive a value that can be compared against a critical value for a given alpha. The probability of observing a test statistic, under H_0, that is more extreme than the one we computed from our data is called the p-value. The p-value decides the statistical significance of our results compared to the null hypothesis. In the previous example, we can find $p = 2 \times P(T_{n-1} > |t_{obs}|)$ where t_{obs} is the observed value of the statistic, and T_{n-1} denotes a random variable following the t-distribution with $n-1$ degrees of freedom. If the resulting p-value is smaller than the significance level, for example, $\alpha = 0.05$, then we can say the test result is significant, indicating strong evidence against the null hypothesis.

In the previous section, we use graphical tools to assess data distributions but we can now also use statistical hypothesis testing to validate data properties. For instance, the Jarque-Bera test can be utilized to assess the validity of the normality assumption. This widely recognized statistical method evaluates whether the sample data skewness and kurtosis are consistent with those expected in a normal distribution, thereby determining if the return distribution adheres to normality.

2.5 Serial Covariance, Correlation, and Stationarity

For time-series forecasting, we make predictions based on historical observations from previous time stamps. While increments in financial time-series are close to independent random variables, and are indeed often modeled by stochastic processes such as Geometric Brownian Motion (GBM), it is still possible to identify and exploit small dependencies to make predictions. We can measure such dependence with serial covariances (autocovariances) or serial correlations (autocorrelations).

Serial covariance refers to the measure of how two variables change together over time within a time-series. In the context of financial time-series, it specifically measures the covariance between different observations of the same financial variable at different points in time. Intuitively, autocovariance tells us how two instances of a time-series (x_t, x_s) at different time points move together. Understanding serial covariance is beneficial for identifying patterns and predicting future values based on historical data. For example, if the price of a stock today is positively correlated with its price yesterday, this might indicate a future upward trend.

Correlation quantifies both the magnitude and the orientation of the linear association between two time-series. In contrast to covariance, correlation is both standardized and dimensionless, offering a uniform metric for assessing the extent to which two variables vary together. The correlation coefficient spans from -1 to 1, where 1 signifies a flawless positive linear association, -1 denotes a perfect negative linear relationship, and 0 implies the absence of any linear relationship. Formally, we can define covariance and correlation as:

$$\text{Covariance: } Cov(X_s, X_t) = E[(X_s - E(X_s))(X_t - E(X_t))],$$
$$= E(X_s X_t) - E(X_s)E(X_t), \tag{6}$$
$$\text{Correlation: } Corr(X_s, X_t) = CoV(X_s, X_t)/\sqrt{Var(X_s)Var(X_t)}.$$

Correlation is essential for many applications in financial time-series analysis. By evaluating the extent to which two assets fluctuate together, investors are able to design portfolios that reduce risk while optimizing returns. For instance, when two assets exhibit low or negative correlations, a portfolio combining the two can achieve lower overall volatility compared to portfolios consisting of highly correlated assets. Correlation analysis is also used for detecting market inefficiencies and arbitrage opportunities. For example, if two assets are expected to be highly correlated due to economic or financial reasons but deviate significantly at some point, one could speculate that this deviation will shrink again.

We can check how a time-series relates to previous observations (at various time lags) using Autocorrelation Function (ACF) plots and Partial Autocorrelation Function (PACF) plots. The ACF measures the correlation between a time-series and its own lagged (i.e., past) values. It indicates the degree to which past values of a series influence its current values, providing insights into the internal structure and patterns of the data. The ACF is especially effective in detecting trends, seasonal patterns, and various cyclical behaviors within a dataset. Mathematically, the ACF at lag k for a time-series X_t is defined as:

$$\rho_k = Corr(X_t, X_{t+k}) = \frac{Cov(X_t, X_{t+k})}{\sigma^2}, \tag{7}$$

where $Cov(X_t, X_{t+k})$ is the covariance between X_t and X_{t+k}, and σ^2 is the variance of the time-series. The values of the ACF span from -1 to 1, where values approaching 1 signify a robust positive correlation, those nearing -1 indicate a strong negative correlation, and values around 0 imply minimal to no correlation. A correlogram depicts the autocorrelation of a time-series as a function of time lags. This plot can help identify the appropriate model for time-series forecasting, such as an Autoregressive Moving Average model (ARMA), in which the autocorrelation structure guides the selection of model parameters.

The PACF serves as an additional instrument in time-series analysis, quantifying the correlation between a time-series and its lagged values while also eliminating the linear effects of intermediate lags. Unlike the ACF, which includes the cumulative effect of all previous lags, the PACF isolates the direct effect of a specific lag. For instance, the PACF at lag k measures the correlation between X_t and X_{t+k} after removing the effects of lags 1 through $k-1$. This allows for a clearer understanding of the underlying relationship at each specific lag, making it easier to identify the appropriate number of lags to include in an autoregressive model.

Mathematically, we can define the PACF at lag k as the correlation between X_t and X_{t+k} that is not accounted for by their mutual correlation with $X_{t+1}, X_{t+2}, \cdots, X_{t+k-1}$. We can obtain PACF values by fitting a linear model with X_t and the regressors standardized:

$$X_t = \alpha + \phi_{k,1} X_{t-1} + \phi_{k,2} X_{t-2} + \cdots + \phi_{k,k} X_{t-k}, \tag{8}$$

where $\phi_{k,k}$ is the PACF value for lag k, and ranges from -1 to 1. With standardization, the regression slopes become the partial correlation coefficient, as correlation is effectively the slope we get when both the response and predictors have been reduced to dimensionless "z-scores." The PACF plot is used in conjunction with the ACF plot to identify the order of an autoregressive (AR) model. While the ACF helps in understanding the overall autocorrelation structure, the PACF helps pinpoint the specific lags that should be included in the AR component of an ARMA model, ensuring a more accurate estimation.

In summary, the ACF and PACF are powerful tools that enable a deeper understanding of time-series data, guiding the development of robust and effective forecasting models. Their combined use allows for the precise identification of temporal structures, leading to improved predictions and better decision-making in fields where time-series data is prevalent. Figure 2 shows an example of ACF and PACF plots for the same underlying data. The shaded area in the plot represents an approximate confidence interval around zero correlation. In other words, it is a visual guide for checking which autocorrelation

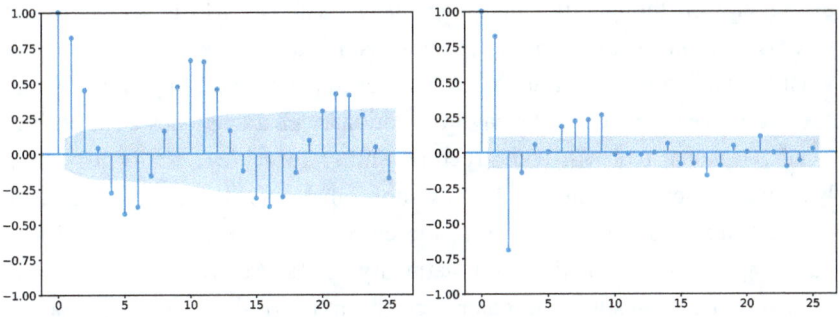

Figure 2 **Left:** ACF plot; **Right:** PACF plot.

(or partial autocorrelation) lags are statistically significant from zero. We can make these plots using the following code:

```
from statsmodels.graphics.tsaplots import plot_acf, plot_pacf
import matplotlib.pyplot as plt

fig, ax = plt.subplots(1,2, figsize=(12,4))
plot_acf(df['ret'], lags=30, ax=ax[0])    # ACF
plot_pacf(df['ret'], lags=30, ax=ax[1])   # PACF
plt.show()
```

Next, we discuss another concept that is commonly used in time-series known as stationarity. Stationarity refers to the statistical property of a time-series where its key characteristics, such as mean, variance, and autocovariance structure, remain constant over time. This consistency makes stationary time-series easier to analyze and model, as their behavior is predictable and stable. In financial markets, where data often exhibit complex patterns, achieving stationarity is helpful for accurate modeling, forecasting, and risk management.

There are two forms of stationarity: strict stationarity and weak stationarity. We say that a time-series process is strictly stationary if the joint distribution $f(X_{t_1}, \cdots, X_{t_k})$ is identical to the joint distribution $f(X_{t_1+\tau}, \cdots, X_{t_k+\tau})$ for all collections $t_1, \cdots, t_k$ and separate values τ. However, this assumption is very restrictive and very few real-world examples meet this requirement. Differently, we say that a time-series process is weakly stationary if:

- $E(X_t) = \mu < \infty$ where the mean of a time-series is constant and finite,
- $Var(X_t) = \sigma^2 < \infty$ where the variance of a time-series is constant and finite,
- the autocovariance and autocorrelation functions only depend on the lag:

$$\gamma_{t,t+\tau} = Cov(X_t, X_{t+\tau}) = \gamma_\tau,$$
$$\rho_{t,t+\tau} = Corr(X_t, X_{t+\tau}) = \rho_\tau. \qquad (9)$$

A considerable number of statistical and econometric models operate under the assumption that the underlying time-series remains stationary. These models depend on the stability of statistical characteristics to generate precise forecasts. In finance, stationarity ensures that historical risk measures, such as volatility and correlation, remain relevant for future periods. In practice, financial time-series frequently display non-stationary characteristics as a result of trends, seasonal patterns, and structural shifts. To achieve stationarity, analysts use various techniques. For example, they might use differencing to subtract previous observation from the current observation with the aim of removing trends and achieving a stationary series. Additionally, they might remove a deterministic trend component from a series (detrending) or apply transformations like logarithms to stabilize the variance.

2.6 Time-Series Models

We have introduced ACF and PACF which can be used to determine the order of AR and ARMA models. But what exactly are these models? In simple words, these are classical time-series models that form a crucial aspect of analyzing sequential data, particularly in fields such as finance, economics, and environmental science. By identifying patterns and correlations in historical price data, we can employ time-series models to develop quantitative trading strategies by exploiting patterns for profit. AR models, for instance, can help in detecting momentum or mean-reversion patterns, which are commonly used in algorithmic trading.

Beyond financial markets, time-series models are vital for economic policy and planning. Central banks and governmental bodies employ these models to predict key economic metrics, including GDP expansion, inflation levels, and unemployment figures. Accurate forecasts help make informed policy decisions that can stabilize the economy and promote growth. Within the spectrum of time-series models, the Autoregressive model (AR), moving average model (MA), and Autoregressive Moving Average model (ARMA) models are among the most fundamental due to their simplicity and effectiveness. These models are capable of capturing the underlying patterns and dynamics of time-series data, making them powerful tools for analysts and researchers aiming to model and forecast temporal data accurately.

The AR is among the most basic and extensively employed time-series models. It describes the current value of a series as a linear aggregate of its past values combined with an independent random error component. If an AR model takes p previous observations, we denote the model as AR(p) and its functional form is given as follows:

$$X_t = \phi_1 X_{t-1} + \cdots + \phi_p X_{t-p} + \epsilon_t, \tag{10}$$

where X_t is the value at current time stamp t, $\phi_1, \cdots, \phi_p$ are the model parameters that represent the effects of past values on the output value, and ϵ_t is an error term. For a given order p, we can fit the model and find the optimal coefficients ϕ_1 in the same way as we would fit a linear regression, with the lagged values $(X_{t-1}, ..., X_{t-p})$ being the predictors and X_t the target. In order to decide which order p to use, we can look at the PACF plot. For example, considering the time-series presented in Figure 2, the PACF suggests that an AR(3) model would probably capture most of the dependence, while it might be useful to consider an AR(9) model to capture further dependence.

The AR model captures how the current observations depend on their past values, making it suitable for modeling time-series with strong autocorrelations. This model is particularly effective when the underlying process is driven by its own past values, which can be the case for stock prices or interest rates. For example, an AR(1) model, where the output depends only on the immediate past observation, is defined as:

$$X_t = \phi_1 X_{t-1} + \epsilon_t, \qquad (11)$$

where the model suggests that the current value of the time-series is influenced directly by the observation at time $t-1$.

Differently than the AR model, the MA model represents the current value of a time-series as a linear combination of its previous error terms. The MA model of order q, symbolized as MA(q), is defined as:

$$X_t = \mu + \epsilon_t + \theta_1 \epsilon_{t-1} + \theta_2 \epsilon_{t-2} + \cdots + \theta_q \epsilon_{t-q}, \qquad (12)$$

where μ is the mean of the series, $\epsilon_t, \cdots, \epsilon_q$ are error terms, $\theta_1, \cdots, \theta_q$ are the model parameters that represent the influence of past errors on the current value. The MA model captures the influence of past shocks or disturbances on the current observation, making it useful for modeling time-series with short-term dependencies. This model is effective when the series is subject to random shocks that have a lasting but diminishing impact over time. For instance, an MA(1) model defines that the observation at time t is only influenced by the immediate past error:

$$X_t = \mu + \epsilon_t + \theta_1 \epsilon_{t-1}, \qquad (13)$$

although, in practice, we can include several terms to model output. To decide the order of a MA model, we check the ACF plot and obtain the estimated point at which the correlation diminishes.

The ARMA model integrates features from both AR and MA models, offering a more adaptable and thorough methodology for time-series analysis. The ARMA model with order (p,q), represented as ARMA(p,q), is defined as:

$$X_t = \sum_{j=1}^{p} \phi_j X_{t-j} + \epsilon_t + \sum_{j=1}^{q} \theta_j \epsilon_{t-j}, \qquad (14)$$

where an ARMA model proficiently models long-term dependencies via its AR components and addresses short-term disturbances through its MA components.

In financial time-series analysis, precise forecasting is important for informed investment choices and the formulation of effective trading strategies. AR, MA, and ARMA models provide systematic ways to predict future price movements based on historical data. An AR model can forecast future stock prices by considering the past price movements, while an MA model can evaluate the impact of past market shocks on future prices. ARMA models are often used to estimate future volatility, an essential component of pricing derivatives and constructing risk-hedging strategies.

Given that the aforementioned models are linear, they should always serve as a benchmark before testing any of the more complex, nonlinear deep learning models that are described in later sections. Linear models also have the added benefit of being easy to interpret. This helps form a better intuition for any investment ideas, before moving to more powerful but less interpretable deep learning models.

2.7 Extras

Alpha and Beta In quantitative finance, the notions of alpha and beta are very important to understanding and evaluating the performance of investment strategies. These metrics are derived from the Capital Asset Pricing Model (CAPM) and are used to measure the returns and risk associated with individual assets or portfolios relative to a benchmark, typically a market index. In quantitative trading, where strategies are often driven by mathematical models and algorithms, alpha and beta provide essential insights into the effectiveness and characteristics of trading approaches.

Alpha assesses an investment's performance relative to a benchmark index. More specifically, it represents the surplus return that an investment or portfolio achieves beyond the expected return predicted by the CAPM. In other words, alpha signifies the additional value that a trader or investment strategy contributes over what is anticipated based on the asset's systematic risk. Conversely, beta measures an investment's responsiveness to market fluctuations. It quantifies the relationship between the investment's returns and those of the overall market or benchmark, indicating the extent to which the investment's returns are expected to vary in reaction to changes in the market index. Mathematically, we define alpha (α) and beta (β) as:

$$\alpha = R_i - [R_f + \beta(R_m - R_f)], \tag{15}$$

where R_i is the return of the investment, R_f is the risk-free rate and R_m is the return of the market. A positive alpha signifies that the investment has surpassed the benchmark, whereas a negative alpha indicates underperformance. In quantitative trading, generating alpha is the primary goal as it reflects the ability of a trading strategy to consistently beat its benchmark through superior stock selection, timing, or other factors. Beta values have different meanings. A beta exceeding 1 signifies that the investment is more volatile than the market, indicating it tends to amplify market movements in response to changes. Conversely, a beta below 1 indicates that the asset's returns are less sensitive to market movements than the market index itself. If an investment has a negative beta, it means that the investment moves inversely to the benchmark. We can also think of beta as the covariance between strategy and market returns scaled by the market's variance.

A strategy that consistently generates positive alpha is considered successful, as it indicates the ability to surpass the market performance on a risk-adjusted basis. On the other hand, beta helps traders understand the risk profile of their strategies and manage risk exposure to market volatility. For instance, a trader seeking to minimize risk might construct a low-beta portfolio, while one aiming for higher returns might opt for higher-beta assets. By utilizing alpha and beta metrics, quantitative traders can make well-informed decisions and enhance their trading performance.

Volatility Clustering Volatility clustering is an extensively observed phenomenon in financial markets, characterized by sequences of high volatility periods that are succeeded by similarly high volatility periods, and periods of low volatility that are followed by similarly low volatility periods. This characteristic implies that volatility is not constant over time but instead exhibits temporal dependencies, forming clusters. This is one of the reasons why financial returns deviate from the normal distribution. This observation is known as heteroskedasticity and describes the irregular pattern of the variation of a process.

Figure 3 shows the returns of the S&P 500, and we can clearly see that large returns tend to cluster. This means that large fluctuations in prices tend to occur together, persistently amplifying the amplitudes of price changes. Such behavior contradicts the assumption of constant variance in traditional models like the classical linear regression model and calls for models that can accommodate changing variances, in order to make reliable predictions.

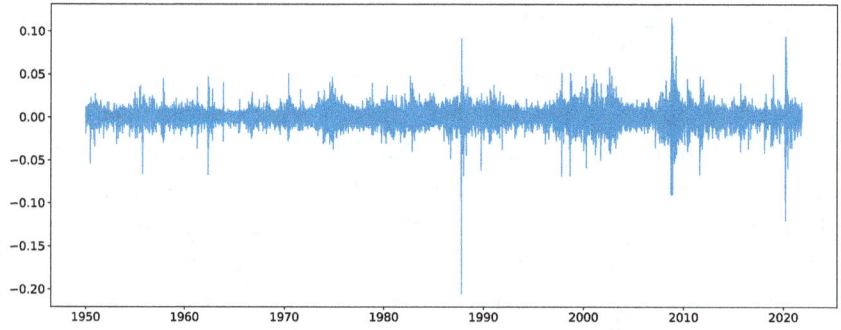

Figure 3 Returns of the S&P 500 over 60 years.

There are two popular models used to capture and analyze volatility clustering: the Autoregressive Conditional Heteroskedasticity (ARCH) model and the Generalized Autoregressive Conditional Heteroskedasticity (GARCH) model. These models help in capturing the changing variance over time and provide a better fit for the distribution of returns. Instead of predicting returns R_t, we now model the variance of returns. An ARCH(p) process of order p is defined as:

$$Var(R_t|R_{t-1}, \cdots, R_{t-p}) = \sigma_t^2 = \alpha_0 + \alpha_1 R_{t-1}^2 + \cdots + \alpha_p R_{t-p}^2, \qquad (16)$$

where the variance of the process at time t is determined by observations from the earlier time step. Accordingly, the ARCH model allows for fluctuations in conditional variance over time, effectively capturing volatility clustering.

The GARCH model extends the ARCH model by including past conditional variances into the model, providing a more flexible and parsimonious model for capturing volatility dynamics. We denote a GARCH(p,q) as:

$$\sigma_t^2 = \alpha_0 + \sum_{j=1}^{p} \alpha_j R_{t-j}^2 + \sum_{j=1}^{q} \beta_j \sigma_{t-j}^2, \qquad (17)$$

where the GARCH model presents a dual dependence that is better at modeling both short-term shocks and sustained persistence in volatility over time.

In practical terms, volatility clustering means that markets experience periods of turmoil and periods of calm. ARCH and GARCH models offer powerful methods for analyzing this phenomenon, enabling more accurate forecasting, risk management, and pricing of financial instruments. By recognizing the temporal dependencies in volatility, these models enable us to better understand market behavior and enhance decision-making in various financial applications.

3 Supervised Learning and Canonical Networks

In this section, we explore the essential concepts of supervised learning, an important subset of machine learning that identifies relationships between input data and output labels using example input-output pairs. Supervised learning is extensively applied in a variety of domains, including image recognition, natural language processing, financial forecasting, and medical diagnosis. By mastering the fundamentals of supervised learning, we can proficiently train models to generate accurate predictions and make informed decisions based on new, unseen data.

Supervised learning entails training a model on a labeled dataset, in which each input is paired with its corresponding correct output. The model then learns to associate inputs with outputs by minimizing the discrepancy between its predictions and the actual results. This methodology includes choosing suitable algorithms, adjusting hyperparameters, and assessing the models' effectiveness. In this section, we will examine these concepts comprehensively, establishing a robust foundation for comprehending and implementing supervised learning methodologies.

Additionally, we will introduce various neural network architectures, which have become the cornerstone of modern machine learning. Neural networks, modeled after the architecture of the human brain, are composed of interconnected layers of nodes (neurons) that process and transform input data. We will cover canonical neural network models, including feed-forward neural networks and state-of-the-art networks such as transformers, each designed for specific types of data and tasks.

Upon finishing this section, you will have a detailed understanding of the core concepts underpinning supervised learning and will better understand various types of neural networks. This knowledge will equip you with the skills to apply these powerful techniques to a wide range of applications, unlocking new possibilities in data analysis, prediction, and decision-making.

3.1 Supervised Learning: Regression and Classification

Supervised learning is at the core of machine learning and it is a process that essentially learns, or in other words, fits a mapping between an input and an output. Formally, for a regression task, it maps an input $x \in \mathbb{R}^d$ to an output $y \in \mathbb{R}$ through a learned function by training on example input-output pairs. We call this collection of example input-output pairs upon which the model is fitted the training set, and it can be expressed as:

$$\{(x_1, y_1), (x_2, y_2), \cdots, (x_N, y_N)\}. \tag{18}$$

A supervised learning algorithm infers a function f that best defines the interplay between inputs and outputs by utilizing training data. The inferred function can then be used to make estimates for new inputs. The function f can be as simple as a linear function or it can also be a highly nonlinear function as obtained through deep learning models. During training, the true output values (labels) are available, and our goal is to reduce the differences between the predicted results and these actual labels. In mathematical terms, this reads:

$$\min L(y, \hat{y}) \quad \text{with} \quad \hat{y}_i = f(x_i), \tag{19}$$

where L is a choice of metric, known as a loss function or an objective function, that measures the difference between real outputs (y) and predicted values ($\hat{y}$). After learning a functional mapping on the training set, we apply it to unseen test data $\{x'_1, x'_2, \cdots, x'_M\}$ and evaluate the performance of our learned function. In general, a supervised learning problem goes through the following steps:

1. Define the prediction problem,
2. Gather a training set that is representative of the application domain,
3. Carry out an exploratory analysis and select input features,
4. Choose the approximate learning algorithm and decide the model's architecture,
5. Conduct model training on the training set and optimize hyperparameters using a separate validation set,
6. Assess the effectiveness of the trained function using a test dataset.

Depending on outputs y, we can divide supervised learning algorithms into two categories: regression and classification. When the output (y) takes continuous values, it is a **regression** problem. For example, stock prices and the weights and heights of a person are all examples of continuous values that would correspond to a regression task. A **classification** problem deals with discrete outputs, such as whether an image contains a dog or not. The training framework for regression and classification is very similar, with the exception of the design of the objective function. We now discuss each problem type in detail.

Regression One key aspect of supervised learning is the selection of an appropriate loss function – also referred to as a cost or objective function – that measures the discrepancy between a model's predictions and the corresponding true target values. The loss function guides the learning process by providing a measure that the model aims to minimize during training. As previously noted, regression problems focus on the prediction of a continuous variable. For regression problems, one of the most commonly used objective functions is the mean-squared error (MSE):

$$L(y, \hat{y}) = \frac{1}{N} \sum_{i=1}^{N} (y_i - \hat{y}_i)^2, \qquad (20)$$

where the loss is merely the sum of residuals, $\epsilon_i = y_i - \hat{y}_i$, squared which we aim to minimize to obtain a good fit to the data.[5] The MSE loss is symmetric and places greater emphasis on larger errors in the dataset.

---

[5] We can also obtain the MSE for a linear model by a Maximum Likelihood approach, where we start with the likelihood of the data, $\prod_i p(\epsilon_i)$, and assume that the distribution of the residuals $p(\epsilon_i)$ is Gaussian. Maximizing the likelihood of the data is equivalent to minimizing the log-likelihood which, up to a constant, is equivalent to the MSE.

Table 1 Objective functions for regression problems.

Metrics	Formula
Root mean squared error (RMSE)	$\sqrt{\frac{1}{N}\sum_i^N (y_i - \hat{y}_i)^2}$
Mean squared log error (MELE)	$\frac{1}{N}\sum_i^N (ln(1+y_i) - ln(1+\hat{y}_i))^2$
Mean absolute error (MAE)	$\frac{1}{N}\sum_i^N |y_i - \hat{y}_i|$
Median absolute error (MedAE)	$median(|y_1 - \hat{y}_1|, \cdots, |y_N - \hat{y}_N|)$
Huber loss (HL)	$\begin{cases} \frac{1}{N}\sum_i^N \frac{1}{2}(y_i - \hat{y}_i)^2, \text{if } |y_i - \hat{y}_i| \leq \delta \\ \frac{1}{N}\sum_i^N \delta|y_i - \hat{y}_i| - \frac{1}{2}\delta^2, \text{otherwise} \end{cases}$

There are numerous options for objective functions. For example, the mean-squared logarithmic error can be applied to outputs that exhibit exponential growth, imposing an asymmetric penalty that is less harsh on negative errors than on positive ones. Both the mean absolute error (MAE) and the median absolute error (MedAE) are symmetric and do not assign additional weight to larger errors. Moreover, Huber loss, which merges aspects of the mean squared error and the mean absolute error, is resistant to outliers and can be used to stabilize training when working with noisy data. Table 1 summarizes some common loss functions for regression problems. It is also very straightforward to implement these losses:

```
from sklearn.metrics import (mean_squared_error,
            mean_squared_log_error,
            mean_absolute_error,
            median_absolute_error)
from scipy.special import huber
import numpy as np

def huber_loss(y_true, y_pred, delta=1.0):
    y_true = np.array(y_true)
    y_pred = np.array(y_pred)
    return np.mean(huber(delta, y_true - y_pred))

mse = mean_squared_error(y_true, y_pred)
rmse = np.sqrt(mse)
msle = mean_squared_log_error(y_true, y_pred)
mae = mean_absolute_error(y_true, y_pred)
med_ae = median_absolute_error(y_true, y_pred)
huber = huber_loss(y_true, y_pred, delta=1.0)
```

The best choice of objective function depends on the specific task. Sometimes, we can create customized loss functions to ensure that performance metrics best reflect the consequences of incorrect predictions. For example, in applications like medical diagnosis or fraud detection, false negatives may be more costly than false positives. In such cases, loss functions can be tailored to penalize certain types of errors more severely, aligning the model's training with the specific needs of the problem.

Classification Unlike regression, classification aims to place input data into predefined categories or classes. It does so by analyzing a labeled dataset where each example is matched with a class label. Once trained, a classification model can predict labels for unseen data based on the learned patterns and relationships. Classification techniques are commonly applied in fields such as finance, healthcare, and marketing. Classification problems can be broadly categorized into binary classification and multi-class classification. Binary classification involves two distinct classes. Common examples of binary classification include determining whether an email is spam, predicting if a credit card transaction is fraudulent, or diagnosing a patient as healthy or ill. Multi-class problems involve more than two classes, such as classifying handwritten digits (0–9), categorizing types of flowers (e.g., the Iris dataset), or classifying news articles into different topics.

Since classification problems have discrete outputs, we first have to produce scores, or logits, to indicate the likelihoods that an observation belongs to certain classes. These scores can then be normalized across all possible class labels to obtain corresponding probabilities $\hat{p}_i$. After that, we use these scores or probabilities $\hat{p}_i$ to make actual predictions $\hat{y}_i$ either by taking the class with the highest score or by using threshold values. In the simplest case of a binary classification problem, we first define the logistic function

$$\sigma(z) = \frac{1}{1+e^{-z}}, \tag{21}$$

which squashes any real-valued input into the open interval (0,1). We can then model the probability of the prediction being positive as

$$p(y_i = 1|x_i) = \sigma(w^T x_i). \tag{22}$$

The same mapping can be represented by

$$\text{logit}(\hat{p}_i) = \log \frac{\hat{p}_i}{1-\hat{p}_i} = w^T x_i, \tag{23}$$

where the logit of the probabilities is a linear function of input features (x_i). The objective functions for classification problems are different from regression as there are instead finite distinct outcomes. In most cases, we choose cross-entropy loss as the objective function for classification. In the binary case, the cross-entropy is calculated as:

$$-(y \log(p) + (1-y) \log(1-p)), \tag{24}$$

where p is the probability of predicting $y = 1$. The loss function is then computed by summing the cross-entropy of each data point:

$$L(\mathbf{y}, \hat{\mathbf{p}}) = -\sum_{i=1}^{N} (y_i \log(\hat{p}_i) + (1 - y_i) \log(1 - \hat{p}_i)). \qquad (25)$$

The functional form of the cross-entropy loss might be less intuitive than the MSE, but it can still be understood within the context of maximum likelihood estimation.[6] If we deal with a multi-class classification problem ($M > 2$), a separate loss is needed for each class label and a summation is taken at the end:

$$-\sum_{c=1}^{M} y_{oc} \log(p_{oc}), \qquad (26)$$

where $y_{o,c}$ is a binary indicator (0 or 1) that is activated when the model assigns the right label c for observation o, and p is the output from the algorithm which indicates the predictive probability of observation o for class c. The loss of the data is then obtained by summing the multi-class cross-entropy of each point.

Once the predicted probabilities are transformed into predictions of one class or another, we can evaluate model performance through several metrics. To illustrate those metrics we focus on binary classification problems for simplicity. A frequently employed measure is the misclassification rate which can be defined as the fraction of misclassified labels:

$$\text{Misclassification rate} = \frac{1}{N} \sum_{i=1}^{N} I_{y_i \neq \hat{y}_i}. \qquad (27)$$

The confusion matrix is another important tool that can be used to visualize various metrics. Table 2 illustrates a confusion matrix that enumerates the quantities of correct and incorrect predictions for every class. For example, the False Positives in the top right corner represent errors where an actual label is negative but a prediction is positive. In the context of a stock price reversion example, this would be a case when a stock price does not revert but we predicted that it would revert. Such an error is much more costly to us than a False Negative, where a stock does actually revert but we predicted it would not.

Following the notation in the confusion matrix, we can thus introduce other popular evaluation metrics, which are shown in Table 3. For instance, accuracy is computed by summing the diagonal entries in the confusion matrix and then

---

[6] The likelihood of the data is $\prod_i \hat{p}_i^{y_i} (1 - \hat{p}_i)^{1-y_i}$, which merely assigns a probability $\hat{p}_i$ to each point with label $y_i = 1$ and a probability $1 - \hat{p}_i$ to each point with label $y_i = 0$. The negative log-likelihood then corresponds to our loss function.

Table 2 Confusion matrix.

		Actual	
		Positive	Negative
Prediction	Positive	True Positive (*TP*)	False Positive (*FP*)
	Negative	False Negative (*FN*)	True Negative (*TN*)

Table 3 Evaluation metrics for classification problems.

Metrics	Formula
Accuracy	$\frac{TP+TN}{TP+FP+TN+FN}$
Precision	$\frac{TP}{TP+FP}$
Recall	$\frac{TP}{TP+FN}$
F1	$2 \times \frac{Precision \times Recall}{Precision + Recall}$

dividing by the total number of predicted samples. Accuracy thus represents the proportion of total predictions that are correct. Precision indicates the fraction of predicted positives that are truly positive, while recall measures the fraction of actual positives correctly identified. Lastly, the F1 score balances precision and recall by using their harmonic mean.

It is very important to check all evaluation metrics when analyzing model performance since a single performance metric can indicate misleading results. For example, in an unbalanced data set, where 90% of labels are +1, we can get an accuracy score of 90% by simply predicting everything as +1, even though the model has not learned anything. Another issue arises when we assign different importance to different types of errors. For example, a mean reversion strategy usually makes frequent small gains but can make infrequent large losses when a stock does not revert. Such a strategy might demonstrate a high accuracy for predicting stock reversion but still lead to significant losses. To implement these metrics, we can use the following code:

```
from sklearn.metrics import accuracy_score, f1_score,
    confusion_matrix, classification_report

acc = accuracy_score(y_true, y_pred)
f1_macro = f1_score(y_true, y_pred, average='macro')
report = classification_report(y_true, y_pred)
cm = confusion_matrix(y_true, y_pred)

print("Accuracy:", acc)
print("F1 Score (macro):", f1_macro)
```

```
10  print("Classification Report:")
11  print(report)
12  print("Confusion Matrix:")
13  print(cm)
```

Instead of using numerical values to assess model performance, we can also use graphical tools. The receiver operating characteristics (ROC) curve enables us to compare and choose models that are conditioned on their respective predictive performance. For this purpose, we need to compare predicted probabilities with selected thresholds to decide final outcomes. Accordingly, different thresholds yield different results. The ROC curve derives pairs of true positive rates (TPR) and false positive rates (FPR) by examining every possible threshold for classification, and then displays these pairs on a unit square plot. We define TRP and FPR as the following:

$$\begin{aligned} TPR &= \frac{TP}{TP + FN}, \\ FPR &= \frac{FP}{FP + TN}. \end{aligned} \qquad (28)$$

Random predictions, on average, yield a diagonal line on the ROC curve which has equal TPR and FPR rates. This diagonal line is the benchmark case, so if the curve falls on the left side of the diagonal line, the learned model is better than random guessing. The further from the margin, the better the classifier (shown in Figure 4). We refer to the area under the ROC curve as

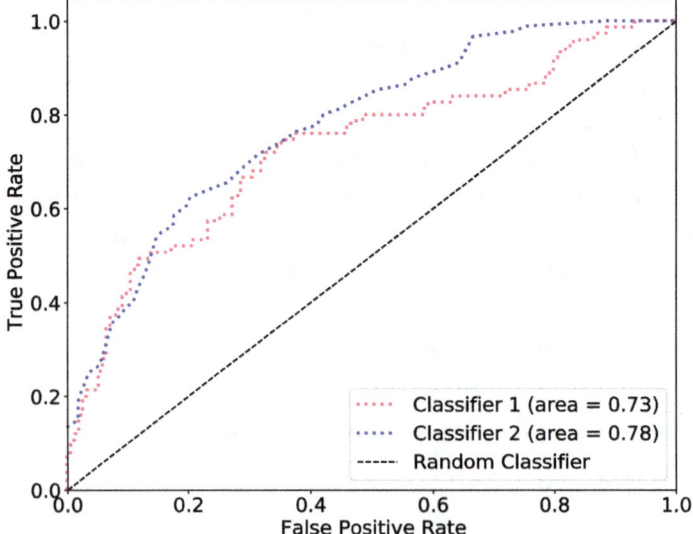

Figure 4 An example of different ROC curves.

AUC and it is a summary measure that tells how good a classifier is. A higher AUC score indicates a better algorithm.

3.2 Fully Connected Networks

After reviewing the basics of supervised learning, we now look at canonical examples of neural network architectures. Fully connected networks (FCNs), also known as multilayer perceptrons, are one of the earliest and most basic neural networks. FCNs are indispensable in the field of deep learning, as they provide the foundational architecture upon which other more sophisticated neural network models are built. FCNs have powerful abilities to approximate complex functions and patterns within data, making them highly versatile and applicable across various domains.

To gain a thorough understanding of FCNs, let us start with a simple linear model, as a linear model can be viewed as a single neuron with a fully connected input layer. Suppose we have an input of vector form $x \in \mathbb{R}^{N_x}$ and a scalar output $y \in \mathbb{R}$. A linear model posits that the prediction for an input vector x can be determined by:

$$y = w^T x + b. \tag{29}$$

This is precisely how a single neuron (in many neural network frameworks) computes its output – via a linear combination of inputs. In neural networks, this single linear neuron can be extended by stacking many such layers (and adding nonlinearities) to get more expressive models. However, at its core, a single neuron's linear component is identical to the linear regression formula. For linear regression under a least squares objective, we can write the objective function as:

$$L = \frac{1}{N} \sum_{i=1}^{N} (y_i - \hat{y}_i)^2, \tag{30}$$

where N is the number of sample points. We can therefore optimize the model parameters by setting the partial derivatives of the L with respect to w and b to 0:

$$\frac{\partial L}{\partial w} = 0 \text{ and } \frac{\partial L}{\partial b} = 0, \tag{31}$$

and the aforementioned can be solved analytically. In fact, by setting $b = 0$ for simplicity, and writing $X = (x_1, ..., x_N)^T$, the solution can easily be obtained as:

$$w = (X^T X)^{-1} X^T y. \tag{32}$$

Moreover, one can directly recover the general case with $b \neq 0$ by noting that we can always interpret the bias b as a weight w_0 of a constant predictor $x_0 = 1$. While the analytical solution provides a direct method to find the optimal parameters, it may not be practical for large-scale problems as numerical matrix inversion can become inefficient. As an alternative, gradient descent offers an iterative approach to approximate the optimal parameters by minimizing the MSE:

$$w = w - \alpha \frac{\partial L}{\partial w},$$
$$b = b - \alpha \frac{\partial L}{\partial b}, \tag{33}$$

where α is the learning rate. This is a rather simple application of gradient descent, especially given that the problem is convex. However, even for a simple linear regression it can be beneficial to use gradient descent. For example, using online gradient descent is a viable strategy for solving cases where the data is so large that it does not fit in memory. Moreover, it is very easy to substitute different loss functions, such as MAE or Huber loss in Table 1.

Note that the notion of learning parameters from data via gradient descent is also the core concept behind more complex neural network training. Understanding how gradients are computed and used to update parameters in linear regression aids in comprehending backpropagation in neural networks. Once again, a single linear neuron is essentially a linear regression with optional activation (defined in the next page). The extension to multiple neurons and stacking them is the essence of deep neural networks.

One of the significant advantages of FCNs is their capacity for universal approximation. According to the Universal Approximation Theorem (Hornik, Stinchcombe, & White, 1989), a single-hidden-layer feed-forward network with an adequately large neuron count can approximate any continuous function. This property makes FCNs incredibly powerful for tasks involving function approximation. Further, many state-of-the-art models, such as convolutional neural networks (CNNs) and recurrent neural networks (RNNs), incorporate fully connected layers as integral components. In CNNs, for instance, FCNs are used in the final stages to consolidate the features from the last hidden layers to make predictions.

In general, FCNs receive an input of vector form $x \in \mathbb{R}^{N_x}$ and map it to an output (here a scalar) $y \in \mathbb{R}$ through a function $y = f(x|\theta)$. The vector θ comprises all model parameters, which we iteratively update to achieve the optimal function approximation. Additionally, an FCN can form a chain structure by stacking multiple layers sequentially. Each layer is a function of the previous layer. The first layer can be defined as:

$$h^{(1)} = g^{(1)}(W^{(1)}x + b^{(1)}), \tag{34}$$

where $h^{(1)} \in \mathbb{R}^{N_1}$ designates the first hidden layer, containing N_1 neurons. Additionally, the quantities $W^{(1)} \in \mathbb{R}^{N_1 \times N_x}$ and $b^{(1)} \in \mathbb{R}^{N_1}$ denote the associated

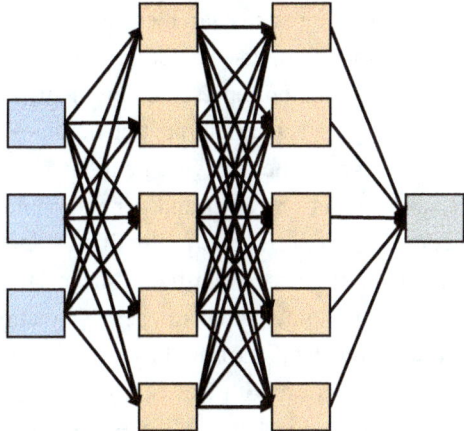

Figure 5 An FCN with two hidden layers in which each hidden layer has five neurons.

weight matrix and bias vector, respectively. The function $g^{(1)}(\cdot)$ is called the activation function. We then define the following hidden layers as:

$$h^{(l)} = g^{(l)}(W^{(l)}h^{(l-1)} + b^{(l)}), \tag{35}$$

where the l-th hidden layer ($h^{(l)} \in \mathbb{R}^{N_l}$) has weights $W^{(l)} \in \mathbb{R}^{N_l \times N_{l-1}}$ and biases $b^{(l)} \in \mathbb{R}^{N_l}$. To better illustrate this, we present an example of an MLP in Figure 5. At its core, each hidden layer computes a linear transformation of the previous layer's output, followed by a nonlinear activation. The ultimate output is determined by the target's nature and is once again derived from the preceding hidden layer. The discrepancy between the model's predictions and the true targets is quantified using a specified loss or objective function. Gradient descent is then employed to adjust the model parameters in an effort to minimize this loss. We can easily build a fully connected network with Pytorch using the following code snippet:

```
import torch.nn as nn

class MLP(nn.Module):
    def __init__(self, seq_length, n_features):
        super(MLP, self).__init__()
        self.flat_dim = seq_length * n_features
        self.net = nn.Sequential(
            nn.Flatten(),
            nn.Linear(self.flat_dim, 64),
            nn.ReLU(),
            nn.Linear(64, 32),
            nn.ReLU(),
            nn.Linear(32, 1)
        )
    def forward(self, x):
        return self.net(x)
```

The activation function requires special attention, as its argument is just a linear combination of the model inputs. Therefore, if the activation function is also linear then the overall function represented by the neural network would also be linear. Thus, making the activation function nonlinear is what allows us to represent complex nonlinear functions with neural networks.[7]

A variety of activation functions exist and general choices include hyperbolic tangent function, sigmoid function, Rectified Linear Units (ReLU) (Nair & Hinton, 2010), and Leaky Rectified Linear Units (Leaky-ReLU) (Maas et al., 2013). Figure 6 plots some of these activation functions. The ReLU function is prevalent in modern applications, and empirical research advises initiating experimentation with ReLU while simultaneously evaluating other activation functions (Mhaskar & Micchelli, 1993). Leaky-ReLUs can also be used to avoid some of the gradient issues caused by the flat part of the ReLU. In broad terms, the selection of activation function to use is dictated by the application context and must be substantiated through validation studies. The same rationale for choosing activation functions likewise applies to other network hyperparameters.

3.3 Convolutional Neural Networks

Convolutional neural networks (CNNs) constitute a class of deep learning architectures meticulously engineered to process images and other structured grid-like data. These networks have fundamentally changed the landscape of computer vision, allowing machines to carry out tasks such as image recognition, object detection, and image segmentation with performance levels that rival human capabilities. Drawing inspiration from the visual cortex of animals, the architecture of CNNs enables them to automatically and adaptively learn spatial hierarchies of features from input data, thereby enhancing their effectiveness in various pattern recognition tasks.

CNNs are arguably the most important network structures as they inspired much of the development of modern deep learning algorithms over the past decade through initial breakthroughs in performance on image recognition problems. Marking a pivotal breakthrough in computer vision, Krizhevsky, Sutskever, and Hinton (2017) introduced the first convolutional neural network successfully applied to large-scale image tasks. Often in image problems, features learned by neural networks have intuitive interpretations such as edges or surfaces. Whereas an FCN would need to relearn a feature for every part of an

---

[7] Mathematical theory shows that a single hidden layer MLP with infinitely many neurons can represent any continuous function. In practice, however, one aims for deeper, rather than wider, networks as they make it easier to learn good feature representations.

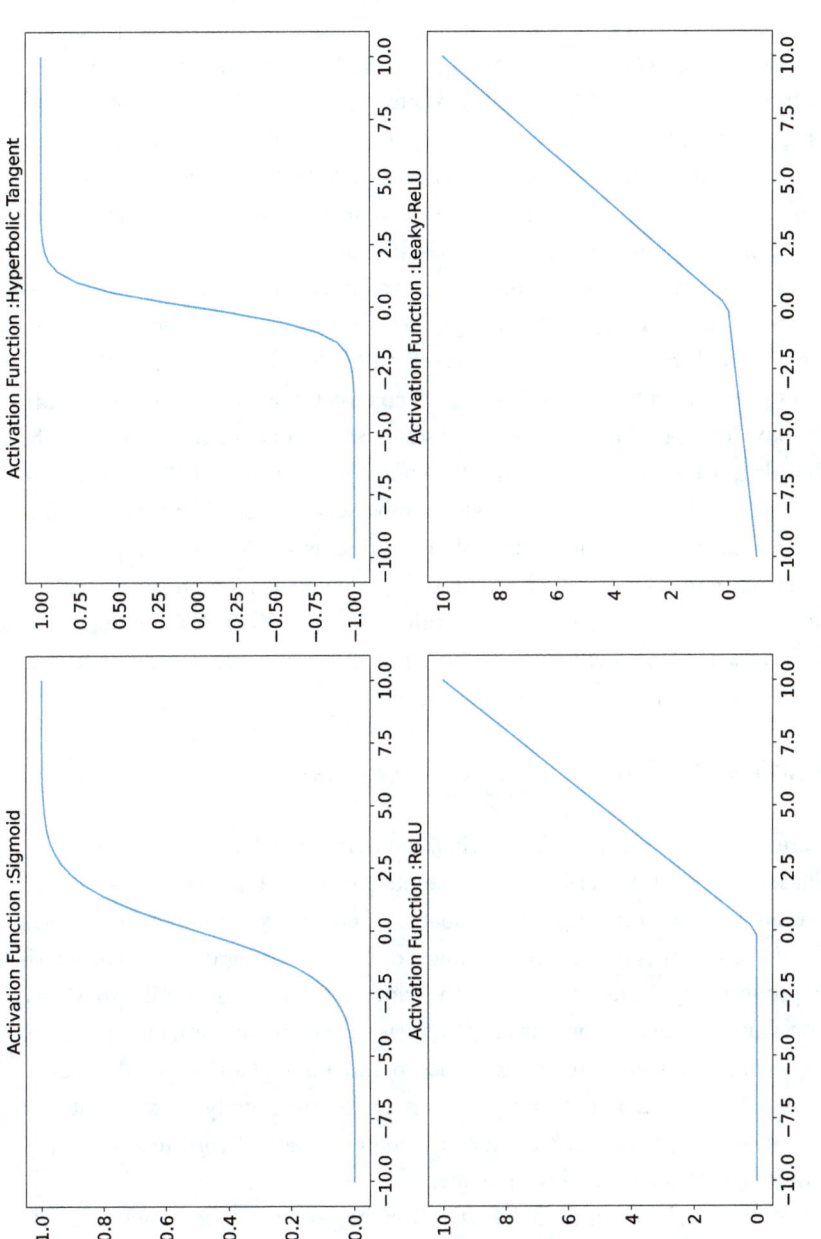

Figure 6 Plots of various activation functions.

image, the CNN architecture enables the model to learn the same feature for different parts of an image by sliding a convolutional filter across it.

Subsequently, CNNs were studied and applied to many domain areas. We now demonstrate how the same concept can be used for time-series problems. Time-series data, characterized by its sequential and temporal nature, can benefit from the unique ability of CNNs to detect patterns and trends over different scales. By adapting the convolutional operations used in image processing to time-series data, CNNs can effectively capture local dependencies and extract representative features. These qualities make them strong tools for time-series forecasting, anomaly detection, and classification.

Unlike MLPs that receive inputs in vector format, CNNs are adept at processing grid-structured input data through the use of two specialized layer types: convolutional layers and pooling layers. Convolutional layers constitute the primary components of a CNN, with each convolutional layer containing multiple convolutional filters designed to extract local spatial relationships from the input data. Convolutional filters, also known as kernels or feature detectors, are designed to traverse and transform input data by detecting specific features or patterns. In essence, a convolutional filter is a diminutive weight matrix that slides across the input data, performing a dot product with each localized region of the input. This procedure is referred to as the convolution operation. We denote a standard convolutional filter as K and it processes the input data $X \in \mathcal{R}^{N_T \times N_x}$ by utilizing a convolution operation:

$$S(i,j) = (X * K)(i,j) = \sum_{m=0}^{M-1} \sum_{n=0}^{N-1} X(i+m, j+n) K(m,n), \qquad (36)$$

where S signifies the resultant matrix (feature map) and (i,j) correspond to the indices of its rows and columns. We denote the convolution process as $*$.

A single convolutional layer is capable of containing multiple filters, each of which convolves the input data using a distinct set of parameters. The matrices produced by these filters are often termed feature maps. Similar to MLPs, these feature maps can be transmitted to subsequent convolutional layers and subjected to activation functions to incorporate nonlinearities into the model. In time-series modeling, the primary strategy involves applying convolutional filters along the temporal axis, thereby enabling the network to discern and learn temporal dependencies and patterns.

Another crucial component of a CNN is the pooling layer, which also features a grid-like structure. This layer condenses the information from specific areas of the feature maps by applying statistical operations to nearby outputs. For example, the widely used max-pooling layer (Y.- T. Zhou & Chellappa, 1988) selects the highest value within a designated region of the feature maps, whereas average pooling computes the mean value of that region. The study by Boureau, Ponce, and LeCun (2010) explores the application of various pooling methods in different contexts. However, in most scenarios, selecting the appropriate pooling technique necessitates domain expertise and empirical experimentation.

Pooling layers are utilized across various applications to make the resulting feature maps relatively invariant to small changes in the input data. This type of invariance is beneficial when the focus is on detecting the existence of particular features rather than their exact positions (Goodfellow, Bengio, & Courville, 2016). For instance, in certain image classification problems, it is only necessary to recognize that an image contains objects with specific characteristics without needing to pinpoint their exact locations. Conversely, in time-series analysis, the precise timing or placement of features is often essential, and therefore the use of pooling layers must be approached with caution.

In addition to convolutional and pooling layers, a CNN has additional possible operations: padding and stride. Padding is employed to preserve the dimensions of the feature maps, as convolution operations would otherwise "shrink" the dimension of original inputs (demonstrated in Figure 7). Padding solves this by adding, or "padding," the original inputs with zeros around the borders (zero-padding) so that the resulting feature maps have the same dimension as before (the top-right figure of Figure 7).

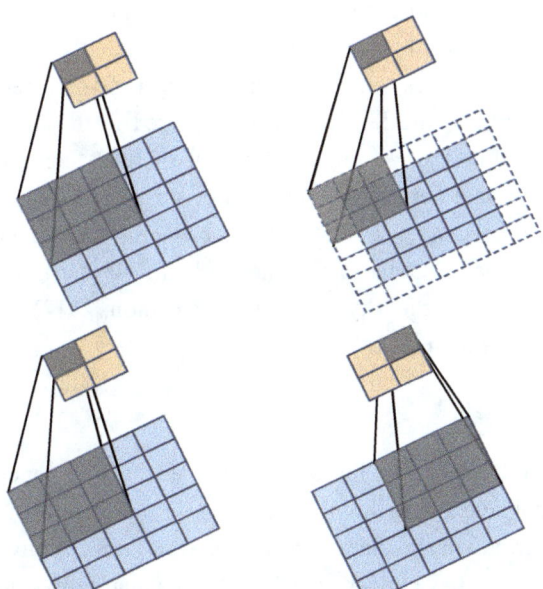

Figure 7 **Top:** an illustration of padding; **Bottom:** an illustration of stride.

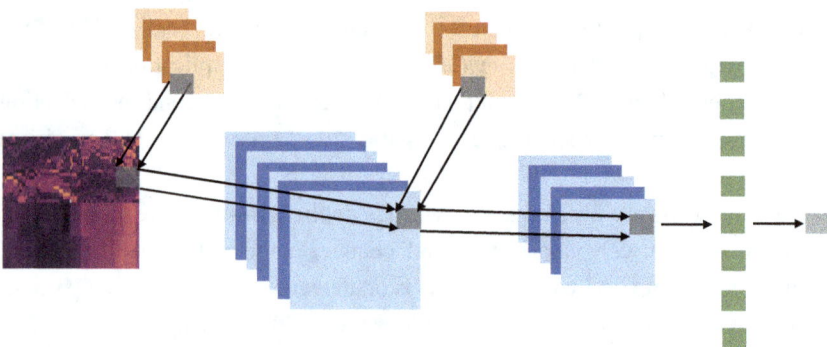

Figure 8 An example CNN network that first goes through a convolutional layer and then a pooling layer with a fully connected layer at the end.

Separately, stride is a commonly utilized parameter that controls how the convolutional filter moves across inputs and can reduce the dimensionality of input data. More concretely, stride defines the number of steps the filter takes as it slides over the input matrix, impacting the dimension of the output feature map and the amount of computational work required. Recall that a convolutional filter "scans" an input and by default moves by a step size of (1,1). Stride defines a different step size. For example, a stride of (2,2) has the effect of moving the filter two steps and thus decreases the original input by half (as shown in Figure 7).

Padding and stride are central concepts within CNNs that manage the spatial dimensions of output feature maps and determine the network's effectiveness in capturing and retaining information from the input data. By carefully choosing padding and stride values, one can balance the trade-offs between computational efficiency and the level of detail captured in the features extracted by the network. Finally, we can combine all of these components to construct a convolutional network. Figure 8 shows a typical example of a CNN and possesses an architecture that is standard and highly popular in image classification problems. Other famous networks for further independent study include "AlexNet" (Krizhevsky, Sutskever, & Hinton, 2012) and "VGGNet" (Simonyan & Zisserman, 2014).

3.4 WaveNet

CNNs are naturally desirable for dealing with stochastic financial time-series as convolutional layers have smoothing properties that facilitate the extraction of valuable information and discard the noise. In addition, a convolutional filter can be configured to have fewer trainable weights than fully connected layers. To some extent, this remedies the problem of overfitting (defined in Section 4).

However, a convolutional filter summarizes information for local regions of the input, so the receptive field from convolutional layers is limited, and in order to consider the entire input sequence, we have to use many layers and such operations could be highly inefficient.

We now introduce WaveNet, an architecture that specifically addresses this issue by using dilated convolutions. A WaveNet is a deep generative model developed by DeepMind (Van Den Oord et al., 2016) which generates raw audio waveforms and represents a substantial milestone in audio synthesis and processing. It is capable of producing highly realistic human speech and other audio signals by directly modeling the raw waveform of the audio, unlike traditional methods that rely on intermediate representations such as spectrograms or parametric models.

WaveNet has proven to be a powerful tool that can be effectively adapted for time-series analysis. Time-series data, characterized by sequential and temporal dependencies, presents a set of challenges that a WaveNet architecture is well-suited to address. By leveraging its strengths to study prolonged dependencies and capture intricate temporal patterns, A WaveNet offers a robust framework for modeling time-series processes. The core of a WaveNet is the dilated causal convolutions which enable the network to consider a broad context of past observations. In essence, the dilated convolutions skip some elements in the input, which allows the networks to access a larger range of inputs. Apart from dilated convolutional layers, other important components of a WaveNet include residual and skip connections and gated activation units.

The work of Borovykh, Bohte, and Oosterlee (2017) proposes that the dilated convolution for a time-series has a large receptive field. Specifically, a dilated convolution is defined as:

$$(w_h^l *_d f^{l-1})(i) = \sum_{j=-\infty}^{\infty} \sum_{m=1}^{M_{l-1}} w_h^l(j,m) f^{l-1}(i - d \cdot j, m), \qquad (37)$$

where M_l denotes the number of channels and d is the dilation factor. A dilated convolutional filter operates with every dth element in the input, therefore, it can access a broad range of inputs compared to standard convolutional filters. The causal nature of the convolutions ensures that the model does not violate the temporal order of the time-series, making it suitable for prediction tasks.

We can stack multiple such layers to extract even longer dependencies. For a network with L dilated convolutional layers, we increase the dilation factor by two at each layer, so that $d \in [2^0, 2^1, \cdots, 2^{L-1}]$, and the filter size w is $1 \times k := 1 \times 2$. As a result, the dilation rate exponentially increases with each layer, allowing the network to efficiently model prolonged dependencies over sequences. An example of a dilated convolutional network that consists

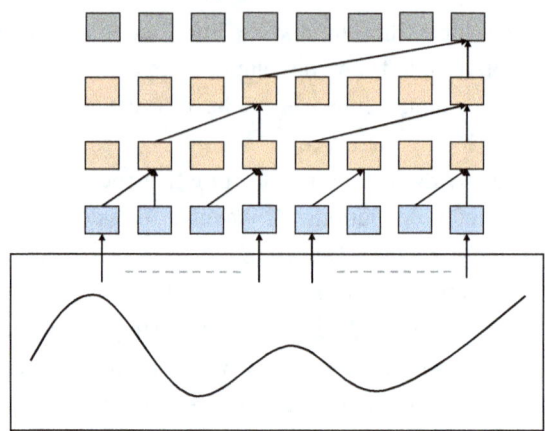

Figure 9 A WaveNet with three layers. The dilation factors for the first, second, and third hidden layers are 1, 2, and 4 respectively.

of three layers is illustrated in Figure 9. To incorporate nonlinearity into the model, we use activation functions after each layer to transform the resulting representations. A WaveNet that uses ReLU has output from layer l is:

$$f^l = [ReLU(w_1^l *_d f^{l-1}) + b, \cdots, ReLU(w_{M_l}^l *_d f^{l-1}) + b], \quad (38)$$

where $*_d$ refers to a convolution performed with a dilation factor of d, $b \in \mathbb{R}$ is the bias term, and f^l indicates the output generated from a convolution using the filters w_l^h for each $h = 1, \cdots, M_l$ within layer l.

In general, a deep network can suffer from an unstable training process if backpropagation becomes unstable during the process of differentiation across multiple layers. This problematic phenomenon is called the degradation problem and was discussed by He, Zhang, Ren, and Sun (2016). The work of He et al. (2016) proposes residual connections to solve this limitation by forcing the network to approximate $\mathcal{H}(x) - x$ instead of $\mathcal{H}(x)$ (the outputs from an intermediate layer). They suggest that optimizing the residual mapping is easier and they implement this technique by adding the inputs and outputs from a neural layer together. In a WaveNet (Figure 10), each dilated convolutional layer is followed by a residual connection. Specifically, the outputs from the activation function undergo a 1×1 convolution (a point-wise convolution) before the residual connection is applied. This approach ensures that both the residual path and the output from the dilated convolution have the same number of channels, allowing multiple layers to be stacked effectively. Finally, we can use WaveNet as an autoregressive model for time-series forecasting. In this context, the expectation for predicting every $t \in \{0, ..., N\}$ is:

$$\mathbb{E}[x_{t+1} | x_t, \cdots, x_{t-r}] = \beta_1 x_{t-r} + \cdots + \beta_r x_t, \quad (39)$$

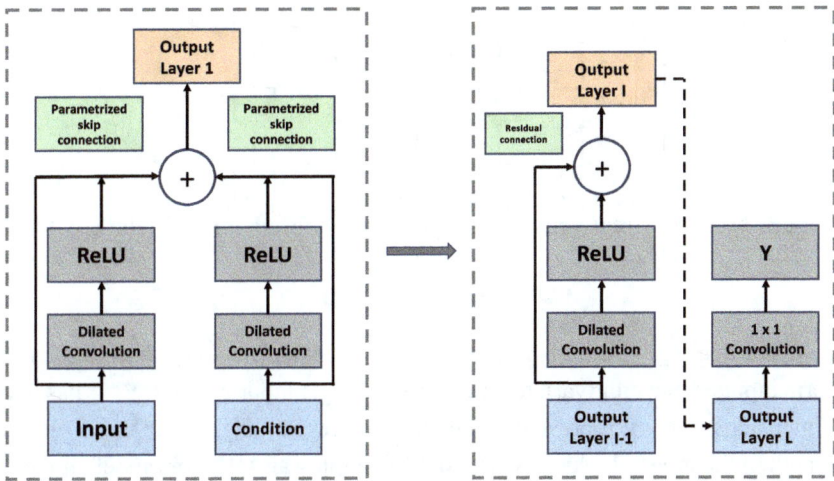

Figure 10 The network structure of a WaveNet. The input is convolved in the first layer and then fed to the following network layer with a residual connection. The **Condition** refers to any other external information that the network uses. This operation is repeated until the output layer $L(M)$ and the final forecast is made.

where β_i are parameters optimized via gradient descent. To create a one-step-ahead prediction, we compute $\hat{x}_{t+1}$ for $t + 1 \geq r$ by inputting the sequence $(x_{t+1-r}, \ldots, x_t)$. These predictions can subsequently be reintroduced into the network to formulate n-step-ahead forecasts. For instance, a two-step-ahead out-of-sample prediction $\hat{x}_{t+2}$ is produced by using the input $(x_{t+2-r}, \ldots, \hat{x}_{t+1})$.

3.5 Recurrent Neural Networks

Recurrent neural networks (RNNs) form a class of neural architectures specifically devised to detect patterns within sequential data, including time-series, natural language, and speech signals. In contrast to conventional feed-forward neural networks which presume independence among inputs, RNNs possess an internal memory structure that captures details of preceding inputs. This design feature enables RNNs to maintain context and appreciate temporal dependencies, rendering them highly suitable for scenarios where the sequential order and context of data are integral.

RNNs have a rich history that dates back to the early days of artificial intelligence and deep learning research. The foundational idea behind RNNs was to create a network that could process sequences of data and retain a memory mechanism to model time-based dependencies, which traditional feed-forward networks could not handle effectively. Given this idea, time-series data that have sequential structures are well suited to the framework of RNNs.

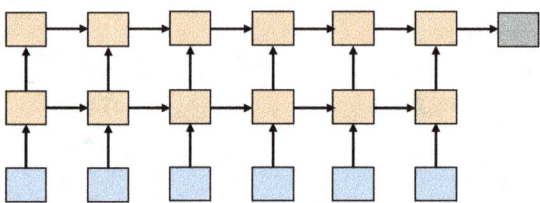

Figure 11 A recurrent network that processes information from the input and the past hidden state.

When dealing with time-series data, we can take previous observations to form inputs. For a multivariate time-series, a single input $x_{1:T} \in \mathcal{R}^{N_T \times N_x}$ has two dimensions where x_t represents the features corresponding to time t, and T is the length of the input's look-back window. To employ an MLP for modeling these processes, the inputs need to be flattened prior to feeding them into the hidden layers. However, this operation could break the existing time dependencies in inputs. To address this potential problem, RNNs have a structure that maintains an internal representation that preserves important temporal relationships

The RNN architecture leverages hidden states that function as a memory mechanism, and recursively update with each new observation at every time step. Consequently, this structure naturally carries information forward from earlier inputs to current ones, extracting temporal patterns from the data. We can define a hidden state as:

$$\begin{aligned} h_t &= f(h_{t-1}, x_t | W, b), \\ &= g(W_h h_{t-1} + W_x x_t + b), \end{aligned} \tag{40}$$

where $W_h \in \mathbb{R}^{N_h \times N_h}$, $W_x \in \mathbb{R}^{N_h \times N_x}$, $b \in \mathbb{R}^{N_h}$ constitute the linear weights and biases for the hidden state, while $g(\cdot)$ designates the activation function. The quantity N_h corresponds to the number of hidden units, and N_x refers to the number of input features observed at any time t. An illustrative example of such an RNN is depicted in Figure 11.

Nevertheless, due to the model's recursive architecture, taking the derivative of the objective function with respect to its parameters involves a sequence of multiplicative terms that could lead to vanishing or exploding gradients for RNNs (Bengio, Simard, & Frasconi, 1994). This issue complicates the back-propagation of gradients, resulting in an unstable training procedure and limiting RNNs' effectiveness in modeling long-term dependencies.

A significant breakthrough came in 1997 when Hochreiter and Schmidhuber (1997) introduced the Long Short-Term Memory (LSTMs) network. LSTM addressed the vanishing gradient problem by introducing memory cells and gating mechanisms that allowed the model to retain and selectively update information over prolonged sequences. This innovation dramatically improved the ability of RNNs to learn and remember over longer time periods, making LSTMs a crucial development in the field.

Much like an RNN, an LSTM maintains a chain of hidden states that undergo recursive updates. However, the LSTM architecture incorporates an internal memory cell, along with three gates – specifically the input gate, forget gate, and output gate – that oversee how information flows into and out of the cell. These gates facilitate the long-term maintenance and adjustment of the network's state over lengthy sequences. We define the gates as follows:

Input gate: $\quad i_t = \sigma(W_{i,h}h_{t-1} + W_{i,x}x_t + b_i)$,

where $W_{i,h} \in \mathbb{R}^{N_h \times N_h}, W_{i,x} \in \mathbb{R}^{N_h \times N_x}$ and $b_i \in \mathbb{R}^{N_h}$,

Output gate: $\quad o_t = \sigma(W_{o,h}h_{t-1} + W_{o,x}x_t + b_o)$,

where $W_{o,h} \in \mathbb{R}^{N_h \times N_h}, W_{o,x} \in \mathbb{R}^{N_h \times N_x}$ and $b_o \in \mathbb{R}^{N_h}$,

Forget gate: $\quad f_t = \sigma(W_{f,h}h_{t-1} + W_{f,x}x_t + b_f)$,

where $W_{f,h} \in \mathbb{R}^{N_h \times N_h}, W_{f,x} \in \mathbb{R}^{N_h \times N_x}$ and $b_f \in \mathbb{R}^{N_h}$, (41)

where we define h_{t-1} as the LSTM's hidden state at time step $t-1$ and apply the sigmoid activation function $\sigma(\cdot)$. The parameters W and b represent the model's weights and biases. The resulting cell state and hidden state at the current time step are then described by:

Cell state: $\quad c_t = f_t \odot c_{t-1} + i_t \odot \tanh(W_{c,h}h_{t-1} + W_{c,x}x_t + b_c)$,

Hidden state: : $\quad h_t = o_t \odot \tanh(c_t)$, (42)

where $\odot$ is the element-wise product, $W_{c,x} \in \mathbb{R}^{N_h \times N_x}, b_c \in \mathbb{R}^{N_h}, W_{c,h} \in \mathbb{R}^{N_h \times N_h}$, and $\tanh(\cdot)$ is the hyperbolic tangent activation function. Figure 12 plots an LSTM cell with all gates mechanisms.

LSTMs have been applied successfully in numerous fields because of their unique properties for dealing with prolonged sequences. For instance, LSTMs

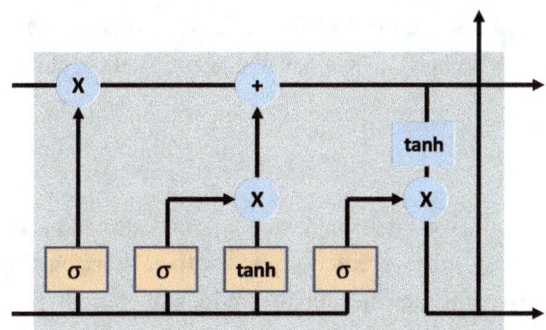

Figure 12 An illustration of an LSTM cell.

are widely used in language modeling, where they predict the next word in a sequence, as well as in machine translation, where they translate text from one language to another. For financial applications, LSTMs are also well studied and there exists a large amount of literature that applies LSTMs to predict financial time-series. Despite their success, LSTMs still suffer from several issues. Firstly, due to the gating mechanism and cell structure, LSTMs are very complex, which leads to a considerable amount of parameters that must be learned. As a result, the problem of overfitting is severe in certain applications. LSTMs are also computationally intensive, requiring lengthy training schedules.

In an effort to address the complications and drawbacks of LSTMs, Cho et al. (2014) proposed the Gated Recurrent Units (GRUs) as a more straightforward alternative. GRUs also aim to mitigate the vanishing gradient problem but do so by utilizing a reduced parameter set. This makes them computationally more efficient while often achieving performance on par with LSTMs. Unlike LSTMs, GRUs merge the forget and input gates into an update gate and also combine the cell and hidden states into a single vector. This results in fewer parameters and a leaner design. In a GRU, there are two primary gates: the update gate and the reset gate. We can summarize the operation of a GRU as follows:

$$\begin{aligned} z_t &= \sigma(W_{z,h}h_{t-1} + W_{z,x}x_t + b_i), \\ r_t &= \sigma(W_{r,h}h_{t-1} + W_{r,x}x_t + b_o), \\ \tilde{h}_t &= tanh(W_h(r_t \odot h_{t-1}) + W_{h,x}x_t), \\ h_t &= (1 - z_t) \odot h_{t-1} + z_t \odot \tilde{h}_t, \end{aligned} \quad (43)$$

where z_t functions as the update gate, r_t serves as the reset gate, $\tilde{h}_t$ denotes the candidate hidden state, and h_t corresponds to the new hidden state.

Overall, GRUs feature a more streamlined architecture than LSTMs, making them less complex to implement and quicker to train. With fewer gates and combined states, GRUs have fewer parameters, reducing the risk of overfitting. GRUs offer an efficient alternative that retains the key advantages of LSTMs. Understanding the differences and trade-offs between LSTMs and GRUs allows practitioners to choose the appropriate architecture for their specific needs.

3.6 Seq2seq and Attention

In previous sections, we focus on a single-point estimation. In other words, our model can only make predictions for a fixed horizon that is specified beforehand. If we are interested in predictions at various horizons, several models need to be fitted, with each requiring independent training. However, information flows from past to future for time-series. We could thus expect that features that are meaningful for short-term predictions could be used for long-term predictions. Therefore it would be a waste to treat them independently. Here, we introduce the Sequence-to-Sequence model (Seq2Seq) and the Attention mechanism that enable us to make multi-horizon forecasts. Both models have an encoder-decoder structure and we can simultaneously forecast all horizons of interest.

3.6.1 Sequence to Sequence Learning (Seq2Seq)

In Sutskever, Vinyals, and Le (2014), the Seq2Seq model was proposed as a significant advancement in the realm of neural networks, especially for NLP applications. The earliest Seq2Seq framework focused on machine translation, whereby text is transformed from one language into another. Prior approaches, such as statistical machine translation, had difficulty handling intricate language patterns and preserving natural fluency. The Seq2Seq model, with its encoder-decoder architecture, provides a more robust framework for handling such tasks.

A standard Seq2Seq model is comprised of two core components: an encoder that encodes an input sequence into a fixed-dimensional representation, and a decoder that leverages this representation to generate an output sequence. Early Seq2Seq implementations typically employed RNNs for both encoding and decoding. However, these RNN-based models struggled with longer input sequences, largely because of issues like vanishing gradients. This led to the adoption of LSTM networks and GRUs, which provided better handling of long-term dependencies.

Seq2Seq architectures were also soon applied to financial time-series. Notably, Z. Zhang and Zohren (2021) introduced an application of Seq2Seq and Attention models in the context of financial time-series. Consider an input sequence $x_{1:T} = (x_1, x_2, \cdots, x_T) \in \mathbb{R}^{T \times m}$, where each $x_t \in \mathbb{R}^m$ is an m-dimensional feature vector at time t and T is the total length of the sequence. The encoder processes these vectors step by step to derive meaningful features, and the resulting context vector captures the relevant information gathered by the encoder. After that, the decoder utilizes the information from the context vector and generates the output $y_{1:k} = (y_1, y_2, \cdots, y_k) \in \mathbb{R}^{k \times n}$ where k is the furthest prediction point. Specifically, given a single $x_{1:T}$, we can derive the hidden state (h_t) with the previous hidden state and current observations (x_t):

Encoder: $\quad h_t = f(h_{t-1}, x_t),$ \hfill (44)

where f can be a simple RNN model or complex recurrent network. The encoder iterates over the input sequence until it reaches the final time step, and its last

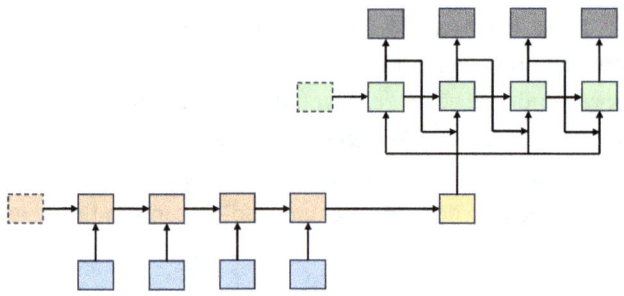

Figure 13 A typical example of a Seq2Seq network.

hidden state serves as a summary of the entire input. In Seq2Seq models, this final hidden state is often taken as the context vector c, functioning as the "bridge" between the encoder and decoder. For the decoder, the hidden state h'_t is defined as:

$$\text{Decoder:} \quad h'_t = f(h'_{t-1}, y_{t-1}, c), \tag{45}$$

and the distribution for output y_t is:

$$P(y_t | y_{t-1}, y_{t-2}, \cdots, y_1, c) = g(h'_t, c), \tag{46}$$

where f and g can be various functions but g needs to produce valid probabilities, which could be achieved through a softmax activation function (Equation 47). Figure 13 shows an example of a standard Seq2Seq network.

$$\text{softmax}(z)_i = \frac{exp(z_i)}{\sum_j^K exp(z_j)}, i = 1, \cdots, K. \tag{47}$$

Seq2Seq models have advanced a wide array of tasks in NLP and other fields. In machine translation, Seq2Seq revolutionized the field by providing more accurate and fluent translations compared to traditional methods. These abilities enabled the generation of concise summaries from long documents, aiding in information extraction and content curation. Further, Seq2Seq models powered early chatbots and virtual assistants, allowing for context-aware responses in dialogues.

A primary drawback of traditional Seq2Seq architectures is that they compress the entire input sequence into one fixed-dimensional context vector. For short sequences, this approach works reasonably well. But, for longer sequences, it becomes problematic as the context vector may not encapsulate all the relevant information. This can potentially lead to a loss of important details and degrade the quality of the generated output. Consequently, the decoder can find it challenging to generate precise and coherent outputs, especially for tasks that require retaining detailed information over extended sequences. These shortcomings led to the subsequent development of the attention mechanism.

3.6.2 Attention

The attention mechanism, introduced by Bahdanau, Cho, and Bengio (2014), enables a model to dynamically attend to different parts of an input sequence instead of relying solely upon a single fixed-size context vector. This approach leverages a system of alignment scores, attention weights, and context vectors to provide the model with greater flexibility, thereby improving its ability to handle longer sequences effectively.

In attention-based models, alignment scores are first calculated to assess the relevance of each encoder hidden state to the current decoder state, indicating how each input token influences the token being generated. These scores are then normalized with a softmax function to yield attention weights, which dynamically control how much emphasis each input token receives at each decoding step. Next, a weighted sum of the encoder hidden states is taken according to these attention weights, resulting in a context vector that highlights the most pertinent aspects of the input. This context vector is then used by the decoder to generate the next token in the output sequence.

The attention mechanism also follows an encoder-decoder architecture. We can denote the encoder's hidden state at time t by $\boldsymbol{h}_t$:

$$\text{Encoder:} \quad \boldsymbol{h}_t = f(\boldsymbol{h}_{t-1}, x_t), \tag{48}$$

where f is a non-linear function that is similar to a Seq2Seq model. The difference lies in the decoder structure as we now need to compute attention weights, alignment scores, and context vectors. Specifically, we define the context vector c_t and attention weights at the time stamp t as:

$$\begin{aligned} \text{Context vector:} \quad & c_t = \sum_{i=1}^{T} \alpha_{t,i} h_i, \\ \text{Attention weight:} \quad & \alpha_{t,i} = \frac{exp(e(\boldsymbol{h}'_{t-1}, \boldsymbol{h}_i))}{\sum_{j=1}^{T} exp(e(\boldsymbol{h}'_{t-1}, \boldsymbol{h}_j))}, \end{aligned} \tag{49}$$

where $e(\boldsymbol{h}'_{t-1}, \boldsymbol{h}_i)$ is the attention score that indicates the weights placed by the context vector on each time step of the encoder. The work of Luong, Pham, and Manning (2015) introduces three methods to compute the score:

$$e(\boldsymbol{h}'_{t-1}, \boldsymbol{h}_i) = \begin{cases} \boldsymbol{h}_i^T \boldsymbol{h}'_{t-1} & \text{dot,} \\ \boldsymbol{h}_i^T W_a \boldsymbol{h}'_{t-1} & \text{general,} \\ tanh(W_a[\boldsymbol{h}_i^T; \boldsymbol{h}'_{t-1}]) & \text{concatenate.} \end{cases} \tag{50}$$

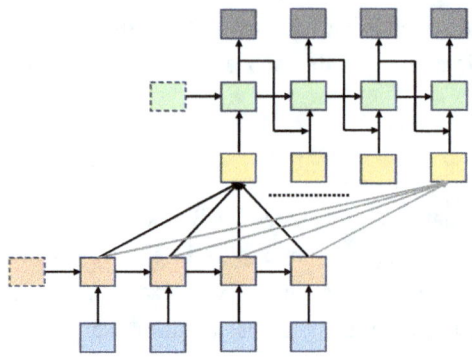

Figure 14 An example of Attention.

Finally, similar to the process for a Seq2Seq model, the context vector c_t is fed to the decoder:

$$\text{Decoder:} \quad h'_t = f(h'_{t-1}, y_{t-1}, c_t), \\ P(y_t | y_{t-1}, y_{t-2}, \cdots, y_1, c_t) = g(h'_t, c_t), \tag{51}$$

where h'_t denotes the hidden state at time t and the activation function is denoted by g. An illustrative example of the Attention mechanism is shown in Figure 14.

In essence, the attention mechanism was conceived to address the drawbacks of Seq2Seq models – namely, their dependence on a fixed-size context vector and the ensuing information bottleneck. By enabling the model to selectively focus on different regions of the input sequence, attention mechanisms substantially improve the handling of lengthy inputs and the retention of crucial contextual information.

By granting the decoder access to all the encoder hidden states, rather than relying on a single fixed-size context vector, the information bottleneck issue is significantly alleviated. Moreover, attention mechanisms promote better gradient flow during training, helping to mitigate the vanishing gradient problem in RNNs and enhancing the model's capacity to capture long-range dependencies.

3.7 Transformers

The attention mechanism is very powerful as it enables context vectors to incorporate information across longer sequences. However, such a model possesses a chain structure that is very slow to train. This problem worsens as input lengths increase. To address this issue, the Transformer network was designed by Vaswani et al. (2017) and represents a major advancement in leveraging attention mechanisms.

Unlike Seq2Seq models which have a recurrent structure that is slow to train, the Transformer architecture introduces a parallelizable attention mechanism that allows it to process entire sequences simultaneously. Transformers substantially reduce training and inference times by leveraging parallel processing, which makes them more efficient when dealing with large datasets. The parallel efficiency of the Transformer model originates from the self-attention mechanism (also referred to as scaled dot-product attention). As the foundational component of the Transformer architecture, self-attention enables the model to evaluate the relationships between all tokens within the input sequence at once, independent of their positional distance. This capability is especially beneficial for capturing long-range dependencies and makes Transformers highly scalable and versatile.

Recent architectures have consistently delivered state-of-the-art results and top-tier performance across a variety of tasks, including language translation, text summarization, and question-answering. Such models can contain billions of parameters and handle extremely large-scale datasets. For example, BERT, introduced by Devlin, Chang, Lee, and Toutanova (2018), was a groundbreaking model in natural language processing that revolutionized the way language models understand text. OpenAI's GPT series comprises autoregressive language models that have also markedly pushed forward developments in the field of natural language generation.

In this section, we carefully introduce the Transformer designed by Vaswani et al. (2017). A solid grasp of the foundational Transformer components is crucial, as many cutting-edge models extend from them. A typical Transformer architecture follows an encoder-decoder design. The encoder includes input embedding, positional encoding, and an attention mechanism. Specifically, the attention module consists of a stack of N layers, each containing a multi-head self-attention sub-layer and a position-wise fully connected feed-forward sub-layer. The decoder mirrors this structure with its own stack of layers – often of the same depth as the encoder – but each decoder layer incorporates three main sub-components: masked multi-head self-attention, encoder-decoder attention, and a position-wise feed-forward network. Figure 15 shows various components of transformers and we discuss each in detail.

3.7.1 Encoder

In traditional machine learning models, data is often represented in raw, high-dimensional forms. For transformers, this raw data is transformed into dense, continuous representations known as Input Embeddings. In the context of NLP applications, the input embedding layer transforms discrete tokens – like words or subwords – into dense vectors of a predefined dimension d_{model}. These vectors capture semantic relationships and contextual meanings of the tokens,

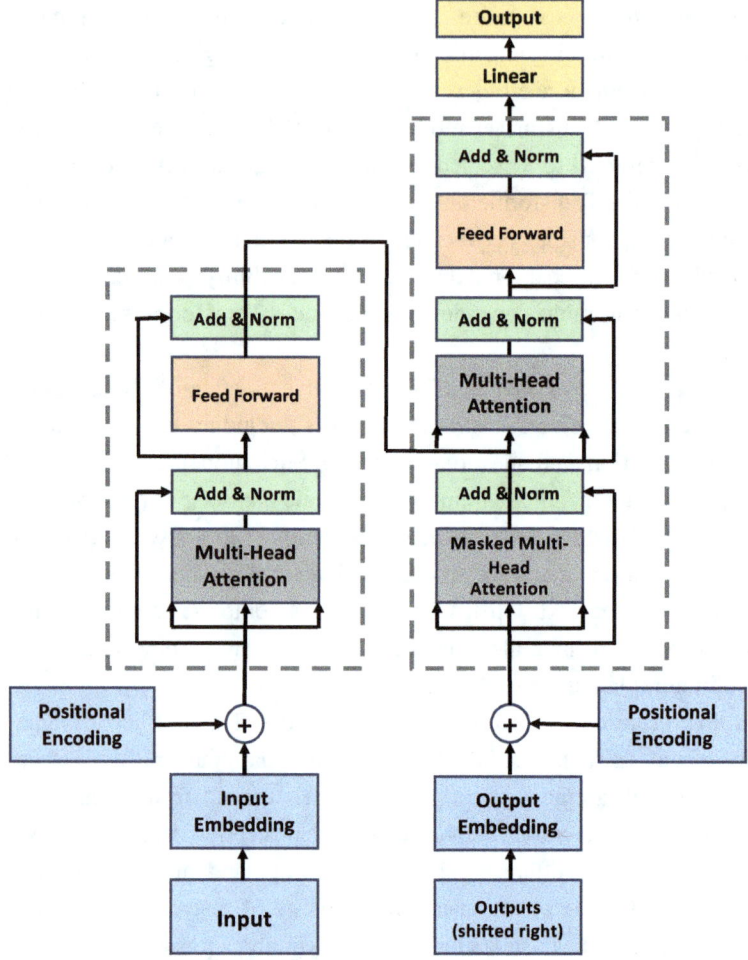

Figure 15 The Transformer model architecture as first introduced in Vaswani et al. (2017).

allowing the model to learn complex dependencies within the data. By mapping tokens into a continuous space, embeddings facilitate more efficient and effective learning and processing by the model. For time-series, we can take, for example, 1-D convolutional layer to carry out the embedding step.

Unlike RNNs or CNNs, transformers do not inherently process data in a sequential manner. This poses a challenge for capturing the order of inputs in a sequence. Transformers address this need by employing Positional Encodings, which are combined with the input embeddings to inject positional context into the model. These encodings are designed to be unique for each position in the sequence and can be generated using various methods, such as sinusoidal functions:

$$PE_{pos,2i} = sin(pos/10000^{2i/d_{model}}),$$
$$PE_{pos,2i+1} = cos(pos/10000^{2i/d_{model}}),$$
(52)

where i is the dimension and *pos* is the position. This function is used as we inspect that this simple form allows the model to study the relative position of inputs. Position encodings ensure that the model can distinguish between different positions in the sequence, thereby preserving the order and relational information that is vital for understanding positional information.

Together, input embeddings and position encodings enable transformers to handle sequential data with high flexibility and efficiency. They transform raw features into meaningful representations and incorporate positional information, allowing transformers to model intricate interconnections and dependencies. This combination is a key factor behind the impressive performance of transformers across a variety of tasks in NLP problems and beyond.

The core strength of the Transformer is rooted in the attention mechanism, specifically self-attention, which enables the model to assign varying levels of significance to different elements of the input sequence when encoding each token. Leveraging well-established mathematical foundations, this mechanism effectively manages long-range dependencies. Within the encoder, the Self-Attention Mechanism allows the model to assign varying degrees of importance to different segments of the input sequence for each token. The first step in this process consists of linear projections:

$$Q_i = W^Q x_i,$$
$$K_i = W^K x_i,$$
$$V_i = W^V x_i,$$
(53)

where each token's embedding is transformed into Query (Q), Key (K), and Value (V) vectors via learned weight matrices. Here x_i represents the internal representation of a single token for NLP tasks or a single timestamp for time-series problems.

Attention scores are determined by the dot product of the Query and Key vectors, scaled by the square root of the Key vector dimension d_k to keep the variance close to 1. These scaled scores are then passed through a softmax function to produce the attention weights:

$$\text{attention weights}(x_i, x_j) = \text{softmax}\left(\frac{Q_i^T K_j}{\sqrt{d_k}}\right),$$
(54)

where the final representation for each token is computed as a weighted sum of the Value vectors:

$$\text{output}_i = \sum_j \text{attention weights}(x_i, x_j) \cdot V_j.$$
(55)

To capture multiple aspects of token relationships, Transformers use multi-head attention. Each head performs self-attention with different sets of weight matrices:

$$\text{head}_h = \text{Attention}(\boldsymbol{Q}^h, \boldsymbol{K}^h, \boldsymbol{V}^h), \tag{56}$$

where outputs from each attention head are concatenated and then passed through a learned weight matrix:

$$\text{Multi Head} = \text{Concat}(\text{head}_1, \cdots, \text{head}_H)\boldsymbol{W}^O, \tag{57}$$

where H indicates the parallel heads. After the self-attention step, each token in the sequence is independently processed by a position-wise feed-forward network, introducing additional nonlinearity and enhancing the transformer's capacity to capture complex features beyond what self-attention alone can achieve. This network is composed of two linear transformations with a ReLU activation in between. Formally, for each token, this can be represented as:

$$\text{FFN}(x) = max(0, x\boldsymbol{W}_1 + \boldsymbol{b}_1)\boldsymbol{W}_2 + \boldsymbol{b}_2, \tag{58}$$

where $\boldsymbol{W}_1$ and $\boldsymbol{W}_2$ are trainable weight matrices, $\boldsymbol{b}_1$ and $\boldsymbol{b}_2$ are learnable biases, and $max(0, \cdot)$ represents the ReLU activation function. The FFN is applied independently to each position (i.e., each token embedding) and transforms the embeddings into a different feature space. In a two-layer FFN, the first linear transformation is often used to expand the dimensionality, while the second rescales it back to the original size.

Both the self-attention and feed-forward sub-layers incorporate residual connections and layer normalization, which help stabilize training and enhance overall performance. Layer normalization is a technique used to stabilize training by normalizing activations within each training example across the features of a given layer. Through these residual connections, the input to each sub-layer is added directly to its output, and layer normalization is applied to the sum to maintain numerical stability and convergence:

$$\text{LayerNorm}(x + \text{Sublayer}(x)). \tag{59}$$

Together, these components enable the Transformer encoder to effectively process and encode sequences. By leveraging self-attention to capture dependencies and FFNs to learn complex feature mappings, the Transformer architecture establishes a versatile and powerful foundation for numerous applications.

3.7.2 Decoder

The decoder in a Transformer architecture is integral to generating output sequences for purposes such as machine translation, text generation, and sequence-to-sequence tasks. The decoder processes representations from the encoder and produces sequential output tokens. Its design integrates key elements such as masked self-attention, multi-head attention, and position-wise feed-forward networks, all of which are instrumental in enhancing the decoder's overall effectiveness.

The decoder's masked self-attention mechanism enforces that the prediction at any position in the sequence relies only on the previously observed positions, thus maintaining the autoregressive property essential for sequence generation. To achieve this, a mask is applied to the attention weights to block the model from attending to future tokens. At each position i in the decoder, the attention scores are calculated as:

$$\text{score}(x_i, x_j) = \boldsymbol{Q}_i^T \boldsymbol{K}_j, \tag{60}$$

where $\boldsymbol{Q}_i$ and $\boldsymbol{K}_j$ are the Query and Key vectors, respectively. To prevent the leakage of future information, a mask M is applied to the scores:

$$\text{masked score}(x_i, x_j) = \frac{\boldsymbol{Q}_i^T \boldsymbol{K}_j}{\sqrt{d_k}} + M_{i,j}, \tag{61}$$

where $M_{i,j}$ is $-\infty$ if $j > i$, ensuring that the softmax function will yield zero weights for future tokens:

$$\text{attention weights}(x_i, x_j) = \text{softmax}(\text{masked score}(x_i, x_j)), \tag{62}$$

where the output for each token x_i is computed as:

$$\text{output}_i = \sum_j \text{attention weights}(x_i, x_j) \cdot V_j. \tag{63}$$

In the decoder, multi-head attention helps the model capture various aspects of the relationships between the decoder's tokens and the encoder's output. Through cross-attention, the decoder focuses on the encoder's output. For each head h, the cross-attention mechanism computes:

$$\text{head}_h = \text{Attention}(\boldsymbol{Q}_{dec}^h, \boldsymbol{K}_{enc}^h, \boldsymbol{V}_{enc}^h), \tag{64}$$

where $\boldsymbol{Q}_{dec}^h$ are the Query vectors from the decoder, and $\boldsymbol{K}_{enc}^h$ and $\boldsymbol{V}_{enc}^h$ are the Key and Value vectors from the encoder. We can concatenate the outputs from each head and transform them as:

$$\text{multi head output} = \text{Concat}(\text{head}_1, \cdots, \text{head}_h) \boldsymbol{W}^o. \tag{65}$$

Each decoder position is individually passed through a position-wise feed-forward network to improve its representational ability. This network is generally comprised of two linear layers with a ReLU activation in between. Formally, for each token x_i, the transformation is:

$$\text{FFN}(x_i) = max(0, x_i W_1 + b_1) W_2 + b_2, \tag{66}$$

where the network enables the decoder to capture complex feature interactions. Residual connections are applied around each sub-layer (self-attention, cross-attention, and feed-forward network), followed by layer normalization. For a given sub-layer output, the layer normalization is:

$$\text{LayerNorm}(x + \text{SubLayer}(x)). \tag{67}$$

By integrating masked self-attention, multi-head attention, and position-wise feed-forward networks, the decoder's architecture empowers it to produce coherent and contextually appropriate output sequences. By attending to past and present tokens and incorporating information from the encoder, the decoder can handle long-range input sequences. The final outputs are generated from the decoder autoregressively, meaning that the model relies upon the encoded input sequence and previously generated tokens to produce each subsequent token.

3.7.3 Transformers-Based Time-Series Models

The usage of transformers for time-series analysis has attracted great popularity. Because time-series problems come with their own unique challenges, such as temporal dependencies, irregular sampling, and varying sequence lengths, there has been a surge of research exploring how to tailor transformers specifically for these use cases (see Y. Wang et al. (2024) for a recent review). Broadly, one can categorize transformers designed for time-series tasks into two main groups: one based on the application domain, and another based on the underlying network architecture. Figure 16 shows the groupings of these models and their respective sub-fields.

From an application-domain perspective, time-series transformers are typically tailored toward four major tasks: forecasting, imputation, classification, and anomaly detection. Our main focus here is on forecasting, but we briefly mention all tasks for completeness. Forecasting involves predicting future values based on historical data patterns. Transformers excel here by capturing long-range temporal dependencies that classical models might miss. Imputation deals with filling in missing or corrupted data points. The self-attention mechanism helps the model learn relationships across different time steps to recover lost information. For the classification of sequences, transformers can leverage learned feature embeddings to distinguish between categories or labels associated with entire sequences or specific time intervals. Finally,

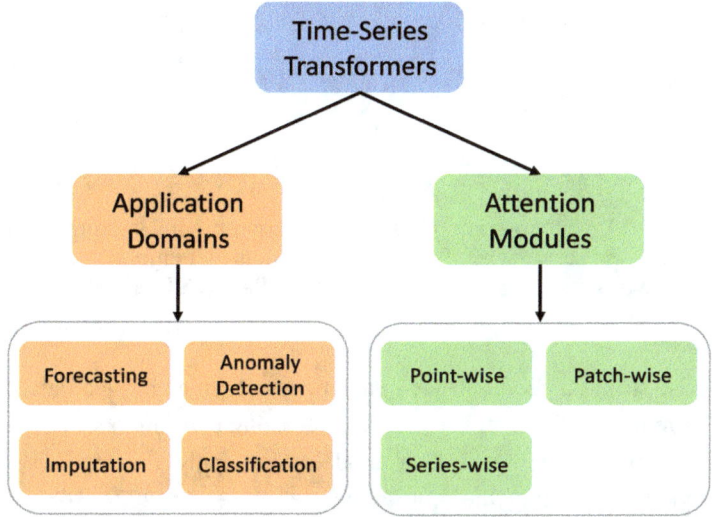

Figure 16 Groups of time-series transformers based on application domains and attention modules.

anomaly detection involves identifying unusual patterns or outliers in the data. Here, transformers can highlight subtle deviations from normal behavior by comparing attention-weighted signals across multiple timestamps.

We can also group models in terms of how attention is employed. Here we distinguish between point-wise, patch-wise, and series-wise. Point-wise attention treats each time step as an individual token, learning direct pairwise relationships across all time steps. This granular approach can capture intricate local patterns, though it might become computationally heavy for very long sequences. Patch-wise attention groups consecutive time steps into patches or segments, reducing the overall sequence length before applying attention. This strategy trades some resolution for improved efficiency and can still preserve local correlations within each patch. Finally, series-wise attention considers the entire sequence as a single unit, using more global operations to learn high-level representations of the data. While this can be extremely efficient, it risks losing some of the fine-grained temporal detail that is critical to many time-series applications. Figure 17 illustrates these attention modules.

We list each attention module with one representative work. For point-wise attention, the vanilla transformer and the Informer designed by H. Zhou et al. (2021) are illustrative examples of earlier transformer models for time-series. A good example for patch-wise attention is PatchTST designed by Nie, Nguyen, Sinthong, and Kalagnanam (2022). The series-wise attention can be found in the recently introduced iTransformer (Y. Liu et al. (2023)). There is a trade-off between the benefits from moving from point-wise to sequence-wise attention.

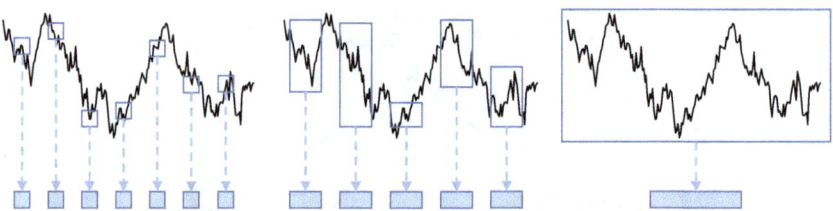

Figure 17 Categorization based on attention modules: point-wise, patch-wise, and series-wise. Examples of models that employ each of those attention types respectively are the Informer, PatchTST, and iTransformer.

Patch-wise strikes a good balance in this trade-off which has led PatchTST to outperform many other architectures in forecasting benchmarks.

Besides, there are many other models that apply one of these attention modules, including the Autoformer (H. Wu et al., 2021), Crossformer (Y. Zhang & Yan, 2023), and others. Readers might also find some of the earlier works in this area useful. These are widely covered in an earlier survey paper by Lim and Zohren (2021). Note that there are still interesting modules that we have not covered here. For example, the work of Lim, Arık, Loeff, and Pfister (2021) on the Temporal Fusion Transformer (TFT) designed a transformer architecture specifically for multi-horizon forecasting, combining the strengths of transformers with recurrent layers to handle both static and time-varying features.

Overall, we think that it is important to recognize the scope and progress that has been made on the development of transformers for time-series applications. It has become clearer which Transformers are best suited for specific time-series challenges, whether that involves capturing nuanced local trends for anomaly detection or learning broad seasonal patterns for long-term forecasting. The interplay between the nature of the data and the chosen architecture continues to shape ongoing innovations in transformer-based time-series modeling. This will continue to pave the way for increasingly accurate and robust models. For interested readers, the aforementioned recent review paper (Y. Wang et al., 2024) is a good place to start any further reading.

3.8 Graph Neural Networks and Large Language Models

In this section, we introduce some recent developments that have gained great popularity. Note that these materials are more advanced and we include them to demonstrate some directions of future development for applying deep learning models to quantitative finance. In this section, we discuss the intuition of the usage of these methods and introduce various promising resulting applications.

3.8.1 Graph Neural Networks

In the realm of machine learning, the advent of graph neural networks (GNNs) has marked a significant evolution in our ability to process, analyze, and derive insights from data that can be modeled by graphs. Graph representations, with nodes that represent entities and edges that represent their relationships, pervade numerous domains including social networks, molecular chemistry, transportation systems, and communication networks. Traditional neural network models, despite their prowess, fall short when it comes to capturing the dependencies and relational information inherent in graph data. GNNs are a groundbreaking class of neural networks engineered to explicitly handle graph structures and have led to a leap forward in areas such as node classification, link prediction, and graph classification.

In finance, we can often naturally represent the interactions among entities (such as individuals, institutions, and assets) as graphs. GNNs provide a framework to process such graph-structured data. Research on the application of GNNs in quantitative finance has been active in the past few years. The works of Pu, Roberts, Dong, and Zohren (2023); C. Zhang, Pu, Cucuringu, and Dong (2023) adopt GNNs to build momentum strategies and to forecast multivariate realized volatility. Soleymani and Paquet (2021); Sun, Wei, and Yang (2024) combine GNNs with reinforcement learning to tackle the problem of portfolio construction. For a nice review on GNNs in various financial applications, interested readers are pointed to the work of J. Wang, Zhang, Xiao, and Song (2021). Here, we introduce the basics of networks and, in particular, we describe the most prevalent GNN model, graph convolutional neural networks (GCNs).

Basics of Networks and Graphs The core strength of GNNs stems from their capacity to learn representations of nodes (or entire graphs) that encapsulate not only their features but also the rich context provided by their connections. Such operations are achieved through mechanisms like message passing, aggregating information across neighboring nodes, and iteratively refining their representations. This process allows GNNs to capture both local structures and global graph topology, offering a nuanced understanding of graph-structured data. Before delving into GNNs, we need to understand the basics of networks and graphs. To start, we define a graph $\mathcal{G}$ as:

$$\mathcal{G} = (\mathcal{V}, \mathcal{E}), \tag{68}$$

where $\mathcal{V} = \{v_1, \cdots, v_n\}$ denotes the set of n nodes and $\mathcal{E}$ represents the set of edges. An edge $e_{ij} = (v_i, v_j) \in \mathcal{E}$ indicates a connection between nodes v_i and v_j.

Nodes (also called vertices) represent the entities or objects in a graph. In different contexts, a node could represent a computer in a network, a person in a social network, a city in a transportation map, or a neuron in a neural network. Edges (also called links) represent the connections or relationships between these nodes. Edges can be undirected, indicating a bidirectional relationship, or directed, indicating a one-way relationship (these form a directed graph or digraph). Edges may also have weights, which quantify the strength or capacity of the connection, such as the distance between cities, bandwidth in a network, or the strength of a social tie.

In order to describe a graph, we need a way to represent nodes and edges in a compact form. This is done in the form of an adjacency matrix. An adjacency matrix $\mathbf{A}$ is a $n \times n$ matrix, where $\mathbf{A}_{ij}$ indicates the connectivity status between node v_i and v_j. Depending on the nature of the problem, there are many types of graphs:

- Undirected graphs: These are graphs with edges that lack direction, meaning each connection between two nodes is inherently bidirectional.
- Directed Graphs (Digraphs): Graphs in which edges carry a direction, representing a one-way relationship from one node to another. For example, $e_{ij} = (v_i, v_j) \in \mathcal{E}$ denotes an edge pointing from node v_i to node v_j.
- Bipartite Graphs: This is a distinct type of graph in which nodes are divided into two separate groups, and every edge connects a node from one group to a node in the other group, with no edges existing within the same group.
- Homogeneous graphs: Graphs where all nodes and edges are of a single type.
- Heterogeneous Graphs: Graphs that contain multiple types of nodes and/or edges. For example, we can denote a graph as $\mathcal{G} = (\mathcal{V}, \mathcal{E}, t : \mathcal{V} \to \mathcal{A}, \tau : \mathcal{E} \to \mathcal{R})$, where each node $v_i \in \mathcal{V}$ is assigned a type $a_i \in \mathcal{A}$ by function t and each edge $e_{ij} \in \mathcal{E}$ is assigned a type $r_{ij} \in \mathcal{R}$ by function τ.
- Dynamic graph: A dynamic graph is defined as a sequence of graphs $\mathcal{G}^{seq} = \{\mathcal{G}_1, \cdots, \mathcal{G}_T\}$, where each $\mathcal{G}_i = (\mathcal{V}_i, \mathcal{E}_i)$ for $i = 1, \cdots, T$. In this sequence, $\mathcal{V}_i, \mathcal{E}_i$ represent the sets of nodes and edges for the i-th graph, respectively.

Graph Convolutional Neural Networks In the work of Z. Wu et al. (2020), GNNs are classified into four main categories: convolutional graph neural networks, graph auto-encoders, recurrent graph neural networks, and spatial-temporal graph neural networks. In this section, we introduce graph convolutional neural networks (GCNs) which have become the most widely adopted and extensively utilized GNN models.

As previously mentioned, CNNs have seen tremendous success in handling data with established grid-like structures, such as images. The fundamental principle of CNNs lies in the convolution operation, which entails moving a filter (or kernel) across the input data (e.g., an image) to generate a feature map. This feature map highlights the presence of particular features or patterns at various positions within the input. This process is inherently suited to data with a regular, grid-like structure where the relative positioning of data points (e.g., pixels in images) is consistent and meaningful.

GCNs (Kipf & Welling, 2016) extend the concept of convolution to graph-structured data, where the data points (nodes) are connected by edges in a non-Euclidean domain. Unlike the regular, grid-like topology of images, graphs are irregular, and the number of neighbors for each node can be different. GCNs address this by defining convolution in terms of feature aggregation from a node's neighbors, allowing them to capture the structural information of the graph. The fundamental operation in a GCN is this aggregation of features from a node's neighbors, and it can be mathematically represented as:

$$H^{l+1} = \sigma(\hat{D}^{-\frac{1}{2}} \hat{A} \hat{D}^{-\frac{1}{2}} H^{(l)} W^{(l)}), \qquad (69)$$

where the matrix of node features at layer l is denoted as $H^{(l)}$ and $H^{(0)}$ is the input feature matrix X. We write $\hat{A} = A + I_N$ as the addition between the adjacency matrix A and identity matrix I_N, allowing nodes to consider their own features in aggregation. $\hat{D}$ is the degree matrix of $\hat{A}$, where $\hat{D}_{ii} = \sum_j \hat{A}_{ij}$, and $W^{(l)}$ is the weight matrix for layer l. Here σ denotes a nonlinear activation function, such as ReLU.

Simply put, much like traditional CNNs are constructed from convolutional layers, GCNs are built by stacking multiple graph convolutional layers. Each graph convolutional layer receives the node vectors from the previous layer (or the initial input feature vectors for the first layer) and generates new output vectors for each node. To illustrate this process, Figure 18 depicts how a graph convolutional layer aggregates the vectors from each node's neighbors.

In Figure 18, the vector for node A, labeled x_A, is combined with the vectors of its neighboring nodes, x_B and x_C. This combined vector is then transformed or updated to produce node A's vector in the next layer, denoted as h_A. This process is uniformly applied to every node in the graph. This technique is commonly referred to as message passing, where each node "passes" its vector to its neighbors to facilitate the updating of their vectors. The "message" from each node is its associated vector. The specific rules for aggregation and updating are detailed in Equation 69.

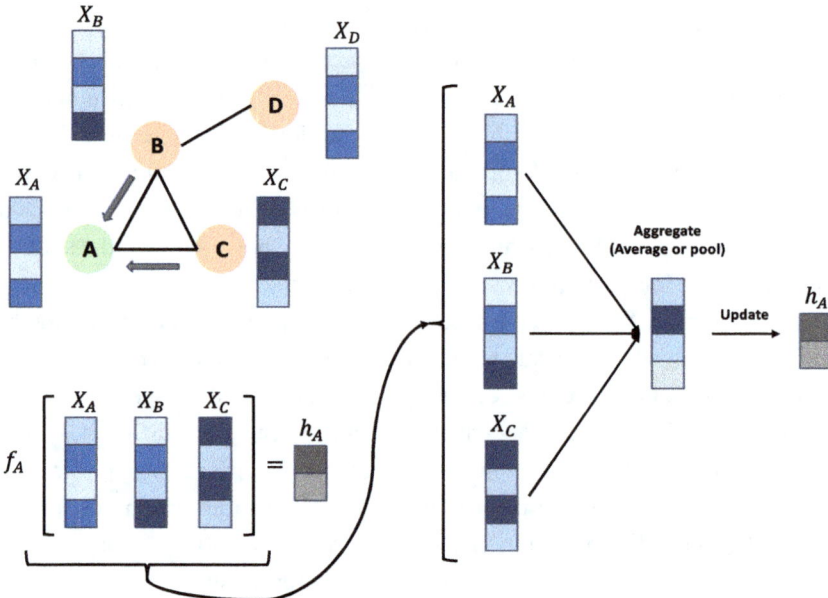

Figure 18 A graph convolution layer that pools information for node A from its neighbors.

Once we stack several graph convolutional layers, we form a typical GCN as shown in Figure 19. The output of a GCN depends on the problem at hand. Graph prediction tasks are commonly classified into three categories: graph-level, node-level, and edge-level. When dealing with a node-level task, such as classifying individual nodes, the vectors generated for each node can serve as the final outputs of the model. In the case of node classification, these output vectors may represent the probabilities that each node belongs to specific classes. This is illustrated in the top section of Figure 20.

Alternatively, we might focus on a "graph-level" task, where the objective is to generate a single output for the entire graph rather than producing outputs for each individual node. For example, the goal could be to classify entire graphs instead of classifying each node separately. In this case, the vectors from all nodes are collectively input into another neural network (such as a simple multilayer perceptron) that processes them together to produce a single output vector. This is illustrated in the bottom part of Figure 20.

Edge-level tasks focus on predicting properties or attributes related to the edges in a graph. These tasks are important for understanding and interpreting the relationships between entities represented by the nodes in a graph. For example, we can predict whether a link (edge) should exist between two nodes, even if it is not present in the observed data. This task is fundamental in

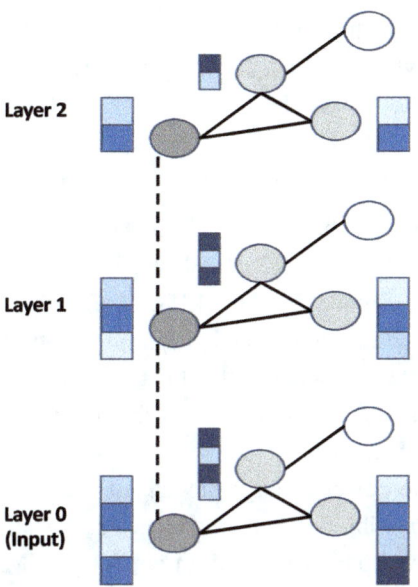

Figure 19 A GCN that consists of multilayers.

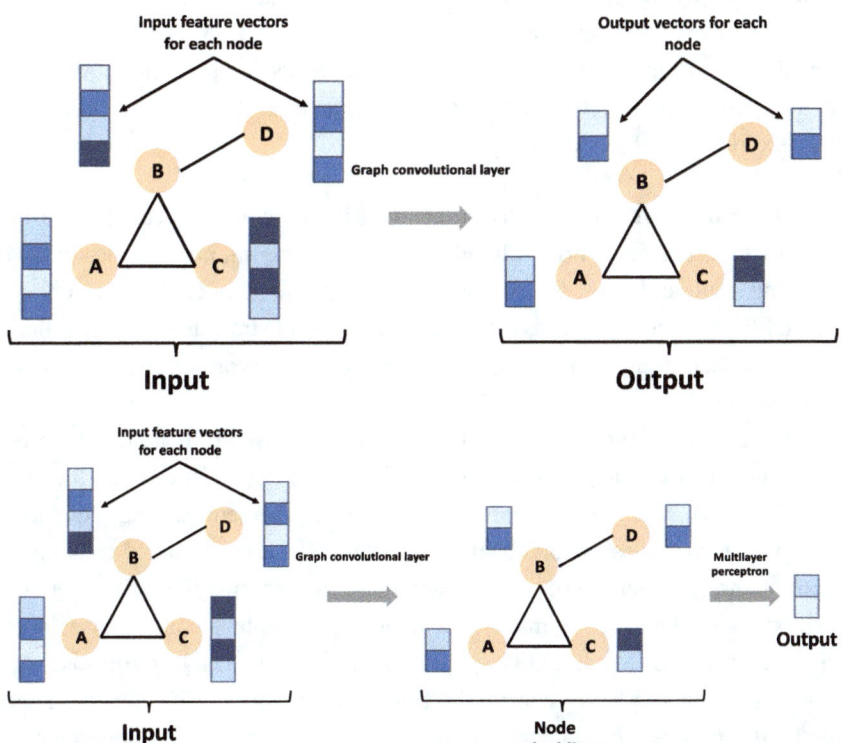

Figure 20 Top: a "node-level" prediction task; **Bottom:** a "graph-level" prediction task.

various applications, such as recommending friends in social networks, predicting interactions between proteins in biological networks, or inferring missing connections in knowledge graphs.

3.8.2 Large Language Models and Generative AI

Recent developments of the GPT-3 and GPT-4 models behind ChatGPT, a breakthrough generative language model, stand as a pinnacle of innovation in the domain of large language models (LLMs), offering a compelling glimpse into the future of human–computer interaction. ChatGPT, along with other models such as Bard and Claude, without a doubt, has revolutionized not only our daily lives but also the way we work, ushering in a transformative period for human-computer interaction.

By leveraging the power of large language models, ChatGPT has opened up unprecedented possibilities in the financial sector and has inspired a wave of research and development focused on applying LLMs to tackle complex challenges in finance. Some examples include automating customer service, market analysis, fraud detection, and more. We next introduce you to the evolution of large language models and discuss the rationale behind the strength of LLMs. However, the development and cointegration of LLMs and quantitative finance are still in the early stages. We also present some potential limitations of applying current state-of-the-art LLMs to quantitative finance and potential future directions of work.

Evolution of LLMs   The evolution of language models has been marked by significant milestones, primarily advancements in neural network design and learning methodologies. Starting with RNNs, the journey to develop models like BERT and the GPT series showcases a remarkable trajectory of innovation, with each leap strengthening the models' capabilities to capture and understand language at scale.

RNNs were among the first neural architectures used to handle sequential data, such as text. Their design allows information to persist through the network's hidden states, theoretically enabling them to remember long sequences of inputs. Nonetheless, in practical applications, RNNs encountered challenges with maintaining long-term dependencies due to problems like vanishing and exploding gradients. This made it challenging to capture context over large spans of text. LSTMs and GRUs, variants of the basic RNN, introduced gating mechanisms to better control the flow of information. This addresses the issue of long-term dependencies to a significant extent. These improvements allowed for more effective learning from longer sequences, leading to better performance on a wide range of NLP tasks.

Subsequently, BERT introduced an innovative method by pre-training a deeply bidirectional model that simultaneously incorporated both left and right contexts across all layers. This approach marked a significant shift from earlier models, which typically processed text in only one direction. Leveraging the Transformer architecture's attention mechanism, BERT effectively understands a word's context by taking into account its entire surrounding environment. This led to notable improvements in tasks like question answering and language inference. Finally, GPT series, starting with GPT-1 and extending to GPT-3 and beyond, emphasized generative pre-training of transformer-based models (only using the decoder part) on a diverse corpus of text, followed by fine-tuning on specific tasks. GPT models demonstrated remarkable text generation capabilities, understanding and generating human-like text across various genres and styles. Their scalable architecture enabled them to learn from vast datasets, capturing deep linguistic patterns.

The evolution from RNNs to sophisticated models like BERT and GPT demonstrates a quantum leap in the field of NLP. Each step in this journey introduced innovations that significantly expanded the capabilities of language models, moving from basic text processing to understanding context, nuance, and even generating coherent and contextually relevant text. These advancements have not only pushed the boundaries of what is possible with machine understanding of language but have also opened up new avenues for human-computer interaction, making machines better conversationalists, writers, and analysts. The future of language models promises even greater integration into daily technology use, making it difficult to distinguish between content created by humans and that generated by machines

What Made LLMs So Powerful? LLMs have become incredibly powerful due to a combination of factors that include algorithmic developments, advancements in computational capabilities, and access to extensive amounts of textual data for training. Following are the primary factors that enhance the effectiveness of large language models.

LLMs are trained on extensive corpora that encompass a wide range of human knowledge and language use, from literature and websites to scientific articles and social media content. This broad coverage enables the models to learn a diverse set of language patterns, idioms, and domain-specific knowledge. The sheer volume of data ensures that the model encounters numerous examples of language use, facilitating the learning of complex linguistic structures and nuances. In addition, LLMs are often pre-trained on a general corpus and then adapted for particular applications using smaller, specialized datasets. This approach, called fine-tuning, allows the models to apply their broad understanding of language to particular domains or applications, significantly enhancing effectiveness in activities such as text classification, responding to questions, and generating written content.

The creation of advanced neural network frameworks, especially the Transformer architecture, has been pivotal. Transformers utilize self-attention mechanisms to handle data sequences. This allows the model to assess the significance of various words within a sentence or document. This ability to understand context and relationships between words significantly enhances the model's understanding of language. Specifically, the adoption of attention mechanisms allows LLMs to focus on relevant parts of the input data when making predictions or generating text. This capability allows the model to study the broader context of a word or phrase and lead to more accurate and coherent outputs.

Training large language models demands considerable computational power, often utilizing clusters of GPUs or TPUs for periods that extend from weeks to several months. Advances in hardware and the availability of cloud computing resources have made it feasible to train models with billions or even trillions of parameters. The scale of these models allows them to capture a vast range of linguistic patterns and knowledge, contributing to their effectiveness. Furthermore, the iterative development of LLMs, in which each new version builds upon the learnings and feedback from previous iterations, has steadily improved their performance. Additionally, the engagement of the research community and industry in developing, testing, and deploying these models has led to rapid advancements and innovative applications.

In summary, the power of large language models lies not just in their size but in the convergence of these technological and methodological advancements. They represent a synthesis of data, computational resources, and cutting-edge algorithms, resulting in tools that are able to comprehend and create text that closely mimics human language with exceptional skill.

LLMs for Time-Series Forecasting and Quantitative Finance LLMs have already sparked significant interest in quantitative finance and time-series analysis in general. Although LLMs models are trained largely on textual corpora, researchers have begun adapting them for forecasting problems by "translating" numerical or temporal patterns into a format that LLMs can process. The core idea is that LLMs have learned powerful sequence-modeling capabilities, which can be harnessed beyond natural language. By carefully encoding time-series data as a pseudo-text input, an LLM can in principle capture long-range dependencies, temporal structures, and contextual nuances in much the same way it understands linguistic patterns (X. Zhang et al., 2024).

One notable approach along these lines is Time-LLM (Jin et al., 2023). This method cleverly reprograms a large language model to treat time-series observations as tokens in a sequence. Specifically, the time-indexed data points are formatted into a textual prompt in which the LLM is asked to "complete" the sequence effectively performing a forecast. Despite being originally designed for language tasks, this work provides an example of how the LLM's internal attention mechanisms and capacity for pattern recognition can be extended to temporal prediction. Time-LLM has shown promising results on a variety of benchmarks, demonstrating that large language models can be repurposed for time-series forecasting with relatively minimal changes to their architecture. By leveraging training on massive text corpora, Time-LLM highlights a new direction for cross-domain learning, where the underlying skills of an LLM are refocused on numerical patterns and trends over time.

Despite their advanced capabilities, the usage of LLMs in quantitative finance is still in the early stage. In the second part of this Element, we will discuss how LLMs can be used for volatility forecasting and portfolio optimization. In this section, we discuss some limitations that LLMs face when applied to the domain of quantitative finance. These limitations stem from the unique challenges and requirements of the financial sector, including the need for precise numerical analysis, real-time decision-making, and understanding of complex financial instruments and markets.

LLMs excel at processing and generating text but often struggle with understanding and manipulating numerical data to the extent required in quantitative finance. Financial analysis often involves complex mathematical models and statistical methods that are beyond the current capabilities of language-based models. Integrating LLMs with specialized numerical processing systems remains a challenge. Furthermore, the financial markets are dynamic, with conditions that change rapidly. LLMs trained on historical data may not adapt quickly enough to real-time data or sudden market shifts. The latency in processing new information and updating models can be a limitation in time-sensitive financial applications.

On the one hand, LLMs can be fine-tuned with financial texts to understand domain-specific language. However, truly grasping the intricacies of financial instruments, regulatory environments, and market mechanisms requires a level of expertise that LLMs may not achieve solely through language training. This gap can lead to inaccuracies or oversimplified analyses when processing complex financial scenarios. On the other hand, there is a continual concern with respect to overfitting, a scenario where a model excels on its training dataset but fails to perform well with new, unseen data as future market conditions can differ significantly from historical patterns. Ensuring that LLMs generalize well to new, unseen market conditions without overfitting to past data remains a challenge. Also, most existing LLMs are trained up-to-date, so they can not be used for historical backtests because of the look-ahead bias due to the information leakage problem.

While large language models hold strong potential for revolutionizing many aspects of quantitative finance, addressing these limitations is important for their effective and responsible application. Ongoing research and development efforts are focused on overcoming these challenges and show promise for the improvement of the capabilities of LLMs in financial analysis, prediction, and decision-making.

3.8.3 Other Recent Developments: State-Space Models and xLSTM

State-space models provide a framework for modeling dynamic systems by representing a system's evolution over time with a set of latent variables. Also, state-space models are the underlying mathematical framework that the Kalman filter (Kalman, 1960) operates on. These models are also very popular in time-series analysis because they can seamlessly incorporate various sources of uncertainty and are adaptable to complex systems. Recent work, Mamba (Gu & Dao, 2023) marks a noteworthy breakthrough in the area of sequence modeling, particularly for time-series data. Traditional sequence models often face challenges because of their computational complexity and capturing long-range dependencies in data. Mamba addresses these issues by leveraging selective state spaces to model sequences efficiently.

The core of Mamba is the concept of selective state spaces, which enables the model to hone in on the sequence's most critical elements while discarding extraneous or less important information. This selective attention mechanism is key to Mamba's ability to operate in linear time, a crucial feature for handling large-scale time-series data where computational efficiency is paramount. By narrowing the state space to only the most important components, Mamba can maintain high accuracy in sequence predictions while significantly reducing the computational overhead.

The linear-time complexity of Mamba is particularly beneficial for real-world applications where speed and scalability are critical. For instance, in financial markets, where vast amounts of noisy high-frequency data need to be processed in real-time, Mamba's approach allows for rapid and accurate modeling of sequences without sacrificing performance. Additionally, the model's ability to selectively study relevant states makes it robust to noise and capable of adjusting to a wide range of time-series data types, from economic indicators to sensor readings in IoT devices.

Another recent work proposed by Beck et al. (2024) designed xLSTM which expands upon a traditional LSTM network to tackle certain inherent shortcomings of standard recurrent networks while enhancing their capabilities for complex sequence modeling tasks. While LSTMs have shown to be very effective in sequential modeling, they can sometimes struggle with certain types of data patterns, especially when tackling very long sequences or when the relationships between data points are highly nonlinear and intricate.

One of the key innovations in xLSTM is the ability to dynamically adjust its memory and learning mechanisms based on the complexity and nature of the data it encounters. Traditional LSTMs use fixed gates for controlling the flow of information, which can be limiting when faced with varying data characteristics. In contrast, xLSTM introduces adaptive mechanisms that allow the network to modulate its memory retention and forgetfulness more effectively. This adaptability enables xLSTM to maintain a high level of performance even when dealing with sequences that have non-stationary patterns or when the relevant information spans a wide range of time steps. By extending the core LSTM architecture, xLSTM is better equipped to capture complex dependencies that might be missed by more rigid models.

The introduction of xLSTM is a significant breakthrough in the ongoing development of neural network architectures for sequence modeling. Kong, Wang, et al. (2024) builds on xLSTM to particularly model multivariate time-series. They improve and revise the memory storage of xLSTM to fit with time-series analysis and adopt patching techniques to ensure that long-term dependencies can be studied.

4 The Model Training Workflow

Having discussed basic descriptive analyses of financial time-series as well as supervised learning frameworks in the context of financial applications, we now present a comprehensive pipeline for the model training workflow. Overall, developing a quantitative trading strategy with deep networks requires a systematic approach to properly evaluate model performance and adjust model configurations. Ensuring that this procedure is transparent and replicable is crucial for successful deployment. This section covers common frameworks to design and train networks in various settings.

Essentially, we can divide the whole process into six parts: problem setup, data collection and cleaning, feature extraction, model construction, cross-validation and hyperparameter tuning, and final deployment. This framework, as illustrated in Figure 21, outlines the essential steps of formulating, training, tuning, and evaluating model performance in a systematic way. We now briefly

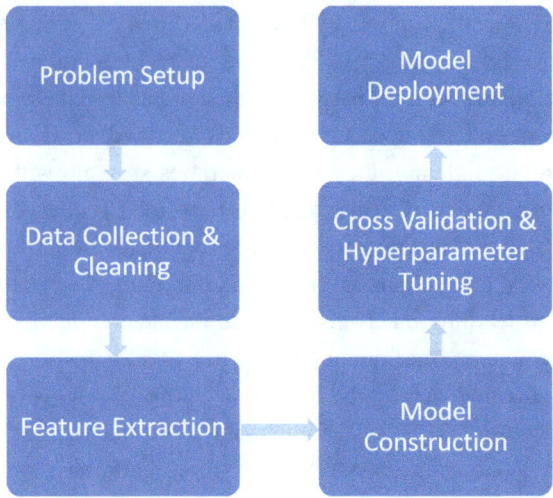

Figure 21 Key steps of the model training workflow.

introduce each of these steps and discuss cross-validation and hyperparameter tuning specific to financial time-series in detail.

4.1 Problem Setup

The starting point for any application is to scope out the ultimate objective and clearly define the stages of the work process. If, for example, our goal is to generate a predictive signal, we need to consider various aspects of the desired signals, including frequency, asset type, and turnover. Even if it is difficult to build an exhaustive list, it is always better to consider these points beforehand. In this section, we provide a prediction task as an example and introduce the stages of generating a signal for trading. Note that the introduced workflow is not tied only to prediction problems but can also be used as a framework for many other applications. In particular, the sections on cross-validation and hyperparameter tuning can be applied across problems.

In the previous section, we explored how supervised learning can be grouped into two main categories: regression and classification. Depending on the desired outputs, the task may be framed as a regression problem aiming to predict returns or as a classification problem placing stocks into performance categories such as return quantiles. Knowing the target format helps us to choose objective functions, features, and proper evaluation metrics.

4.2 Data Collection and Cleaning

After defining our objective, we need to choose an appropriate dataset and carry out cleaning processes to make sure the dataset represents the application of our interest. We have introduced several methods to source market price data in Appendix B and, importantly, we need to choose the frequency of interest and price formats. High-frequency microstructure market data or down-sampled price and volume data are two possible examples specific to quantitative trading. Different formats might influence network architectures and change the amount of training data required.

Beyond obtaining the right dataset, data preparation is a vital step and might affect our model performance in unexpected ways if it is carried out poorly. Missing data is one of the common problems that we might encounter when dealing with time-series. Hence, we need be extremely careful to make sure that there is no leakage of future information (also known as a look-ahead bias) when choosing to impute these missing values. Having access to future information might erroneously boost training performance but will lead to very poor out-of-sample results.

Additionally, it is important to store data in a format that permits swift exploration and iteration. Beyond databases, popular choices are pickle, HDF, or Parquet formats – each with its own advantages and disadvantages. For data exceeding available memory or requiring distributed processing across multiple machines, parallel computing can also be employed.

4.3 Feature Extraction

One of the primary advantages of employing neural networks is the ability to automate feature extraction. However, a model still might not be able to generalize well on out-of-sample data if we feed networks with excessive irrelevant information, especially when the signal-to-noise ratio is very low as is typical in financial applications. We should first get a sense of data that we are working with and understand the relationship between targets and variables. This can help us choose the most appropriate algorithm and carry out transformations as needed. As introduced in Section 2, we can use visualizations such as histograms or QQ-plots to examine our data.

As an example, we aim to predict next-day trading volumes V_{t+1}. When looking at a histogram we observe several issues. Firstly, trading volumes are always positive. To deal with this, one might choose to model the logarithm $\log V_{t+1}$. Furthermore, when plotting this over time we might observe non-stationarities. It is thus advisable to model the next day's volume normalized by a trailing measure of volume, such as the 20-day median volume at day t, $\tilde{V}_t$. We would thus choose to build a model to predict $\log(V_{t+1}/\tilde{V}_t)$ and choose similar normalizations for input features that refer to past volumes, such as $\log(V_{t-d}/\tilde{V}_t)$ for $d = 0, 1, 2, \ldots$.

We can also calculate numerical metrics such as correlation and nonlinear statistics such as the Spearman rank correlation coefficient. A systematic and thorough exploratory data analysis is the basis of building a successful predictive signal. Information-theoretic approaches, including mutual information (Vergara & Estévez, 2014), can also be used to better understand variable relationships. After exploring the data, we can begin to design and properly normalize features from a meaningful set that could boost model performance, speed up the training process, and help with convergence.

Nevertheless, feature engineering is a complex process that draws on domain expertise, statistical and information theory principles, and creative insights. It involves clever data transformations aimed at uncovering the systematic links between input and output variables. Practitioners can employ numerous approaches, such as outlier detection and remediation, functional transformations, and integrating multiple variables. We can also even leverage unsupervised learning. Although the focus of this Element is not on feature engineering, we emphasize that this plays a central role in building quantitative trading strategies, and in practice, it is sometimes learned through trial and error.

4.4 Model Construction

We have introduced a wide range of neural network architectures, ranging from canonical examples such as multilayer perceptrons and CNNs to state-of-the-art transformer-based architectures for time-series. In general, neural networks are flexible function approximators that require few assumptions about data distributions. However, they often need a large dataset to calibrate model weights to successfully model the relationships between inputs and targets.

When constructing a network, one of the most important factors to consider is the bias-variance trade-off. Our goal is to evaluate and adjust the model's complexity using estimates of its generalization error. In order to properly tune the model to obtain decent out-of-sample performance, we need be aware of how the bias-variance trade-off relates to under and overfitting. In general, we can break down prediction errors into reducible and irreducible parts. The irreducible part is due to random variation (noise) in the data such as natural variation or measurement errors. This type of error is out of our control and cannot be reduced by model choice.

The reducible portion of generalization error can be divided into bias and variance errors. Both types arise from differences between the true functional relationship and the model's approximation. If a model is too simple to capture a dataset's complex structure, we might get poor results due to the model's inability to capture the complexity of the true functional form. This type of error is called bias. For example, if a true relationship is quadratic, but our model is linear, even an infinite amount of data would not be enough to recover the true relationship. This is exactly the bias part of the bias-variance trade-off.

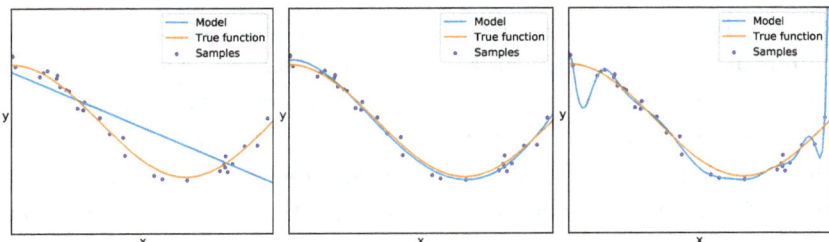

Figure 22 A visual example of under and overfitting with polynomials.

On the contrary, if a model is too complex, it shows superior performance on training data, but might end up overfitting as it starts extracting information from the noise instead of learning true patterns in the data. As a result, it learns idiosyncrasies from training data which likely would not be found in the testing set, and consequently, the out-of-sample predictions will vary widely. This is the variance part of the bias-variance trade-off.

Figure 22 illustrates the concepts of under and overfitting. We assess the in-sample errors when approximating a sine function using polynomials of increasing complexity. Specifically, we generate thirty random samples with added noise and fit polynomials of varying degrees to these data points. The model then makes predictions on new data, and we record the mean-squared error for these forecasts. In the left panel of Figure 22, a first-degree polynomial is fitted to the data, clearly demonstrating that a straight line does not adequately capture the true function. However, the estimated lines remain relatively consistent across different samples drawn from the underlying function. It thus has high bias and low variance. The right panel shows a polynomial of degree 15 fitted to the same data. It closely matches the small sample data but fails to accurately estimate the true relationship because it has overfitted upon the random variations in the sample points. As a result, the learned function is highly sensitive to the specific sample, exhibiting low bias and high variance. The middle panel illustrates that a fifth-degree polynomial provides a reasonably accurate approximation of the true relationship within the interval. It is the Goldilocks example which is just right. It simultaneously has a variance that is only slightly higher than the model on the left and a bias that is only slightly higher than the model on the right, so that the sum of the two yields the lowest generalization error.

4.5 Cross Validation

Once we train multiple models, we need to compare them and choose the most appropriate one. Recall that the ultimate goal for any supervised learning algorithm is to make good predictions on testing data, and that this requires models to generalize performance from the training set to unseen instances. In order to fulfill this goal, we often split data into three sets: training, validation, and testing sets. Model weights are first calibrated on the training data. Then we can take a subset of training data (not used during the training process) to form the validation set which evaluates model performance so that we can compare different algorithms and select the best model architecture based on the bias-variance trade-off.

The reason for using the validation set in addition to the test set is to preserve the test set and not touch it until the final evaluation. Otherwise, we could artificially boost model performance. This occurs because, each time we use our test set for evaluating a model, we are effectively learning from that test set. The more frequently we do this, the more the model learns from the test set and is corrupted. This type of information leakage is especially detrimental for financial time-series as we are attempting to model causal relationships. Besides comparing different network architectures on a fixed validation set, we often resort to systematic cross-validation to perform hyperparameter optimization. Deep networks are sensitive to many hyperparameters, for example, the number of neurons in a layer, learning rate and batch size. We will discuss the exact techniques for choosing hyperparameters in the next section.

In general, K-fold cross-validation is a standard technique used for tuning hyperparameters. However, cross-validation for time-series is nontrivial. The first and most important difference for time-series is that we can not randomly assign samples to either training or validation set because, if so, we might end up training with future information. In other words, temporal dependency exists between observations and we must be sure not to include this during the training process. Otherwise, we could obtain a seemingly "superior" model that in reality has poor generalization ability. To understand this point better, let us give an example. Imagine we had intraday price data at either tick or 1 second frequency and our aim was to make predictions of the future price move over the next 5 minutes, that is, 300 seconds. The sample which includes the future return from t to $t + 300$, and the sample one second later, which includes the return from $t + 1$ to $t + 301$, are highly correlated if not virtually the same. Randomly shuffling the data could end up placing one of these samples in the training data and one in the test set. The effect of this is similar to testing on in-sample data because of the high correlation. In order to solve the aforementioned limitation, we utilize hold-out cross-validation in which samples are chronologically fed into validation sets after being used for training. Specifically, we can start cross-validation on a rolling basis. Figure 24 shows this process where the validation set comes chronologically after the training subset. Note that it is not necessary to gradually increase the training set. We can

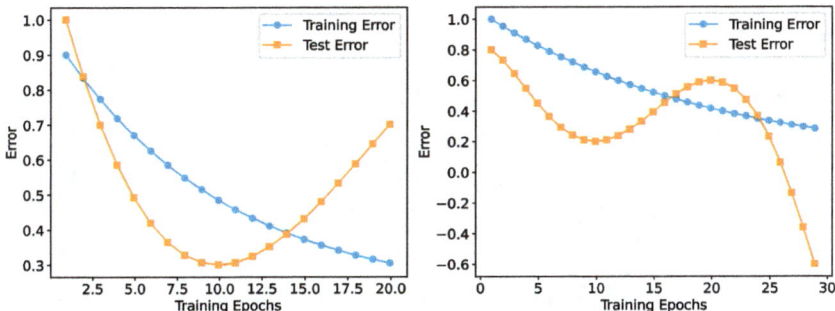

Figure 23 **Left**: traditional U-shaped overfitting curve; **Right**: double descent error curve.

implement this rolling forward cross-validation by Listing 1 in Appendix D and more information can found in our GitHub repository.[8]

Recently, there has been research on a concept called Double Descent which is a phenomenon observed in over-parameterized deep networks where the test error curve exhibits two distinct "descent" phases. Double descent is a phenomenon observed in modern, over-parameterized deep learning models where the test error curve, expressed as a function of model complexity or training time, exhibits not just one but two distinct "descent" phases. Traditionally, one might expect the test error to reach a minimum at some intermediate model complexity and then increase (due to overfitting) as complexity grows. However, with double descent, after initially declining and then peaking around the point where the model just fits the training data (the "interpolation threshold"), the test error goes down a second time as model complexity or training continues to increase. In effect, very large or heavily trained models often end up generalizing better than smaller ones. Figure 23 compares the traditional U-shaped error curve and the double descent error curve. This concept is counter to classic underfitting/overfitting intuition. We have not observed similar patterns within financial time-series but nonetheless it might inspire new possibilities.

4.6 Hyperparameter Tuning

We have briefly mentioned hyperparameters, but we now take a careful look at them as they are important components in the construction of a successful deep neural network. When creating a network, we are presented with many choices. It is nontrivial to set hyperparameter values beforehand and we need a systemic

---

[8] See DeepLearningQuant.com or https://github.com/zcakhaa/Deep-Learning-in-Quantitative-Trading.

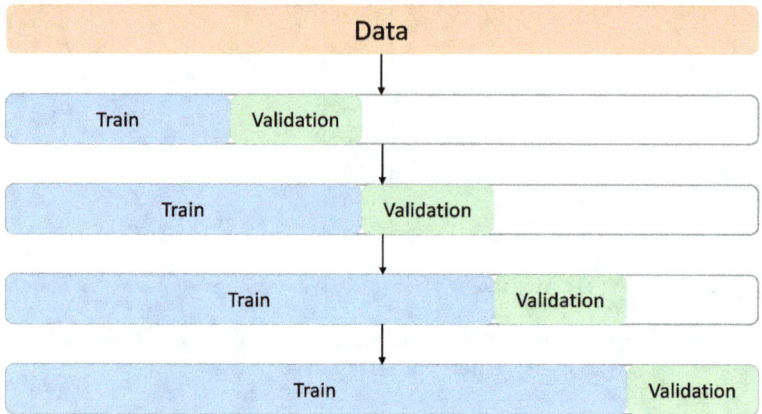

Figure 24 Cross-validation for time-series.

way to search for optimal parameters. This process of searching for optimal parameters is called hyperparameter tuning. These parameters are not part of the so-called "inner" optimization of the model, such as learning the weights of the neural network using gradient descent. During this inner optimization, the hyperparameters are kept fixed. In hyperparameter optimization, which is sometimes also called "outer" optimization we now repeat the inner optimization multiple times for different choices of hyperparameters with the aim of finding the model with the lowest cross-validation error. There are many ways to search for optimal hyperparameters and we introduce three popular methods here.

The most basic hyperparameter tuning method is grid search in which we fit a model for each possible combination of hyperparameters over a grid of possible values. Obviously, if we have a large number of hyperparameters to tune, this method would be extremely time-consuming and inefficient. An alternative to grid search is random search. Random search is different from grid search in the sense that we do not come up with an exhaustive list of combinations. Rather, we can give a statistical distribution for each hyperparameter and sample a candidate value from that distribution. This gives better coverage on the individual hyperparameters. Indeed, empirical evidence suggests that only a few of the hyperparameters matter which makes grid search a poor choice for dealing with a larger number of candidates.

The previous two methods perform individual evaluations of hyperparameters without learning from previous hyperparameter evaluations. The advantage of these approaches is that they allow for trivial parallelization. However, we discard the information from previous evaluations that could otherwise be used to inform regions where we are more likely to find better hyperparameters. For example, if initial evaluations show that the generalization error plateaus quickly after reducing the learning rate, it might be less likely to find better models when reducing the value even further.

Bayesian optimization (Frazier, 2018) is a sequential global optimization (SMBO) algorithm that can be used to inform at which point in the hyperparameter space to evaluate a model's performance next given generalization errors obtained from previous evaluations. It is specifically designed for scenarios in which each evaluation of a target function is complex or expensive to run. To implement such an approach, we first construct a model with some hyperparameters and obtain a score v according to some evaluation metric. Next, a posterior distribution of the hyperparameter is computed and the choices for the next experiment can be sampled according to this posterior expectation. We would then repeat this process until convergence.

In practice, Gaussian Processes (GPs) are often used to model the objective function. An intuitive way of thinking about a GP is as a Gaussian distribution over continuous functions. Any finite number of points on this function are distributed according to a multi-variate Gaussian – thus another way of thinking about the GP is as a multi-variate Gaussian where the number of possible points goes to infinity. The correlation between points is given by a kernel function which depends on the distance between the points. Thus, the closer the points the more correlated they are, which enforces the continuity of the GP.

In Bayesian optimization, one typically starts by specifying a GP prior over the model's generalization error across the hyperparameter space, often with a zero mean and constant variance for simplicity. An initial evaluation is performed on a random hyperparameter setting, after which the posterior distribution is updated based on the observed outcome. This updated posterior then guides the selection of the next hyperparameters to explore, aiming to efficiently locate optimal configurations. Intuitively, when choosing the next point to evaluate the model, we have to trade off exploration and exploitation: It makes sense to search further in regions where the GP indicates that the objective function is improving (exploitation). However, we also want to search in areas where the uncertainty is large and we have no knowledge yet regarding how good the objective might be (explorations).

In practice, we can carry out hyperparameter tuning by using Optuna (Akiba et al., 2019), which is an open-source optimization framework designed for hyperparameter tuning. It leverages techniques such as Bayesian optimization to systematically explore large search spaces and find optimal configurations. We can easily integrate it with cross-validation to ensure that optimizations are evaluated on multiple splits of data for reliable results. By intelligently selecting the most promising hyperparameter settings to evaluate at each step, Optuna minimizes the amount of training required and reduces the need for extensive manual tuning.

4.7 Setting Up Model Pipelines in Practice

The last step before deploying models to production is to have a pipeline that encapsulates the processes mentioned previously and to build a robust framework. It is also important to consider the capability of handling distributed computing, which enables the scalability of our infrastructure. It is thus possible to build the entire framework ourselves if we possess the necessary knowledge and we can tailor each step based upon specific requirements. Otherwise, we can also resort to established tools to build our frameworks. There are generally three popular frameworks, Ray, Dask, and Apache Spark, that facilitate the construction of model pipelines. Each has its own strengths and use cases. The three platforms have different design goals so it is difficult to say which is the best in general. To better understand each platform, we compare them based on performance, scalability, ease of use, ecosystem, and use cases.

Ray is designed for high-performance computing and excels in scenarios requiring real-time execution, such as online learning, reinforcement learning, and serving models. It is highly scalable and capable of handling millions of tasks over thousands of cores with minimal overhead. Dask provides scalable analytics and is optimized for computational tasks that fit into the Python ecosystem, including data manipulation with Pandas and NumPy. It is particularly effective for parallelizing existing Python code and workflows. Apache Spark is renowned for its speed in batch processing and its ability to handle streaming data, courtesy of its in-memory computing capabilities.

In terms of ease of use, Ray offers a Python-native interface that is easy to use for those familiar with Python programming. Its API is flexible, allowing for straightforward integration with other machine learning and deep learning libraries. Dask integrates closely with Python's data science stack, making it accessible to data scientists and analysts already working with Pandas, NumPy, or Scikit-learn. Its lazy evaluation model allows for efficient computation. Apache Spark, while powerful, may have a steeper learning curve, especially for users not familiar with its RDD and DataFrame APIs. However, it provides good documentation and a vast array of functionalities beyond data processing.

Ray has a growing ecosystem and is particularly strong in AI applications with libraries like Ray Tune for hyperparameter tuning and Ray Serve for model serving. It is also part of the Anyscale platform, which simplifies deployment and scaling. Dask is part of the larger Python ecosystem, making it easy to integrate with existing data science and machine learning workflows. It does not have as wide an array of dedicated tools as Spark but excels because of its simplicity and flexibility. Apache Spark boasts a mature ecosystem with built-in libraries for various tasks, including Spark SQL for processing structured data,

MLlib for machine learning, and GraphX for graph processing. Its widespread adoption ensures a wealth of resources and community support.

The choice between platforms depends on the problem to be solved and, in some cases, you might even integrate these platforms to achieve desired outcomes. For example, we could use Ray to build a start-to-finish framework for deep learning models. For initial data preprocessing, we can use Ray's remote functions (@ray.remote) to parallelize data fetching and use libraries like Ray Pandas to normalize or extract meaningful features. Such libraries provide us with Pandas-like operations but on a much larger scale. For deep learning models, Ray integrates seamlessly with frameworks like TensorFlow and PyTorch, distributing the training process and making efficient use of available computational resources. In terms of hyperparameter tuning and cross-validation, Ray Tune is an excellent tool that empowers us to distribute the search for the best model parameters across multiple workers simultaneously. This is particularly beneficial when experimenting with large models or when you need to iterate quickly over many hyperparameter combinations.

PART II: APPLICATIONS

5 Enhancing Classical Quantitative Trading Strategies with Deep Learning

In this section, we embark on an exploration of classical quantitative trading strategies, dissecting their mechanics, applications, and the unique market conditions they respectively best serve. Given the breadth and diversity of these strategies, we divide this journey into three distinct parts.

The **first part** focuses on CTA-style futures and FX strategies in the commodities and foreign exchange markets. To start, we introduce the idea of "volatility targeting," a risk management technique that adjusts investment exposure based on changing market volatility, with the objective of maintaining a consistent risk profile throughout different market conditions. Next, we delve into "time-series momentum" and "trend-following" strategies, as well as simple reversion models. These methods exploit the persistence of price trends over time, whether by capitalizing on the continuation of current market directions or by anticipating reversals. By analyzing historical price data, these strategies seek to predict and profit from future price movements, making them particularly suited to the futures and FX markets where trends can be pronounced and prolonged. We then round out the first part of our exploration by investigating the "carry" strategy. This approach seeks to profit from the interest rate spread between different currencies, capturing the "carry" earned when holding higher-yielding assets financed by borrowing lower-yielding ones.

This strategy highlights the importance of interest rates and funding costs in trading decisions.

The **second part** of the section shifts focus to classical cross-sectional strategies, which are important in the equity market. We explore the "long-short" strategy via cross-sectional momentum, in which long positions are taken in stocks showing strong performance and short positions in those with weak performance. This method aims to capitalize on the relative momentum across different securities, hedging market-wide risk by maintaining balanced portfolio-level long and short exposures. We next discuss "Statistical Arbitrage" (StatArb) strategies, which involve employing statistical models to identify and exploit price inefficiencies between closely related assets. By analyzing historical price relationships and using statistical methods to identify deviations from expected values, traders can execute high-frequency trades to take advantage of temporary mispricings, all while managing risk and exposure through sophisticated mathematical models.

The **third part** is the core of this section, in which we address the transformative potential of deep learning to refine and revolutionize such classical quantitative strategies. By leveraging deep learning algorithms, with their ability to analyze vast datasets, traders can uncover complex nonlinear patterns, and improve the predictive accuracy of models. This section covers how deep learning can be integrated into both futures/FX and equity strategies, from augmenting trend analyses in CTA-style strategies to refining the selection process in long-short equity approaches and improving the detection of arbitrage opportunities in StatArb.

By providing insights into these cutting-edge techniques, this section aims to equip readers with the knowledge to harness the power of deep learning, pushing the boundaries of traditional quantitative trading strategies to achieve enhanced performance and risk management in an increasingly complex market environments.

5.1 Overview of Classical Quantitative Trading Strategies

5.1.1 Classical CTA-Style Futures and FX Strategies

Commodity Trading Advisors (CTAs) play an influential role in futures and foreign exchange (FX) markets, employing a variety of strategies to generate returns and manage risk. This section delves into classical CTA-style strategies, focusing on long-only benchmarks, volatility targeting, time-series momentum, and trend-following strategies. The explanation of each strategy is accompanied by its mathematical underpinnings, so as to provide a deeper understanding of its operational mechanics.

Before diving into specific trading rules, we include a brief introduction to futures contracts. We have also included an extended discussion of futures contracts in Appendix B. Futures possess unique characteristics that must be considered when performing data preprocessing. Futures contracts are standardized legal agreements to buy or sell an asset at a predetermined price on a specified future date, and they have different end dates. Difficulties can arise when joining futures contracts with different settlement dates. There are generally two ways to combine futures contract time-series: nearest futures and continuous futures approaches.

The nearest futures approach is quite straightforward. To start, we select the price series of a contract until its expiration, the next contract is then directly selected, and so on until all contracts of consideration have been selected. However, the time-series generated with the nearest futures approach can not be used for back-testing purposes because it includes significant price distortions due to the price gaps on expiration dates. Figure 25 shows an example with such a distortion where the nearest futures chart shows a large apparent price jump on July 22, 2021. However, this price jump never took place because this is due to contract expiration. In reality, all outstanding contracts are liquidated on (or before) their respective settlement date. To maintain a position, a trader must

Figure 25 **Top**: price series generated by a nearest futures contract approach; **Bottom**: price series generated by a continuous futures contract approach.

"roll forwar" the contract by closing the one set to expire and opening a new one with a future expiry. In essence, if the new contract is 20% cheaper, you would be able to buy 25% more of those, for the same dollar amount.

On the contrary, the continuous futures approach reflects actual price movements by linking successive contracts in a way that eliminates price distortions (price gaps) at rollover points. This alternate linked-contract representation can thus be used for back-testing and more accurately reflects the hypothetical gains and losses of a trader. However, the trade-off is that the price series from continuous futures contracts will not match actual historical prices whereas those generated by the nearest futures approach do. In some cases, we might even observe the negative price series from the continuous futures approach. As a result, the appropriate method to join futures contracts together depends on the specific use case. Generally, the nearest futures contracts should be used if the actual historical price is important, but if the goal is to simulate the gains and losses of a strategy, the continuous contracts approach should be adopted instead.

Long-Only Benchmark The long-only benchmark strategies are common in investment management, and particularly relevant in futures and FX trading. The default position for such strategy is the respective benchmark (S&P 500, BTC, etc.) and that the trader tries to reallocate positions so as to achieve a better (risk-adjusted) return than this benchmark. The strategy is thus evaluated based on its relative performance to the benchmark rather than its absolute performance.

By comparing the returns of actively managed portfolios against a long-only benchmark, investors can gauge the value added by portfolio managers through active selection and timing decisions. Also, the performance of long-only portfolios can reflect broader market sentiments and trends. In bull markets, long-only strategies are likely to perform well, capturing upside potential. Conversely, their performance can suffer in bear markets, highlighting their sensitivity to overall market conditions.

Correlations of these strategies with their benchmarks are also important. For example, pension funds can achieve broad long-only market exposure cost-effectively through cheap passive instruments. However, adding small allocations to uncorrelated strategies like time-series momentum, despite potentially higher fees, enhances diversification and introduces the potential for excess returns due to their differentiated risk-reward profiles.

Volatility Targeting Volatility targeting is a dynamic position sizing method that can be used within strategies. It adjusts the exposure of an asset based on the current or forecasted volatility of that asset or broader market. This ensures that the level of risk remains stable over time. This method is especially significant in the management of futures, FX trading, where market conditions fluctuate significantly. By considering volatility – a primary measure of risk – investors can potentially enhance risk-adjusted returns and better manage the drawdowns associated with periods of high market turbulence.

The core idea behind volatility targeting involves scaling an asset's investment exposure according to the ratio of a target volatility level to the current or expected volatility of that asset. This adjustment factor can be defined as:

$$A = \frac{\sigma_{target}}{\sigma_{current}}, \tag{70}$$

where $\sigma_{current}$ is the current asset volatility typically estimated using the standard deviation of historical returns over a specified look-back period. The target volatility (σ_{target}) is a predetermined level of risk that the investor aims to maintain. Its determination is guided by the investor's risk tolerance, investment timeline, and perspective on market conditions.

The trading positions are then scaled by the adjustment factor A to align the volatility with the target level. Hence, if an asset's current volatility is higher than the target, its exposure is reduced (and vice versa), thereby aiming to stabilize the risk profile. Figure 26 shows an example of a long-only S&P 500 benchmark strategy which has a Sharpe ratio of 0.461. It also includes a version of the strategy that uses volatility targeting (to an annual volatility of $\sigma_{tgt} = 15\%$) to scale positions and consequently increases the Sharpe ratio to 0.632.

In practice, implementing a volatility targeting strategy involves continuous monitoring of market conditions and trading performance. As market volatility

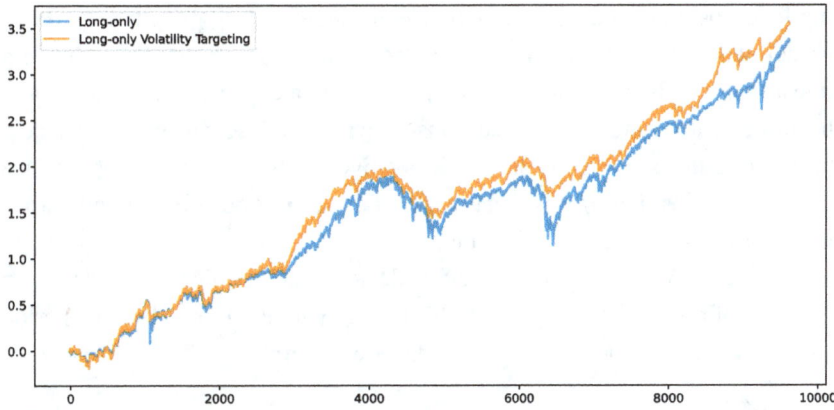

Figure 26 Long-only benchmark S&P 500 strategy and an accompanying version that incorporates volatility targeting of 15% annual standard deviation.

changes, the risk exposure must be periodically adjusted to maintain the target risk level. This dynamic rebalancing requires a disciplined approach and an efficient execution mechanism to minimize transaction costs and slippage. Moreover, investors often employ advanced forecasting tools that consider factors like market sentiment, economic metrics, and geopolitical conditions, that allow them to adjust their risk exposure in anticipation of potential volatility. These models can range from simple historical volatility measures to complex GARCH models and machine learning algorithms.

As we discuss in greater detail in the next section, volatility targeting across multiple instruments can also be interpreted as a simple form of portfolio construction. In particular, when assuming that the covariance matrix of portfolio constituents is a diagonal matrix with respective variances on its diagonal entries, then a standard mean-variance portfolio reduces to volatility targeting. While assuming a diagonal covariance matrix tends to be a poor assumption for equity markets, we can see that the covariance matrix of a universe of future contracts is roughly block-diagonal with very small terms in the off-diagonals (Figure 27).

Time-Series Momentum and Trend Following Time-series momentum (TSM) and trend-following are quantitative trading strategies designed to profit from ongoing market trends. Their core assumption is that assets showing robust performance over a certain timeframe will likely maintain that momentum, while assets underperforming during the same period will continue to lag. These strategies are regularly applied across multiple asset classes – such as futures, foreign exchange, equities, and commodities – and they have played an important role in systematic trading.

A TSM strategy focuses on the autocorrelation of returns. It involves taking long positions in assets that have demonstrated rising price trends over a predefined look-back period and short positions in assets that have shown a downward trends. Specifically, a simple TSM strategy implementation could be implemented as follows: for each instrument s, we assess whether the excess return from the previous (k) periods is positive or negative. If it is positive, we enter a long position; if it is negative, we take a short position. In both cases, the position is maintained for (h) months.

According to Moskowitz, Ooi, and Pedersen (2012), which demonstrates an example of a 12-month ($k = 12$) TSM strategy with a 1-month holding period ($h = 1$), we can define the return of a time-series strategy (TSMOM) as:

$$r_{t,t+1}^{TSMOM,i} = sign(r_{t-k:t}^i)\frac{\sigma_{tgt}}{\sigma_t^i}r_{t,t+1}^i, \qquad (71)$$

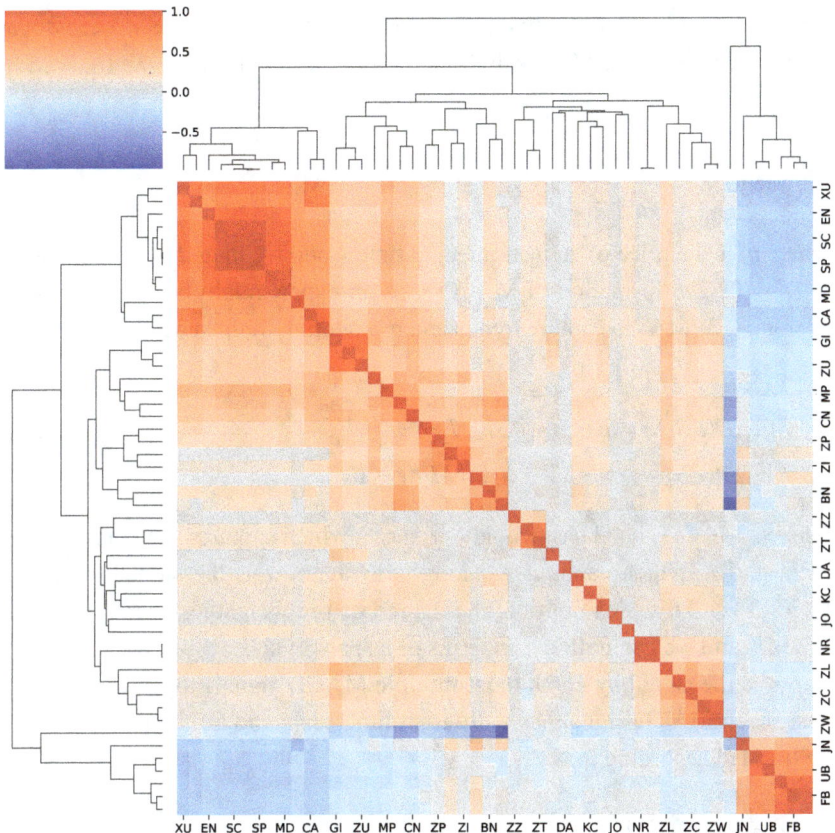

Figure 27 A heatmap of correlation matrix among various futures contracts.

where σ_{tgt} is the annualized volatility target and σ_t^i is an estimate of current market volatility, which can be calculated by using an exponentially weighted moving standard deviation on $r_{t,t+1}^i$. Note that in the previous formulation, when working with returns (and ignoring or only using linear transaction costs), the result does not depend on the actual overall position size. However, in practice, one would actually target a dollar volatility, such as an volatility of $\sigma_{tgt}^{USD} =$ 10 million USD, rather than a percentage volatility of say $\sigma_{tgt} = 15\%$. Then $sign(r_{t-k:t}^i)\sigma_{tgt}^{USD}/\sigma_t^{i,USD}$ would correspond to the actual target trading position in USD.

In this case, $sign(r_{t-k:t}^s)$ is essentially the time-series momentum factor, where we go long if the 12-month return is positive and vice versa. In practice, there are various ways to decide the direction of our positions and we use Y_t to indicate trading directions in a more general case. We here introduce two popular trend-following strategies: simple moving-average crossover (SMA) and moving average crossover divergence (MACD) strategies. The SMA crossover strategy utilizes two SMAs with different look-back periods K_1, K_2 ($K_1 < K_2$):

$$Y_t = SMA(t, K_1) - SMA(t, K_2),$$
$$SMA(t, K) = \frac{1}{K} \sum_{i=0}^{K-1} p_{t-i}, \tag{72}$$

where p_t is the price of an instrument at time t, and we long if $Y_t > 0$ and short if $Y_t < 0$. The formation of MACD uses an exponentially weighted moving average (EWMA) to capture trends and momentum defined as:

$$Y_t(S, L) = MACD(t, S, L),$$
$$MACD(t, S, L) = EWMA(t, S) - EWMA(t, L), \tag{73}$$
$$EWMA(t, S) = \alpha p_t + (1 - \alpha) EWMA(t - 1, S),$$

where a MACD signal has two time-scales S, which captures short-term movement and L, which captures the long-term trend. α is the smoothing factor ($0 < \alpha \leq 1$), which controls the degree of the weighting decrease for the EWMA and we can define α in terms of a span S via $\alpha = \frac{2}{S+1}$. We can further improve the signal by combining multiple MACD signals together. In such a case, each MACD signal has a different time-scale and a final position could be decided according to:

$$\tilde{Y}_t = \sum_{k=1}^{3} Y_t(S_k, L_k), \tag{74}$$

where, for example, $S_k \in \{8, 16, 32\}$ and $L_k \in \{24, 48, 96\}$ days. Note that the long look-back is often chosen to be roughly three times the short look-back.

Carry Carry trading is predominantly employed in the foreign exchange market to exploit interest rate differentials between currencies. The strategy involves going long on a currency that offers a higher interest rate while shorting a currency with a relatively low interest rate. Traders profit from the interest spread, provided that the exchange rate remains favorable. The carry trade strategy gained significant attention in the 1990s and early 2000s, with the Japanese yen (JPY) often selected as the funding currency due to Japan's low interest rates. Accordingly, traders would leverage the low borrowing costs in JPY and allocate those funds into higher interest rate currencies, such as the Australian dollar (AUD) or the New Zealand dollar (NZD).

Persistent interest rate differentials can exist due to many reasons, including differing economic policies, growth rates, and inflation levels across countries. Carry traders that take advantage of these interest rate differences expect that a higher-yielding currency will not depreciate against a lower-yielding currency by an amount greater than the interest rate spread. If we are trading a currency pair, say Currency A (with interest rate i^A) and Currency B (with interest rate i^B), the interest rate differential (IRD) is:

$$IRD = i^A - i^B, \qquad (75)$$

for which going long Currency A and shorting Currency B, we will earn interest on Currency A and pay interest on Currency B. The net interest earned per day (I) on a notional amount of capital C can therefore be calculated as:

$$I = \frac{(i^A - i^B) \times C \times l}{365}, \qquad (76)$$

where l is the leverage that magnifies both potential profits and potential losses. While the interest differential might be positive, there remains a risk that the currency pair's exchange rate moves against the position. If Currency A depreciates against Currency B, it can negate the interest earnings or even lead to a net loss. Accordingly, carry trading in FX markets involves not only a simple interest rate arbitrage but also entails significant exchange rate risk. Traders thus need to account for the possibility that currency movements could wipe out the interest gains. Additionally, leverage, which is frequently employed in carry trades, can magnify returns, but also heightens the potential for losses. This makes it crucial to manage risk effectively in carry trading strategies.

5.1.2 Classical Equity Strategies

In the realm of quantitative finance, strategies in equity markets are popular tools, particularly for hedge funds and institutional investors. Among these, classical equity strategies like long-short, cross-sectional momentum, and statistical arbitrage stand out for their approaches to capturing alpha while managing risk. Before discussing these strategies individually, we first introduce the concept of portfolio optimization, as these strategies are mostly traded in the form of a portfolio. A portfolio is the group of assets and the primary goal of managing a portfolio is to balance risk and return in accordance with the investor's specific objectives. By distributing investments across a variety of asset classes (such as stocks, bonds, and real estate), different sectors, geographic regions, and investment strategies, a portfolio can minimize idiosyncratic risk (also called diversifiable or specific risk). This strategy, known as diversification, helps mitigate the impact of poor performance of any individual investment on the overall portfolio.

The success of a portfolio depends on the allocation of its assets. There are various ways to determine the weightings of a portfolio's constituent assets.

As a simple example, we present an equally weighted long-only portfolio with volatility targeting:

$$r_t^p = \frac{1}{N} \sum_{i=1}^{N} \frac{\sigma_{tgt}}{\sigma_t^i} r_{t,t+1}^i, \tag{77}$$

where N_t denotes the total number of assets within the portfolio, and r_t^i represents the return of the asset i. The upcoming sections will outline traditional trading strategies and illustrate how deep learning models can be utilized to enhance these methodologies.

Equity Long-Short via Cross-Sectional Momentum A popular form of long-short equity strategy involves buying undervalued (long positions) and selling overvalued (short positions) stocks. Long-short strategies seek to generate returns in both upward and downward market conditions, achieving a balance that reduces market exposure and captures alpha through stock selection. In fundamental long-short strategies investors or fund managers conduct thorough research to choose stocks that are undervalued for purchasing and those that are overvalued for short selling. The strategy often employs a fundamental analysis approach, looking at company financials, industry conditions, and economic factors.

By maintaining long and short positions simultaneously, the strategy aims to hedge market risk. Many funds aim for market neutrality by targeting a zero net exposure, which is the difference between long and short exposures and can be defined as:

$$\text{Net Exposure} = \frac{(\text{Value of Long Positions} - \text{Value of Short Positions})}{\text{Portfolio Value}}. \tag{78}$$

This is also called a market-neutral strategy. The portfolio return (r^p) is determined by taking the weighted average of the returns from the long positions (r^L) and subtracting the weighted average of the returns from the short positions (r^S):

$$r^p = w_L \cdot r^L - w^S \cdot r^S, \tag{79}$$

where w_L and w_S are the weights of the long and short positions, respectively. Another strategy for stock selection is the cross-sectional momentum strategy, which capitalizes on the momentum factor across different stocks or sectors. The underlying concept is that stocks that have outperformed their competitors in the past are expected to sustain their strong performance in the short to medium term, while those that have underperformed are likely to continue struggling.

Specifically, this strategy involves ranking stocks based on their past returns and taking long positions in those within the top percentile while shorting those within the bottom percentile. Mathematically, the strategy first ranks stocks based on r^j_{t-1}, which is the return in the previous period. It then goes long stocks with r^j_{t-1} in the top $x\%$ and short stocks in the bottom $x\%$, with a typical value for $x\%$ being 10%. To avoid sector biases and sector-specific exposure, the strategy can be applied within sectors, buying the best performers and selling the worst performers within each sector. Momentum strategies can exhibit considerable variation in their effectiveness based on the chosen time frame for measuring past returns, and often require back-testing to determine optimal parameters. These strategies are staples in the quantitative trading world and are widely applied in today's trading markets.

Statistical Arbitrage (StatArb) Statistical Arbitrage, often referred to as StatArb, is a sophisticated financial strategy that seeks to exploit statistical mispricings of one or more often-related assets. Rooted in the principles of mean reversion and quantitative analysis, StatArb involves complex mathematical and computational techniques and is a subset of arbitrage strategies, which aims to profit from price differences between markets or securities without taking significant risk. Statistical Arbitrage has its roots in the convergence trading strategy developed at Morgan Stanley in the 1980s. The approach was pioneered by a group led by Nunzio Tartaglia, a physicist and mathematician. Initially, it focused on pairs trading, which involves taking opposing positions in two co-integrated stocks. Cointegration is a concept in time-series analysis that applies to nonstationary series whose linear combination turns out to be stationary. More concretely, consider two nonstationary time-series X_t and Y_t. If there exists some constant β such that $X_t - \beta Y_t$ is stationary, we say that X_t and Y_t are co-integrated. Over time, Statistical Arbitrage evolved to incorporate multiple assets and use more sophisticated statistical models, leading to its increased usage in quantitative trading.

In its simplest form, StatArb involves identifying pairs of co-integrated stocks (pairs trading). When the price relationship between such a pair diverges, the trader sells the overperformer and buys the underperformer, betting on the convergence of their prices. For example, if p^i_t and p^j_t are the prices of two co-integrated stocks i and j at time t, we would look for significant deviations in their price ratio or difference. If the price ratio p^i_t/p^j_t increases so that it deviates significantly from its historical mean, traders might short stock i and go long on the stock j, betting on the ratio of their prices to revert toward the mean. In more sophisticated multivariate approaches, a StatArb strategy might involve modeling p_t, a vector of stock prices at time t, using a vector autoregressive or deep learning model. By identifying complex relationships among multiple stocks, traders can then construct portfolios that are expected to be market-neutral and profit from mean reversion across related assets. Because StatArb strategies rely upon subtle, unstable price relationships, they require rigorous and active risk management.

5.2 Enhancing Time-Series Momentum Strategies with Deep Learning

In the previous sections, we introduced several classical trading strategies. We now demonstrate how to combine these strategies with deep learning models to obtain better performance. By incorporating deep learning, we can better analyze, model, and trade markets. Notably, time-series momentum trading, which capitalizes on the continuation of asset price trends over time, greatly benefits from deep learning's ability to analyze extensive historical data and uncover complex patterns that simpler algorithms might miss.

First, we present an end-to-end framework proposed by Lim, Zohren, and Roberts (2019) which utilizes networks to directly optimize performance metrics. This framework, termed Deep Momentum Network, builds upon ideas from time-series momentum strategies (Moskowitz, Ooi, and Pedersen, 2012). In these strategies, a network is trained by optimizing the Sharpe ratio and directly outputs trade positions. Second, we extend Deep Momentum Network with transformers, as proposed by Wood, Giegerich, Roberts, and Zohren (2021). In this framework, the transformers help to extract long term dependencies and can be interpreted to a certain degree by their attention weights. Third, we present an approach designed by Poh, Lim, Zohren, and Roberts (2021a) which further extends cross-sectional momentum trading strategies. In particular, they improve cross-sectional portfolios by integrating learning-to-rank algorithms, recognizing that the effectiveness of a cross-sectional portfolio relies heavily upon accurately ranking assets before portfolio construction.

Traditionally, quantitative trading is often a two-step optimization problem where we first decide the direction and then the positions of the trades. The first step is essentially a prediction problem and various methods, like the previously introduced trend-following strategies can be used to predict price directions. The second step is to determine positions based on these predictive signals and similarly there are established methods for doing this. For example, we could simply select the direction based on the signal's sign and scale the size of the position based on the signal's magnitude.

With deep learning, we can bypass this two-step optimization problem by concurrently learning trend analysis and determining position sizes within a single function. The Deep Momentum Networks (DMN) framework, introduced in Lim et al. (2019), directly output positions based on the objective of maximizing strategy metrics, like returns or Sharpe ratio. Instead of outputting a predictive signal like a standard supervised learning task, we use a network f to output positions w_t^i at any time point for asset i:

$$w_t^i = f(\boldsymbol{u}_t^i; \boldsymbol{\theta}), \tag{80}$$

where $\boldsymbol{u}_t^i$ are market features and $\boldsymbol{\theta}$ are network parameters. In particular, we aim to optimize the average return and the annualized Sharpe ratio using the following loss functions:

$$\begin{aligned}\mathcal{L}_{returns}(\boldsymbol{\theta}) &= -\mu_R, \\ &= -\frac{1}{N}\sum_{\Omega} R(i,t), \\ \mathcal{L}_{sharpe}(\boldsymbol{\theta}) &= -\frac{\mu_R \times \sqrt{252}}{\sqrt{(\sum_{\Omega} R(i,t)^2)/N - \mu_R^2}}, \\ R(i,t) &= w_t^i \frac{\sigma_{tgt}}{\sigma_t^i} r_{t,t+1}^i,\end{aligned} \tag{81}$$

where μ_R represents the average return across the entire universe Ω of size N and $R(i,t)$ denotes the return generated by the trading strategy for asset i at time t. We can employ different network architectures to model the relationship between the position w_t^i and the market features $\boldsymbol{u}_t^i$. The entire computational process is differentiable, which allows for the use of gradient ascent to maximize the objective functions. In practice, we multiply the loss functions by minus one and use gradient descent to minimize them. The following code snippet demonstrates how to construct a negative Sharpe ratio loss function in Pytorch:

```
import torch
import torch.nn as nn

def Neg_Sharpe(portfolio):
    return -torch.mean(portfolio) / torch.std(portfolio)

class SharpeLoss(nn.Module):
    def __init__(self):
        super().__init__()

    def forward(self, outputs_prev, future_rets):
        portflio = outputs_prev * future_rets
        loss = Neg_Sharpe(portflio)
        return loss
```

We include results from Lim et al. (2019) to demonstrate the effectiveness of DMNs. The authors assessed multiple different network architectures by back-testing their performance across eighty-eight ratio-adjusted continuous futures contracts sourced from the Pinnacle Data Corp CLC Database. These contracts contained price data spanning from 1990 to 2015 for a diverse set of asset classes, including commodities, fixed income, and currency futures. The following metrics were used to gauge the trading performance: expected returns ($E(R)$), volatility ($Std(R)$), downside deviation (DD), the maximum drawdown (MDD), Sharpe ratio, Sortino ratio, Calmar ratio, the percentage of positive returns observed (% of +Ret) and the average profit over the average loss ($Ave.P/Ave.L$). The exact definitions of these metrics can be found in Appendix C.

In Table 4, we present the experimental results alongside three classical trading benchmark strategies: long-only, using the sign of past returns for time-series momentum strategies (Sgn(Returns)) and MACD signals. We also test on different network architectures, including a simple linear model, MLP, WaveNet, and an LSTM. The complete testing period extends from 1995 to 2015, during which we optimize the performance metrics for the strategy's returns as outlined in Equation 80. In Table 5, volatility scaling is applied to adjust the overall strategy returns to align with the volatility target (15%). The rescaling of volatility should, in general, increase Sharpe ratio and facilitate comparisons between different strategies.

When reviewing the raw signal outputs (Table 4), the LSTM model optimized for the Sharpe ratio delivers the highest performance, exceeding the Sharpe-optimized MLP by 44% and the Sgn(Returns) strategy – the top classical approach – by more than double. Additionally, the DMN enhances the Sharpe ratio for both the linear and MLP models. This suggests that models capable of capturing nonlinear relationships can achieve superior results by utilizing extended time histories through an internal memory state.

We report the results with the addition of volatility scaling in Table 5. The results clearly demonstrate that the addition of volatility scaling improves performance ratios across strategies. Specifically, the volatility scaling has a greater positive impact on network-based strategies compared to the classical strategies for which the Sharpe-optimized linear models beat reference benchmarks. In terms of risk evaluation metrics, the adjusted volatility also makes downside deviation and maximum drawdown comparable across strategies. The LSTM models optimized for the Sharpe ratio maintain the lowest maximum drawdown among all models and consistently achieve superior risk-adjusted performance metrics.

The Momentum Transformer In the previous section, we observe that network architectures can be successfully used for momentum strategies, and

Table 4 Performance metrics – raw signal outputs.

	E(R)	Std(R)	DD	MDD	Sharpe	Sortino	Calmar	% of +Ret	$\frac{Ave.P}{Ave.L}$
References									
Long Only	0.039	0.052	0.035	0.167	0.738	1.086	0.230	53.8%	0.970
Sgn(Returns)	0.054	0.046	0.032	0.083	1.192	1.708	0.653	54.8%	1.011
MACD	0.030	0.031	0.022	0.081	0.976	1.356	0.371	53.9%	1.015
Linear									
Sharpe	0.041	0.038	0.028	0.119	1.094	1.462	0.348	54.9%	0.997
Ave. Returns	0.047	0.045	0.031	0.164	1.048	1.500	0.287	53.9%	1.022
MLP									
Sharpe	0.044	0.031	0.025	0.154	1.383	1.731	0.283	56.0%	1.024
Ave. Returns	0.064	0.043	0.030	0.161	1.492	2.123	0.399	55.6%	1.031
WaveNet									
Sharpe	0.030	0.035	0.026	0.101	0.854	1.167	0.299	53.5%	1.008
Ave. Returns	0.032	0.040	0.028	0.113	0.788	1.145	0.281	53.8%	0.980
LSTM									
Sharpe	0.045	0.016	0.011	0.021	2.804	3.993	2.177	59.6%	1.102
Ave. Returns	0.054	0.046	0.033	0.164	1.165	1.645	0.326	54.8%	1.003

Table 5 Performance metrics – rescaled to target volatility.

	E(R)	Std(R)	DD	MDD	Sharpe	Sortino	Calmar	% of +Ret	$\frac{Ave.P}{Ave.L}$
References									
Long Only	0.117	0.154	0.102	0.431	0.759	1.141	0.271	53.8%	0.973
Sgn(Returns)	0.215	0.154	0.102	0.264	1.392	2.108	0.815	54.8%	1.041
MACD	0.172	0.155	0.106	0.317	1.111	1.622	0.543	53.9%	1.031
Linear									
Sharpe	0.232	0.155	0.103	0.303	1.496	2.254	0.765	54.9%	1.056
Ave. Returns	0.189	0.154	0.100	0.372	1.225	1.893	0.507	53.9%	1.047
MLP									
Sharpe	0.312	0.154	0.102	0.335	2.017	3.042	0.930	56.0%	1.104
Ave. Returns	0.266	0.154	0.099	0.354	1.731	2.674	0.752	55.6%	1.065
WaveNet									
Sharpe	0.148	0.155	0.103	0.349	0.956	1.429	0.424	53.5%	1.018
Ave. Returns	0.136	0.154	0.101	0.356	0.881	1.346	0.381	53.8%	0.993
LSTM									
Sharpe	0.451	0.155	0.105	0.209	2.907	4.290	2.159	59.6%	1.113
Ave. Returns	0.208	0.154	0.102	0.365	1.349	2.045	0.568	54.8%	1.028

that LSTM networks generally outperform the other networks in DMNs. Nonetheless, LSTMs can struggle to handle long-term patterns and react to major events like market crashes. In time-series contexts, attention mechanisms and learnable attention weights can be used to assess the relevance of past timestamps. This enhances the model's ability to capture and consider long-term dependencies. This approach also allows the model to focus, or place higher attention, on significant events and regime-specific temporal dynamics. Furthermore, the use of multiple attention heads allows for the examination of multiple regimes that occur simultaneously across different timescales.

The works of Wood, Giegerich, et al. (2021); Wood, Kessler, Roberts, and Zohren (2023); Wood, Roberts, and Zohren (2021) follow the DMN framework and design Transformer-based networks that incorporate attention mechanisms. One of the core attributes of the Momentum Transformer (TFT) is its ability to effectively capture attention patterns in time-series data, segmenting the input sequence into distinct regimes. This segmentation process allows the model to focus on specific temporal windows in which market behavior exhibits consistent momentum, thus enabling the TFT to learn and predict trends more effectively. The attention mechanism in TFT dynamically adjusts to different market regimes, helping to distinguish between periods of significant market movements and noise. This segmentation process not only enhances predictive accuracy but also provides insight into how different time periods contribute to overall forecasts, allowing for more interpretable trading strategies.

TFT does not only use attention models, but rather is constructed from a combination of LSTM and attention architectures. In the context of financial markets, where low signal-to-noise ratios persist, the LSTM serves as a tool to summarize local patterns and capture short-term dependencies and trends prior to the application of an attention mechanism. In other words, the LSTM layer acts as a filter that distills relevant information, allowing the attention mechanism to operate more efficiently on a more structured, cleaner representation of the time-series. This approach differs from other applications of transformers, such as in NLP, where raw sequence data might contain more immediately discernible patterns. However, in the context of noisy, stochastic financial markets, the combination of LSTM for local pattern summarization and attention for regime-based segmentation enables the TFT to outperform conventional transformers.

Specifically, the aforementioned authors study the following Transformer architectures: Transformer, Decoder-Only Transformer, Convolutional Transformer, Informer (H. Zhou et al., 2021) and Decoder-Only TFT (Lim et al., 2021). They adhere to the experimental framework outlined in Lim et al. (2019) by examining the test results over three periods: overall performance from 1995 to 2020 to evaluate general performance; underperformance period from 2015 to 2020, a timeframe during which both classical strategies and LSTM-optimized DMNs exhibited underperformance; and the COVID-19 crisis period spanning the COVID-19 pandemic period, characterized by market regime shifts that included a market crash and a subsequent bull market.

In Table 6, we display the experimental findings in terms of the performance metrics of the strategy over the portfolio of 88 futures for the aforementioned periods. Notably, the Decoder-Only TFT achieves the highest performance across all risk-adjusted evaluation metrics for both scenarios 1 and 2. When compared to the LSTM-optimized model, the Sharpe ratio increases by 50% for the period from 1995 to 2020 and by 109% for the period from 2015 to 2020. During the COVID-19 crisis, the LSTM model experienced significant losses but transformer models still deliver decent results, however, the TFT performs less well than the other transformer models. Overall, the different variants of the momentum transformer have higher returns and lower risks, indicating their ability to better model price dynamics.

In Figure 28, we display the return plots for experimental periods 2 and 3. These plots clearly show that LSTM models were ineffective during the period of market instability from 2015 to 2020 and throughout the COVID-19 crisis. In contrast, transformer architectures were capable of adapting smoothly to sudden changes in market regimes, and outperformed LSTM models significantly. Additionally, the nonhybrid transformer models excelled during the Bull market that followed the COVID-19-induced market crash, capitalizing on this sustained momentum of this regime.

To trade with DMNs, it is important to comprehend the reasoning behind how the model selects positions. The attention mechanism within the TFT not only highlights important segments of the time-series but also assigns greater weight to specific key dates, such as those when significant market events occurred. This feature provides transparency into the model's decision-making process, making it easier for traders and analysts to understand why particular predictions were made. By focusing on key dates, the TFT helps users interpret how past market events influence future predictions, offering valuable insights into the driving forces behind market momentum. In Table 7, we present the significance of input variables for the Decoder-Only TFT, for the years 2015–2020 and the COVID-19 crisis period. Overall, across both periods, the daily return feature is assigned the highest weight, indicating that the TFT pays the most attention to market movements over that past day as compared to longer lookbacks.

It is also notable that daily data plays a less significant role during the COVID-19 crisis than it does during the 2015–2020 period. This is likely

Table 6 Performance metrics – raw signal outputs.

	E(R)	Std(R)	DD	MDD	Sharpe	Sortino	Calmar	% of +Ret	$\frac{Ave.P}{Ave.L}$
Average 1995 - 2020									
Long Only	0.024	0.049	0.035	0.125	0.51	0.73	0.21	52.4%	0.988
TSMOM	0.043	0.044	0.031	0.063	1.03	1.51	0.94	54.2%	1.002
LSTM	0.027	0.016	0.011	0.021	1.70	2.66	1.68	55.1%	1.091
Transformer	0.031	0.024	0.016	0.029	1.14	2.13	1.53	54.7%	1.051
Decoder-Only Trans.	0.029	0.026	0.017	0.034	1.11	1.69	1.09	53.5%	1.051
Conv. Transformer	0.029	0.027	0.018	0.038	1.07	1.60	0.98	53.5%	1.041
Informer	0.023	0.013	0.008	0.014	1.72	2.67	1.79	54.8%	1.103
Decoder Only TFT	0.040	0.015	0.009	0.013	2.54	4.14	3.22	57.3%	1.154
Average 2015 - 2020									
Long Only	0.017	0.050	0.035	0.114	0.37	0.51	0.15	51.9%	0.982
TSMOM	0.009	0.043	0.031	0.082	0.24	0.33	0.12	52.8%	0.931
LSTM	0.012	0.018	0.013	0.035	0.82	1.19	0.66	53.3%	1.004
Transformer	0.019	0.012	0.008	0.010	1.53	2.32	1.86	54.7%	1.071

Table 6 (cont.)

	E(R)	Std(R)	DD	MDD	Sharpe	Sortino	Calmar	% of +Ret	Ave.P/Ave.L
Decoder-Only Trans.	0.013	0.019	0.013	0.026	0.72	1.03	0.60	52.7%	1.012
Conv. Transformer	0.018	0.019	0.007	0.031	0.98	1.47	0.77	52.9%	1.056
Informer	0.016	0.011	0.008	0.017	1.51	2.30	1.44	54.3%	1.089
Decoder Only TFT	0.019	0.012	0.006	0.017	1.71	2.61	2.06	55.7%	1.073
COVID-19									
Long Only	-0.014	0.067	0.056	0.123	-0.19	-0.22	-0.12	57.2%	0.720
TSMOM	0.009	0.047	0.031	0.041	0.21	0.32	0.22	50.0%	1.041
LSTM	-0.041	0.028	0.025	0.053	-1.50	-1.67	-0.78	52.2%	0.643
Transformer	0.042	0.012	0.008	0.008	3.38	5.55	7.31	64.8%	1.066
Decoder-Only Trans.	0.080	0.025	0.014	0.010	3.01	5.55	8.56	58.8%	1.243
Conv. Transformer	0.031	0.019	0.014	0.016	1.81	2.74	3.17	57.4%	1.058
Informer	0.043	0.016	0.010	0.010	2.71	4.45	4.28	59.6%	1.137
Decoder Only TFT	0.018	0.017	0.013	0.021	1.22	1.74	1.57	60.3%	0.831

Deep Learning in Quantitative Trading

Table 7 Decoder-Only TFT average variable importance.

	2015–2020	**COVID-19**
r_{day}	30.8%	24.4%
r_{month}	13.6%	10.6%
$r_{quarter}$	8.9%	14.0%
$r_{biannual}$	8.9%	8.5%
r_{annual}	11.9%	13.5%
$M(8, 24)$	9.1%	9.7%
$M(16, 48)$	10.3%	11.9%
$M(32, 98)$	6.5%	7.3%

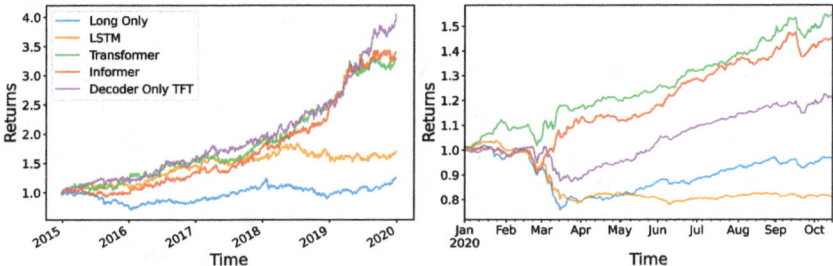

Figure 28 These figures compare the performance of variants of the momentum transformer strategy with benchmarks for the 2015–2020 period (left) and the COVID-19 crisis (right). In each plot, we display cumulative returns adjusted to an annualized volatility level of 15%.

because the 2015–2020 timeframe was highly non-stationary, whereas 2020 included a substantial market crash followed by a distinct upward trend. Accordingly, it is not surprising that during the COVID-19 crisis, the TFT assigned quarterly returns greater weight. Additionally, MACD ($M(S, L)$) indicators of all lookbacks were assigned above-average importance, further demonstrating the TFT's ability to adapt to each specific scenario.

To further demonstrate the interpretability of transformers we show feature importances for forecasting Cocoa futures prices in Figure 29. Cocoa provides a representative example of the model's behavior when trading a commodity future, displaying a series of well-defined regimes throughout the observed period. This variation in variable importance for trading Cocoa futures is illustrated over time from 2015–2020 in Figure 29. These varying feature importances are a result of the model's ability to effectively combine different components at different moments, adapting its approach in response to significant events.

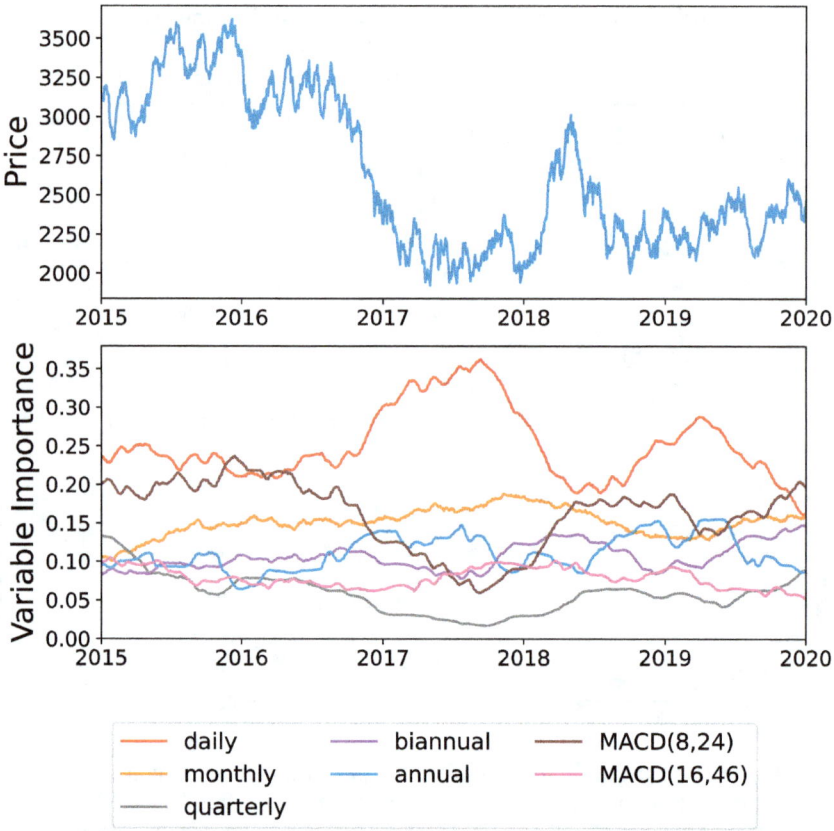

Figure 29 Variable importance for Cocoa futures during out-of-sample forecasting from 2015 to 2020 is illustrated in the accompanying figures. The upper plot displays the price series, while the lower plot showcases the Decoder-Only TFT model. To emphasize the most significant features, we highlight the seven variables with the highest average weights.

5.3 Enhancing Cross-Section Momentum Strategies with Deep Learning

As previously discussed, cross-sectional strategies are a widely adopted form of systematic trading, that can be applied to many asset classes. These strategies aim to capture risk premia by engaging in relative trading between assets – purchasing those with the highest expected returns while shorting those with the lowest. For a portfolio of securities that is rebalanced on a monthly basis, the returns for a cross-sectional momentum (CSM) strategy at time t can be represented as follows:

$$r_{t,t+1}^{CSM} = \frac{1}{N} \sum_{i=1}^{N} X_t^i \frac{\sigma_{tgt}}{\sigma_t^i} r_{t,t+1}^j, \tag{82}$$

where $r_{t,t+1}^{CSM}$ represents the realized portfolio returns from time t to $t + 1$, N denotes the number of stocks within the portfolio, and $X_t^i \in \{-1, 0, 1\}$ defines the cross-sectional momentum signal or trading rule for security i. The overarching framework of the CSM strategy consists of the following four components:

Score Calculation: $Y_t^i = f(u_t^i)$, (83)

where u_t^i denotes the input vector for asset i at time t, and the strategy's predictive model f generates the corresponding score Y_t^i. For a cross-sectional universe consisting of N assets, the collection of scores for the assets of consideration is represented by the vector $Y_t = \{Y_t^1, \cdots, Y_t^N\}$. The second step involves ranking these scores. Each score ranking can be determined as:

Score Ranking: $Z_t^i = \mathcal{R}(Y_t^i)$, (84)

where $Z_t^i \in \{1, \cdots, N\}$ signifies the ranking position of asset i after the scores are sorted in ascending order using the operator $\mathcal{R}(\cdot)$. The third step is the selection process and typically involves applying a threshold to retain a specific proportion of assets, which are then used to construct the corresponding long and short portfolios. Equation 85 follows the assumption that the strategy utilizes standard decile-based portfolios, meaning that the top and bottom 10% of assets are selected:

Security Selection: $X_t^i = \begin{cases} -1 & Z_t^i \leq (0.1 \times N), \\ 1 & Z_t^i > (0.9 \times N), \\ 0 & \text{Otherwise.} \end{cases}$ (85)

The last step is **portfolio construction**. For example, we might construct an equally weighted portfolio scaled by volatility targeting as shown in Equation 82. Most cross-sectional momentum strategies conform to this framework and are generally consistent in the final three steps: ranking scores, selecting assets, and constructing the portfolio. However, it can differ in the choice of prediction models f used to calculate the asset scores, ranging from simple heuristic methods to advanced models that incorporate a wide array of macroeconomic inputs. While there are numerous techniques available for scores computation, we typically focus on three primary approaches: classical momentum strategies, Regress-then-Rank, and Learning to Rank.

For classical momentum strategies, we calculate scores with time-series momentum factors or signals, such as MACD. Equation 86 illustrates how an asset could be scored based on its raw cumulative returns calculated over the preceding 12 months:

Score Calculation: $Y_t^i = r_{t-252,t}^i$, (86)

where $r^j_{t-252,t}$ represents the unadjusted returns of asset i over the 252-day period ending at time t.

Differently, the regress-then-rank approach first requires a predictive model, such as a standard regression or deep learning model. A score is then calculated so that:

Score Calculation: $Y^i_t = f(u^j_t; \theta),$ (87)

where f denotes a prediction model that receives an input vector u^j_t and is parameterized by θ. We then designate a target variable, such as volatility-normalized returns, and train the model by minimizing the MSE loss:

$$\mathcal{L}(\theta) = \frac{1}{N} \sum_{\Omega} (Y^i_t - \frac{r^i_{t,t+1}}{\sigma^i_t})^2,$$ (88)

where Ω denotes the collection of all N possible forecasts and target pairs across the set of instruments and their corresponding time steps.

Learning to Rank (LTR) (T.- Y. Liu et al., 2009) is a research domain in Information Retrieval that emphasizes the use of machine learning techniques to develop models for executing ranking tasks. To introduce the framework of LTR, we borrow examples from document retrieval. For training purposes, we are provided with a collection of queries $Q = \{x_1, \cdots, x_N\}$. Each query x_i is linked to a set of documents $\{x^1_i, \cdots, x^m_i\}$ that must be ranked according to their relevance to the respective query. An accompanying set of document labels $y_i = \{y^1_i, \cdots, y^m_i\}$ is provided to indicate the relevance scores of the documents. The goal of LTR is essentially to learn a ranking function f that takes as input a pair (x_i, x^j_i) and outputs a relevance score $f(x_i, x^j_i)$ that can then be used to rank the j-th item for query i. There are several ways to train LTR algorithms, but we choose to introduce the framework here using the point-wise approach. We can treat each query-item pair (x_i, x^j_i) as an independent instance and train the model with the objective of minimizing the mean squared error between the estimated scores and the actual relevance scores, expressed formally as:

$$L_{point\ wise} = \sum_{i,j} (f(x_i, x^j_i) - y^j_i)^2.$$ (89)

The studies by Poh et al. (2021a); Poh, Lim, Zohren, and Roberts (2021b, 2021c); Poh, Roberts, and Zohren (2022) adopt the concept of Learning to Rank and introduce a framework for integrating LTR models into cross-sectional trading strategies. To apply this framework to momentum strategies, we can equate each query to a portfolio rebalancing event. In this analogy, each associated document and its corresponding label can be viewed as an asset and its

Deep Learning in Quantitative Trading

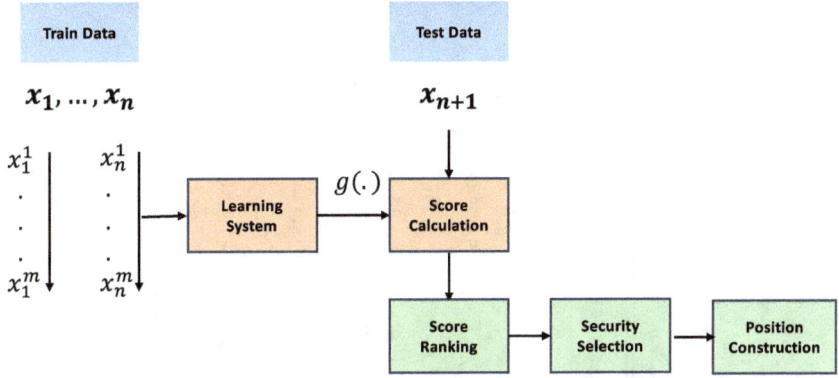

Figure 30 LTR for cross-sectional momentum strategy.

designated decile for the next rebalance. This decile is based on a performance metric, typically returns.

Figure 30 illustrates a schematic representation of this adaptation. Following this framework, for the training process, let $\mathcal{B} = \{x_1, \cdots, x_N\}$ represent a sequence of monthly rebalancing events. At each rebalancing point x_i, there is a collection of equity instruments $x_i = \{x_i^1, \cdots, x_i^m\}$ along with their corresponding assigned deciles $y_i = \{y_i^1, \cdots, y_i^m\}$. With all rebalance-asset pairs, we can form the training set $\{(x_i, x_i^j), y_i\}_{i=1}^N$ to obtain a trained function g to produce scores. During testing, we inject out-of-sample data to obtain scores and then rank these scores to select securities. Accordingly, we construct portfolios that invest in the assets projected to deliver the highest returns and divest from those expected to generate the lowest.

As a concrete example, Poh et al. (2021a) applied this approach to actively trade companies listed on the NYSE from 1980 to 2019. At each rebalancing interval, 100 stocks – representing 10% of all tradable stocks – were selected and actively traded according to multiple different LTR algorithms. These include RankNet (RNet), LLambdaMART (LM), ListNet (LNet), and ListMLE (LMLE). To verify the effectiveness of LTR, they include four benchmarks: a random selection of stocks (Rand), classical time-series momentum strategies that use past returns (TM) or MACD signals (MACD) to calculate scores, and a regress-then-rank technique that uses a MLP network (MLP).

The out-of-sample effectiveness of these different strategies can be evaluated by the results shown in Figure 31 and Table 8. Figure 31 displays the strategies' cumulative returns, while Table 8 presents the strategies' principal financial performance indicators. To enhance the comparability of each strategy's performance the overall returns are standardized to an annualized 15% portfolio-level volatility target for all strategies. In this analysis, all returns are calculated

Table 8 Performance metrics – rescaled to target annualized volatility of 15%.

	E(R)	Std(R)	DD	MDD	Sharpe	Sortino	Calmar	% of +Ret	$\frac{Ave.P}{Ave.L}$
Benchmarks									
Rand	0.024	0.156	0.106	0.584	0.155	0.228	0.042	54.5%	0.947
TM	0.092	0.167	0.106	0.328	0.551	0.872	0.281	58.2%	1.114
MACD	0.112	0.161	0.097	0.337	0.696	1.157	0.333	59.1%	1.184
MLP	0.044	0.165	0.112	0.641	0.265	0.389	0.068	55.1%	1.001
Learning to Rank Models									
RNet	0.243	0.162	0.081	0.294	1.502	3.012	0.828	69.3%	1.407
LM	0.359	0.166	0.067	0.231	2.156	5.321	1.555	76.2%	1.594
LNet	0.306	0.155	0.068	0.274	1.970	4.470	1.115	71.5%	1.679
LMLE	0.260	0.162	0.071	0.236	1.611	3.647	1.102	68.1%	1.534

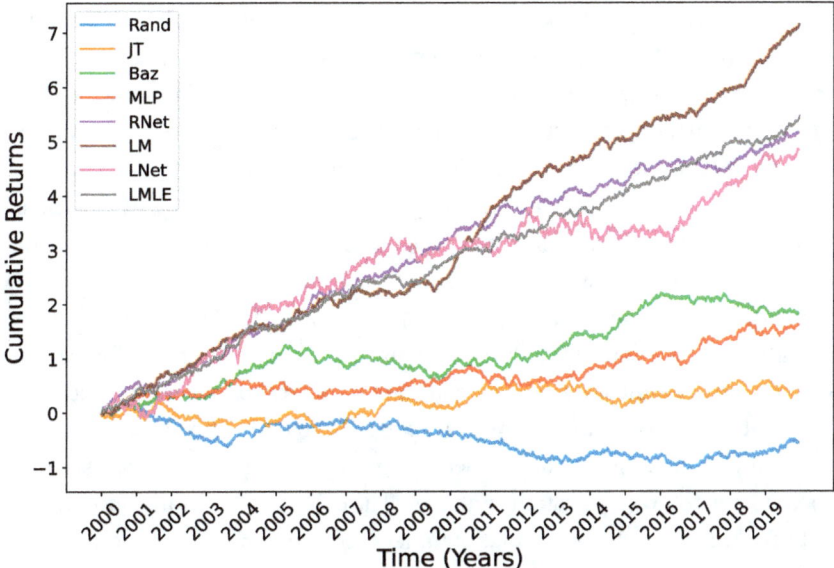

Figure 31 Cumulative returns – rescaled to target volatility annualized volatility of 15%.

without accounting for transaction costs, focusing on the models' inherent predictive capabilities. Both the graphical data and the statistical metrics clearly indicate that the LTR algorithms surpass the benchmark group across all performance criteria, with LambdaMART achieving the highest scores on the majority of the evaluated metrics.

More generally, the ranking algorithms notably enhance profitability, demonstrating both higher expected returns and the rate percentages. Even the least effective LTR model significantly surpasses the top reference benchmark across all evaluated metrics. Although all models have been adjusted to maintain similar levels of volatility, LTR-based strategies tend to experience fewer severe drawdowns and reduced downside risks. Moreover, the leading LTR model achieves substantial improvements across various performance indicators. This pronounced difference in performance highlights the value of learning cross-sectional rankings, as it can lead to better results for momentum strategies.

6 Deep Learning for Risk Management and Portfolio Optimization

In this section, we will introduce concepts and practical tools for evaluating risk in financial markets, as well as techniques to optimize portfolios for various objectives. We begin by examining traditional risk metrics, such as the standard deviation and Value at Risk (VaR), which have long been employed to capture both the volatility and potential downside of asset returns. These metrics are foundational concepts for understanding market risk and inform a wide range of decision-making processes in financial institutions. Next, we delve into classical models for volatility forecasting – covering established approaches such as the HAR (Heterogeneous Auto-Regressive) model – that provided financial practitioners with insights into how market fluctuations evolve over time. While these methods remain useful, they may not always capture the complex structures present in modern, high-frequency financial market data. Consequently, we also introduce deep learning models for volatility forecasting, emphasizing how neural networks can learn intricate, nonlinear dynamics from large datasets in ways that traditional econometric tools often cannot.

Following this discussion of measuring and forecasting risk, we shift our focus to portfolio optimization strategies. The essence of portfolio optimization is to find an asset allocation that optimizes for some investment performance criteria. For example, a portfolio manager might aim to minimize volatility or maximize the Sharpe ratio. The main benefit of investing in a portfolio is the diversification which decreases overall volatility and increases return per unit risk. We continue by exploring the classic mean–variance framework pioneered by Markowitz (1952), which remains a foundational element of modern portfolio theory. This approach weighs expected returns against the portfolio's variance (risk), enabling investors to construct an efficient frontier of optimal risk–return trade-offs. We then discuss maximum diversification, a strategy designed to spread risk across diverse assets or factors, and consequently achieve a more stable performance profile across varying market conditions.

Moving beyond these traditional methods, we next demonstrate how deep learning algorithms can be applied to portfolio optimization. Based on two works C. Zhang, Zhang, Cucuringu, and Zohren (2021); Z. Zhang, Zohren, and Roberts (2020), we present an end-to-end approach that leverages deep learning models to optimize a portfolio directly. Instead of predicting returns or constructing a covariance matrix of returns, the model directly optimizes portfolio weights for a range of objective functions, such as minimizing variance or maximizing the Sharpe Ratio. Deep learning models are adaptable to portfolios with distinct characteristics, allowing for short selling, cardinality, maximum position, and several other constraints. All constraints can be encapsulated in specialized neural network layers, enabling the use of gradient-based methods for optimization.

By bringing risk measurements, volatility forecasting, and portfolio optimization together in one section, we underscore the integral connection between these topics. Accurately forecasting volatility is vital not only for effective risk management but also for informing the dynamic allocation of assets in a portfolio. When market volatility patterns are well understood, practitioners can align their portfolio strategies in a way that accounts for fluctuating levels of uncertainty. In other words, volatility forecasting is not merely an isolated exercise and it provides a predictive lens through which portfolio decisions can be refined. Combining these topics ensures a holistic perspective, from quantifying and forecasting market risk to deploying those insights in a systematic strategy that seeks to balance returns and risk.

6.1 Measuring Risk

We start this section by reviewing the main concepts of risk in quantitative trading, as risk measurement is crucial for developing, evaluating, and executing trading strategies. There are many different ways to quantify risk, for example, Value at Risk (VaR), expected shortfall, drawdown, Sharpe ratio, and Sortino ratio. Each metric provides us with a unique perspective to understand the potential losses of a trading strategy. This section combines risk and portfolio optimization. We typically view risk in the context of portfolio optimization as the uncertainty of returns, focus on the variability of asset prices and the potential for investment loss. To do so, we tend to look at the following metrics:

- Standard deviation (Volatility): The standard deviation of returns remains one of the most widely used risk metrics in portfolio optimization. It measures how much returns fluctuate from their mean, indicating the variability of performance. Hence, a larger standard deviation implies a higher level of risk.
- Covariance and Correlation: These metrics capture the relationship between the movements of two assets. Covariance indicates the direction of the relationship, while correlation provides both direction and strength. Understanding the relationships between assets is crucial for diversification, and is accordingly a key concept in portfolio optimization.
- Beta: Beta measures how an asset's returns move in response to overall market changes. When beta is above 1, the asset's returns tend to amplify market movements, while a beta below 1 means the asset's returns are less sensitive to market swings. In a portfolio context, assessing the portfolio's overall beta offers insights into its exposure to market fluctuations.
- Value at Risk (VaR) and Conditional Value at Risk (CVaR): VaR quantifies the maximum potential loss over a specified time horizon at a chosen

confidence level. In other words, with probability (for example) 95%, losses will not exceed the VaR figure. When VaR is used as a risk constraint, it effectively places a limit (threshold) on the acceptable level of potential loss. CVaR extends this by indicating the expected loss beyond the VaR. Thus, CVaR focuses specifically on the distribution's tail, capturing the average magnitude of losses that surpass the VaR.
- Downside Risk: This measures the potential for loss in adverse scenarios, focusing on negative returns. Metrics like the Sortino ratio, which is the ratio of the asset's return relative to its downside risk, are particularly useful in this context.

These risk metrics are popular indicators in both academia and industry. Thus, a good understanding of these metrics provides us with the foundation for managing our portfolio risks. Note that risk measurement is not a set-and-forget process. Continuous monitoring is vital as market conditions, asset correlations, and volatilities evolve. Consistent reviews are imperative to maintain alignment between the portfolio and an investor's risk preferences and objectives. By applying diverse risk metrics and regularly monitoring and adjusting their holdings, investors can improve the likelihood of meeting their financial targets while effectively managing their risk exposure.

6.2 Classical Methods for Volatility Forecasting

We focus on volatility, as it is one of the most commonly used risk measures. Volatility is computed via the standard deviation of price changes. These changes can be either percentage changes in price, that is, returns, or price differences. The former yields a volatility in percentage terms, for example, 15% volatility per year, while the latter yields a dollar volatility, that is, $10 million volatility per year. Different methods can be used to estimate standard deviations. For example, we can simply take the weighted average of historical volatility to represent current market conditions. We can also resort to sampling methods such as Monte Carlo which relies upon random sampling and statistical techniques to approximate the probability distribution of returns. To go yet a step further, we can use predictive models to forecast the future variability of returns on a financial instrument.

We first delve into some classical methods to predict future volatility. In particular, we focus on the Heterogeneous Autoregressive (HAR) model for daily volatility forecasts and the HEAVY (High-frequency based Auto-regressive and Volatility) model, which further utilizes intraday data to improve its forecasts.

The HAR model is a popular approach for forecasting daily volatility. It was introduced to account for the regularly observed enduring memory effect, which suggests that volatility shocks can have prolonged effects over time. The HAR model incorporates lagged values of daily, weekly, and monthly volatilities to predict the next day's volatility. In doing so, the model's structure acknowledges that market participants operate on different "heterogeneous" time horizons. The predicted daily volatility $v_{d,t+1}$ is denoted as:

$$v_{d,t+1} = \beta_0 + \beta_1 v_{d,t} + \beta_2 v_{w,t} + \beta_3 v_{m,t} + \epsilon_t, \tag{90}$$

where $v_{d,t}, v_{w,t}, v_{m,t}$ represent the daily, weekly, and monthly volatilities respectively, and β coefficients are the parameters that need to be inferred. The linear HAR model is straightforward to estimate and interpret, which makes it a valuable tool for capturing the dynamics of financial market volatilities.

While the HAR model is an effective method, the HEAVY model is designed to forecast volatility using high-frequency data, which provides more granular insights into the market's behavior compared to traditional low-frequency data. HEAVY models are commonly used for modeling volatility from high-frequency data like tick-by-tick or minute-by-minute price movements. In order to estimate volatility from high-frequency data, we introduce the notion of realized volatility (RV_t). A common estimate for realized volatility is:

$$RV_t = \sqrt{\sum_i^m (r_{t_i}^2)}, \tag{91}$$

where $r_{t_i}^2$ are the high-frequency returns, and m represents the number of high-frequency intervals within a day (e.g., minutes). RV is used as a measure of the total variance in asset prices over a specific time interval, and the idea is that volatility can be obtained from the squared returns of the high-frequency price series. We can then express the HEAVY model as the following:

$$v_{d,t+1} = \alpha + \beta v_{d,t} + \gamma RV_t + \epsilon_t, \tag{92}$$

where the realized volatility is used to capture the short-term volatility from high-frequency data and the lagged volatility component is used for the long-term trends. The benefits of leveraging high-frequency data allow for more accurate volatility estimation, and HEAVY models are well-equipped to handle the phenomenon of volatility clustering.

However, microstructure noise exists and the HEAVY model remains sensitive to certain market effects, such as bid-ask spreads, and sampling frequency. It is nontrivial to eliminate the noise, which could affect the accuracy of volatility estimates and predictions.

6.3 Deep Learning Models for Volatility Forecasting

While largely effective, traditional volatility models sometimes struggle to capture complex, nonlinear patterns in financial time-series data. Deep learning offers an alternative approach that is able to model such intricate dependencies and nonlinearities. One of the innovative applications in this domain is HARnet (Reisenhofer, Bayer, & Hautsch, 2022), which integrates the WaveNet architecture with the original HAR model to enhance volatility forecasting. In the original HAR model, daily, weekly, and monthly features are used to increase the receptive field of the model. Similarly, as previously covered in the Foundations section, WaveNet is a deep learning architecture with similarly capabilities, but a higher level of complexity that enables it to capture non-linearities. The proposed HARnet is able to leverage both models' strengths to capture sequential patterns with long memory properties in volatility data.

A typical HARnet comprises an input layer, stacked dilated convolutions, skip connections, and a final output layer. A HARnet receives different lagged volatilities (daily, weekly, and monthly) and injects this input data to stacked dilated convolutions which process input volatilities to capture dependencies across different time scales. Because of its dilation factor, WaveNet can exponentially extend its receptive field as the depth of the network increases. This facilitates the incorporation of information from long sequences without a significant increase in computational complexity. After a subsequent series of neural layers, a final output layer is used to predict future volatility. While the aforementioned WaveNet-based architecture is interesting, its usage shows few improvements, as it still only incorporates daily data. It is also somewhat counterintuitive to simultaneously use WaveNet and daily, weekly, and monthly inputs.

A much better use case for WaveNet is forecasting volatility from intraday data. First, the dynamic range is much larger, stretching from minutes to months. Second, intraday data has more potential to contain interesting nonlinear patterns that can be exploited. Accordingly, Moreno-Pino and Zohren (2024) introduces DeepVol, a model that adopts the WaveNet architecture to predict volatility from high-frequency financial data. This network is composed of a stack of dilated causal convolution layers and a subsequent dense layer that produces the volatility forecast. The use of dilated convolutions allows the network to efficiently increase its receptive field (i.e., the range of time steps it can consider when making a prediction) without having to increase the number of layers or computational cost. The work's results show that these properties allow the model to efficiently make use of past intraday data to enhance its predictions.

The application of deep learning to volatility forecasting represents a significant advancement in financial modeling. By leveraging architectures like WaveNet, deep learning-based models can better handle nonlinear relationships in data, a valuable attribute when dealing with financial markets. Deep networks are also particularly adept at capturing long memory characteristics of volatility through dilated convolutions and attention layers. As financial data continues to expand in volume and complexity, deep learning will likely play an increasingly central role in the development of such advanced analytical tools.

6.4 Classical Methods for Portfolio Optimization

Portfolio optimization is a cornerstone of modern finance, providing a structured approach to selecting investments that balance risk and return according to an investor's objectives. In this section, we review two important approaches: mean-variance optimization and maximum diversification. Each method offers a unique perspective on how to construct a portfolio to achieve specific investment goals. Mean-variance optimization, developed by Markowitz (1952) in the 1950s, is a foundational component of modern portfolio theory. This approach focuses on constructing a portfolio that aims to maximize returns for a specified level of risk or, conversely, minimize risk for a specified level of return. They introduce the concept of the efficient frontier, which represents the portfolio construction that yields the highest expected return for each level of risk. This is achieved through mathematical optimization by maximizing returns and minimizing variances (or volatility which represents risk).

To construct such a portfolio, consider a set of n assets, where each asset has an expected return r_i and variance σ_i^2. The portfolio weights are represented by $w = (w_1, w_2, \cdots, w_n)^T$ where w_i is the proportion of the portfolio invested in asset i. One way to formulate the optimization problem is to identify portfolios that achieve the highest possible expected returns for a specified level of risk. This can be expressed as:

$$\max_{w} r_p = w^T r, \text{ s.t.,}$$
$$\sigma_p^2 = w^T \Sigma w = \sigma_{p,0}^2, \text{ and } w^T \mathbf{1} = 1, \tag{93}$$

where Σ is the covariance matrix of asset returns with σ_{ij} representing the covariance between asset i and j. $\sigma_{p,0}^2$ denotes a target level of risk and $\mathbf{1}$ is a vector of ones ensuring that the weights sum to 1 (i.e., fully invested portfolio). In solving the constrained maximization problem outlined earlier, one determines the optimal portfolio weights that maximize returns while keeping risk at a given level. An alternative formulation of the mean-variance problem focuses on minimizing portfolio risk while enforcing a specified target for expected returns. This would be expressed as:

$$\min_{w} \sigma_p^2 = w^T \Sigma w, \text{ s.t.,}$$
$$r_p = w^T r = r_{p,0}, \text{ and } w^T \mathbf{1} = 1, \tag{94}$$

where $r_{p,0}$ denote a target expected return level. To solve this formulation of the constrained optimization problem, we introduce Lagrange multipliers λ and γ for the constraints. The Lagrangian $\mathcal{L}$ is:

$$\mathcal{L}(w, \lambda, \gamma) = w^T \Sigma w + \lambda(r_{p,0} - w^T r) + \gamma(1 - w^T \mathbf{1}). \tag{95}$$

To find the optimal solution, we take the partial derivatives of $\mathcal{L}$ with respect to w, λ and γ and set each of them to zero:

$$\frac{\partial \mathcal{L}}{\partial w} = 2\Sigma w - \lambda r_{p,0} - \gamma \mathbf{1} = 0,$$
$$\frac{\partial \mathcal{L}}{\partial \lambda} = r_{p,0} - w^T r = 0, \tag{96}$$
$$\frac{\partial \mathcal{L}}{\partial \gamma} = 1 - w^T \mathbf{1} = 0,$$

where the solution obtained provides the optimal portfolio allocation that minimizes the portfolio risk for a given expected return. By setting the partial derivatives equal to zero, we are essentially finding the point where the rate of change of the objective function with respect to each asset weight is zero, implying that the portfolio has reached an optimal balance between risk and return. The Lagrange multiplier in this context represents the trade-off between the expected return and the risk of the portfolio. It provides insight into how much additional return can be achieved by increasing the overall level of risk in the portfolio. The solution essentially tells us the proportion of wealth to allocate to each asset in order to achieve the best risk-return trade-off, considering both the covariance between asset returns and the constraints set.

The strategy of maximum diversification is based on the premise that a portfolio that diversifies across a wide range of assets will typically have a lower risk than the sum of its individual components. Accordingly, the objective is to trade a selection of assets that effectively lowers unsystematic risk, thereby minimizing the overall portfolio's volatility. As a result, maximum diversification considers the correlations between assets rather than just their individual risks. By holding assets with low or negative correlations, the aggregate risk of a portfolio can be meaningfully reduced. A central measure for this approach is the diversification ratio (DR), defined as the ratio between the sum of the individually weighted asset volatilities and the total volatility of the portfolio. A larger value therefore indicates more effective diversification. In mathematical terms, we define DR as:

$$DR = \frac{w^T \sigma}{\sqrt{w^T \Sigma w}}, \tag{97}$$

where w is again the weight vector and $w^T \sigma$ represents the weighted sum of the individual asset volatilities. The goal is to maximize the diversification ratio with respect to the weights vector w, and can be expressed as:

$$\max_{w} \frac{w^T \sigma}{\sqrt{w^T \Sigma w}}, \quad s.t.\ w^T \mathbf{1} = 1, \tag{98}$$

where $\mathbf{1}$ is a vector of ones, ensuring the weights sum to 1. The optimization problem is a fractional programming problem due to the ratio in the objective function. We can simplify this by maximizing the numerator while holding the denominator constraint. This reformulation constrains the portfolio variance to be constant (usually set to 1), and focuses on maximizing the weighted average volatility. One approach to tackle this optimization problem is to again employ Lagrange multipliers:

$$\mathcal{L}(w, \lambda, \gamma) = w^T \sigma - \lambda(w^T \Sigma w - 1) - \gamma(w^T \mathbf{1} - 1), \tag{99}$$

where λ and γ are Lagrange multipliers for the constraints. We optimize the portfolio weights by differentiating with respect to w, λ and γ:

$$\begin{aligned}
\frac{\partial \mathcal{L}}{\partial w} &= \sigma - 2\lambda \Sigma w - \gamma \mathbf{1} = 0, \\
\frac{\partial \mathcal{L}}{\partial \lambda} &= w^T \Sigma w - 1 = 0, \\
\frac{\partial \mathcal{L}}{\partial \gamma} &= w^T \mathbf{1} - 1 = 0.
\end{aligned} \tag{100}$$

Intuitively, an investor allocates capital across a variety of assets that have low or negative correlations with each other to achieve maximum diversification (MD). Following the same logic, this strategy aims to minimize unsystematic risk, capitalizing on the unique price movements of each asset. The key advantage of MD is risk reduction without a proportional decrease in potential returns, which is particularly appealing during turbulent market conditions. This diversification can help protect against significant downturns in any single investment or asset class as negatively correlated assets are unlikely to all move in the same direction.

Although MPT and MD are popular, their underlying assumptions have been widely questioned and frequently do not hold true in real financial markets. In particular, MPT presupposes normally distributed asset returns and assumes that investors are rational, risk-averse, and chiefly focused on mean and variance. Nevertheless, financial datasets frequently exhibit highly erratic behavior, making them prone to deviating from these assumptions, particularly during episodes of sharp market fluctuations (see for instance (Cont & Nitions, 1999; Z. Zhang, Zohren, & Roberts, 2019b)). Additionally, MPT assumes a static view of risk and return, ignoring the dynamic nature of asset performance and market conditions. The estimates of expected returns, variances, and covariances are also very difficult to obtain, and small errors in these estimates can lead to significant discrepancies in the model results and consequently over- or under-allocation to certain assets.

6.5 Deep Learning for Portfolio Optimization

We now tackle the problem of portfolio optimization from the perspective of deep learning. Returns and their covariance matrices are often unstable and difficult to estimate. However, these challenges can be addressed through the application of deep learning algorithms. Specifically, C. Zhang et al. (2021) and Z. Zhang et al. (2020) propose an end-to-end framework that leverages deep learning models to directly optimize a portfolio. Unlike the conventional two-step process of forecasting and then optimizing, this approach bypasses the need for estimating future returns and the covariance matrix by directly outputting optimal portfolio weights.

The proposed framework is highly flexible and capable of dealing with different objectives and constraints. We take a general mean-variance problem as an example to demonstrate the framework. In a general mean-variance problem that permits short selling, we seek to maximize:

Objective (1) *Mean Variance Problem*:

$$\max_{\mathbf{w}_t} E(r_{p,t+1}) - \frac{\lambda}{2} Var(r_{p,t+1}), \text{ s.t. } ||\mathbf{w}_t||_1 = \sum_{i=1}^{n} |w_{i,t}| = 1, \tag{101}$$

where $r_{p,t+1} = \mathbf{w}_t^T \mathbf{r}_{t+1}$ represents the portfolio return, while $\mathbf{r}_t = (r_{1,t}, \cdots, r_{n,t})^T$ denotes the vector of returns for n assets at time t, with $r_{i,t}$ referring to the return of asset i ($i = 1, \cdots, n$). The index t can be any chosen interval, such as minutes, days, or months. λ is the risk aversion rate that controls the trade-off between returns and risks, and $\mathbf{w}_t = (w_{1,t}, \cdots, w_{n,t})T$ represents the portfolio weights that need to be optimized. In order to obtain $\mathbf{w}_t$, we adopt a deep neural network (f) that outputs portfolio weights:

$$\mathbf{w}_t = f(\mathbf{X}_t), \tag{102}$$

where X_t denotes the inputs to the network. Figure 32 depicts the proposed end-to-end framework, which contains two main components: the **score block** and the **portfolio block**.

Deep Learning in Quantitative Trading

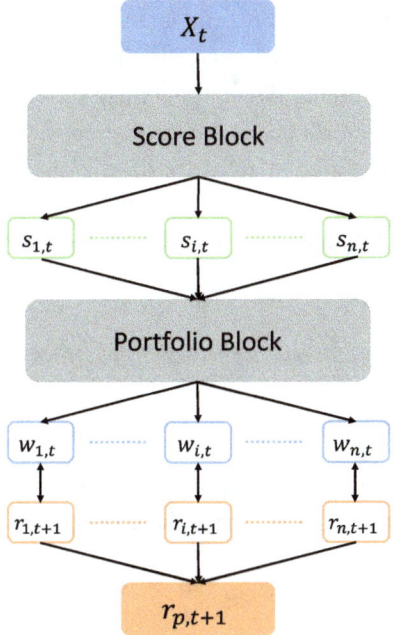

Figure 32 Architecture of the proposed end-to-end framework.

The **score block** maps inputs to portfolio scores. Inputs can be any market information that might be useful for adjusting portfolio weights. For example, past returns up to lag p ($r_{t-p}, \ldots, r_t$), momentum features (MACD). More specifically, a neural network maps the input data to fitness scores for each asset. Higher fitness scores indicate a greater likelihood of receiving larger portfolio weights. We denote this network as f_{scores} and the resulting fitness scores as:

$$s_t = (s_{1,t}, \ldots, s_{N,t})^T = f_{scores}(X_t), \tag{103}$$

where f_{scores} can be any stack of neural layers, such as convolutional, recurrent, or attention layers.

Within the **portfolio block**, we transform previously derived scores s_t into portfolio weights that meet the constraints of the relevant differentiable functions $f_{weights}(\cdot)$. We then calculate the realized portfolio return $r_{p,t+1}$ from the underlying asset returns r_{t+1} and derive the loss based on the chosen objective function. In the context of Equation 101, which allows short selling and stipulates that the sum of absolute weights must be one, the fitness scores require the following transformation:

$$\begin{aligned} w_{i,t} &= f_{weights}(s_{i,t}), \\ &= \text{sign}(s_{i,t}) \times \frac{e^{s_{i,t}}}{\sum_{j=1}^{N} e^{s_{j,t}}}, \end{aligned} \tag{104}$$

where the entire framework is differentiable so gradient ascent can be used to optimize model parameters. In practice, investors have different risk tolerance and face different constraints. We can optimize different objective functions and adjust the portfolio block ($f_{weights}$) to meet these various constraints as long as these operations are differentiable. Specifically, we examine the following objective functions and constraints:

Objective (2) *Global Minimum Variance Portfolio* (GMVP):

$$\min_{w_t} Var(r_{p,t+1}), \qquad (105)$$

Objective (3) *Maximum Sharpe Ratio Portfolio* (MSRP):

$$\max_{w_t} \frac{E(r_{p,t+1})}{Std(r_{p,t+1})}, \qquad (106)$$

Constraint (1) *Long-only* and $\|w_t\|_1 = 1$: To ensure nonnegative weights, we apply the softmax activation function to the scores. For $i = 1, \ldots, n$, we define:

$$w_{i,t} = \frac{e^{s_{i,t}}}{\sum_{j=1}^{n} e^{s_{j,t}}}, \qquad (107)$$

where Listing 2 in Appendix D demonstrates how to construct this constraint in Pytorch.

Constraint (2) *Maximum Position* and $\|w_t\|_1 = 1$: To ensure the weights automatically satisfy the upper bound u, we transform the scores using a generalized sigmoid function $\phi_a(x) = a + \frac{1}{1+e^{-x}}$ (where $a \geq 0$). Upon setting $a = \frac{1-u}{nu-1}$, we obtain $w_{i,t} \leq u$ as follows:

$$w_{i,t} = \text{sign}(s_{i,t}) \times \frac{\phi_a(|s_{i,t}|)}{\sum_{j=1}^{n} \phi_a(|s_{j,t}|)}, \qquad (108)$$

if we set the maximum position u to 1, $\phi_a(x)$ reduces to the standard sigmoid function.

Constraint (3) *Cardinality* and $\|w_t\|_1 = 1$: To handle cardinality, we begin by defining a sorting operator $\Pi(\cdot)$ that takes $s_t \in \mathbb{R}^n$ and generates a permutation matrix $\Pi(s_t) \in \mathbb{R}^{n \times n}$. As a result, $\tilde{s}_t = \Pi(s_t)$ is the vector s_t arranged in descending order. Based on this ordering, we take long positions in the top k assets and short positions in the bottom k to form our portfolio:

$$w_{i,t} = \frac{1}{2} \times \frac{1_{\{s_{i,t} > d_u\}} e^{|s_{i,t}|}}{\sum_{j=1}^{n} 1_{\{s_{j,t} > d_u\}} e^{|s_{j,t}|}} - \frac{1}{2} \times \frac{1_{\{s_{j,t} < d_l\}} e^{|s_{i,t}|}}{\sum_{j=1}^{n} 1_{\{s_{i,t} < d_l\}} e^{|s_{j,t}|}},$$
$$d_u = \tilde{s}_t[k], \quad d_l = \tilde{s}_t[n-k], \quad k = \left\lfloor \frac{n}{2} \right\rfloor + 1, \qquad (109)$$

where $\tilde{s}_t[k]$ denotes the k-th entry of $\tilde{s}_t$, that is, the k-th largest value in s_t. To calculate the sorting operator, we first introduce a square matrix $\Lambda_{i,j}^t$ derived from the fitness score s_t as follows:

$$\Lambda_{i,j}^t = (n + 1 - 2i)s_{j,t} - \sum_m |s_{j,t} - s_{m,t}|. \tag{110}$$

According to previous works (Blondel et al., 2020; Cuturi, Teboul, & Vert, 2019; Grover, Wang, Zweig, & Ermon, 2018; Ogryczak & Tamir, 2003), the permutation matrix $\Pi(s_t)$ can be constructed as:

$$\Pi(s_t)_{i,j} = \begin{cases} 1, & \text{if } j = \text{argmax}(\Lambda_{i,:}^t), \\ 0, & \text{otherwise.} \end{cases} \tag{111}$$

Since the argmax function is not differentiable, Grover et al. (2018) introduce a NeuralSort layer that substitutes argmax with softmax, producing a differentiable approximation of $\Pi(s_t)$:

$$\widehat{\Pi(s_t)}_{i,:} = \text{softmax}(\Lambda_{i,:}^t). \tag{112}$$

Thus Equation (109) becomes differentiable, allowing for the use of standard gradient descent.

Constraint (4) *Leverage, i.e.* $L\|w_t\|_1 = L$: In line with Equation (104), we scale the overall exposure of the positions by a factor of L:

$$w_{i,t} = L \times \text{sign}(s_{i,t}) \times \frac{e^{|s_{i,t}|}}{\sum_{j=1}^n e^{|s_{j,t}|}}. \tag{113}$$

To illustrate the performance of this deep learning framework for portfolio optimization, we use daily data from 735 stocks within the Russell 3000 Index. The dataset spans from 1984/01/03 to 2021/07/06 and the testing period is designated as 2001 to 2021. When reporting the performance, we include evaluation metrics from previous sections, as well as Beta, to gauge the portfolio's correlation with the S&P 500 Index. This metric is useful to consider because it measures the sensitivity of a portfolio's return to that of a market index. Ideally, we would like a portfolio that is less correlated with the market, as this helps limit risk during market downturns.

Table 9 displays the experimental results, which are divided into four sections. The first section (Baselines) comprises four benchmark strategies: the S&P 500 Index, an equally weighted portfolio (EWP), the maximum diversification (MD) portfolio, and the global minimum variance portfolio (GMVP) (Theron & Van Vuuren, 2018). The second block (MSRP) of Table 9 compares the classical mean-variance optimization approach (MPT) with the proposed deep learning algorithms (E2E) optimizing Sharpe ratio. For MPT, we first predict assets' returns by minimizing the mean squared loss and then substitute these estimates to obtain optimal portfolio weights. For deep learning models, gradient ascent is used to directly optimize the Sharpe ratio. We test on several models in this part including a linear model (LM), a multilayer perceptron (MLP), an LSTM network, and a CNN model.

Table 9 Performance metrics.

	E(R)	Std(R)	DD	MDD	Sharpe	Sortino	Beta	% of +Ret
Baselines								
S&P 500	0.061	0.196	0.140	0.568	0.402	0.563	1.000	54.1%
EWP	0.130	0.212	0.148	0.548	0.682	0.973	1.000	54.6%
MD	0.439	0.239	0.141	0.519	1.641	2.785	0.599	54.8%
GMVP	0.080	0.081	0.059	0.408	0.992	1.360	0.257	56.4%
MSRP								
MPT-LM	0.004	0.015	0.011	0.062	0.290	0.414	0.009	50.4%
MPT-MLP	0.008	0.027	0.019	0.140	0.299	0.424	0.036	51.5%
MPT-LSTM	0.014	0.017	0.011	0.043	0.858	1.259	0.014	52.0%
MPT-CNN	0.007	0.017	0.012	0.093	0.426	0.609	0.014	51.3%
E2E-LM	0.049	0.044	0.030	0.168	1.116	1.649	0.011	54.6%
E2E-MLP	0.044	0.026	0.016	0.073	1.688	2.657	0.008	55.2%

E2E-LSTM	0.060	0.023	0.013	0.017	2.604	4.448	0.017	57.8%
E2E-CNN	0.023	0.024	0.017	0.084	0.931	1.365	0.046	53.1%
Other Objective Functions								
E2E-LSTM-GMVP	0.001	0.011	0.008	0.060	0.047	0.067	-0.004	50.4%
E2E-LSTM-MVP$_{\lambda=10}$	0.064	0.317	0.207	0.878	0.349	0.534	0.342	51.8%
E2E-LSTM-MVP$_{\lambda=20}$	0.179	0.169	0.115	0.380	1.055	1.555	0.195	54.8%
E2E-LSTM-MVP$_{\lambda=30}$	0.168	0.116	0.076	0.187	1.394	2.149	0.060	55.2%
Constraints								
E2E-LSTM-MSRP-Long	0.368	0.197	0.125	0.253	1.691	2.666	0.767	56.6%
E2E-LSTM-MSRP-LEV	0.321	0.112	0.068	0.151	2.540	4.203	0.132	57.6%
E2E-LSTM-MSRP-CAR	0.032	0.056	0.039	0.167	0.588	0.844	-0.011	52.0%
E2E-LSTM-MSRP-MAX	0.057	0.021	0.012	0.026	2.683	4.459	0.021	57.8%

The third block (other objective functions) indicates the results for the application of deep learning to different objective functions including global minimum variance portfolio (GMVP) and mean-variance problem in Equation 101. The final section (Constraints) explores the influence of multiple constraints by constructing a strictly long portfolio aimed at maximizing the Sharpe ratio (MSRP-LONG), a leveraged portfolio (LEV) with $L = 5$, a cardinality-constrained strategy (CAR) that selects 20% of the instruments thereby going long on the top decile and shorting the bottom decile, and lastly a portfolio that imposes a 5% maximum position limit for each instrument (MAX).

In the second block of Table 9, the end-to-end (E2E) deep learning methods outperform both the MPT and baseline models. The third block highlights how varying objective functions influence model performance. Specifically, GMVP not surprisingly provides the lowest variance. Additionally, adjusting the risk aversion parameter λ in the mean-variance approach allows users to control their preferred risk level – raising λ increases the penalty on risk, thereby reducing variance. The final block presents results under different constraints, demonstrating the framework's flexibility. Users thus have the ability to customize these constraints to align with their individual requirements and trading conditions.

6.6 Recent Developments on Volatility Forecasting and Portfolio Construction

In this last part of the section, we explore some more recent developments in the application of deep learning to volatility forecasting and portfolio optimization.

6.6.1 Graph-Based Models and LLMs for Volatility Forecasting

It can be helpful to view financial assets as network structures. Supply networks are one helpful example, in which volatility can spill over from one company to another in a network. Moreover, textual information, such as news can also be incorporated in the forecasting task. There has thus been an increased interest in applying graph-based methods and large language modeling to such problems.

We will review and detail some key works that apply these techniques, focusing on how these models offer a deeper understanding of market dynamics and provide more reliable predictions.

Volatility Forecasting with Graph-Based Models Traditional models for volatility forecasting typically focus on single-variate time-series, where the volatility of each asset is predicted independently based on its own historical data. While models that use vector forms provide a way to study multiple time-series simultaneously, they still fall short in capturing the complex relationships and interactions between assets. This is a limitation in financial markets, where assets often exhibit strong correlations and spillover effects that influence their volatility.

We now look at graph-based models that address this issue by explicitly representing these relationships as a graph, where assets are connected based on their correlations or other relevant interactions with one another. By doing so, traders can better capture the intricate dependencies across assets, allowing for a more accurate and holistic approach to volatility forecasting. C. Zhang, Pu, Cucuringu, and Dong (2024) introduces Graph-HAR (GHAR), which lays out a framework to forecast multivariate realized volatility by extending the HAR model with graphs. Suppose we have $v_{d,t} = (v_{d,t}^1, \cdots, v_{d,t}^N)$ as the vector of realized volatility for n assets. Recall that a HAR model incorporates lagged values of daily, weekly, and monthly volatilities to predict the next day's volatility (Equation 90). We can define GHAR as:

$$v_{d,t+1} = \alpha + \beta_d v_{d,t} + \beta_w v_{w,t} + \beta_m v_{m,t} \\ + \gamma_d \tilde{A} \cdot v_{d,t} + \gamma_w \tilde{A} \cdot v_{w,t} + \gamma_d \tilde{A} \cdot v_{d,t}, \quad (114)$$

where $\tilde{A}$ is the normalized adjacency matrix of A. The adjacency matrix A encodes relationships between assets ($A[i,j]$ is the weight of the edge between node i and node j) which can be determined in several ways. For instance, we can resort to correlation-based methods, such as computing the pairwise correlations of returns and adding correlations to edges between assets when their correlations exceed a certain threshold. $\tilde{A} \cdot v_t$ represents the neighborhood aggregation over different horizons and γ represents the effects from connected neighbors. Notably, GHAR assumes a linear relationship between the volatilities of two connected assets. However, we have the ability to introduce nonlinearities by using graph convolutional layers.

This brings us to the GNNHAR network which is a GNN-enhanced HAR model by C. Zhang et al. (2023) which replaces the linear neighborhood aggregation in GHAR (the term $\tilde{A} \cdot v_t$) with GNNs. Specifically, let us define a GNNHAR with l layers:

$$v_{d,t+1} = \alpha + V_t \beta + H^{(l)} \gamma, \\ H^{(l)} = GNN(H^{(l-1)}, A) = \sigma(\tilde{A} H^{(l-1)} W^{(l)}), \quad (115)$$

where $V_t = (v_{d,t+1}, v_{w,t+1}, v_{m,t+1}) \in \mathcal{R}^{n \times 3}$ and $H^{(0)} = V_t$. We define $W^{(l)}$ as the learnable weights and σ denotes the ReLU activation function.

GNNs possess several advantages for forecasting volatility. One key benefit is that a GNN can model both the direct and indirect effects of asset interactions. For example, when one asset experiences a large shock, it can cause volatility to spill over to other assets in the network, even if those assets were not directly affected by the initial event. This phenomenon is known as the spillover effect and can reverberate between assets that are not directly related. In other words, it describes the transmission of financial disturbances, such as price movements, volatility shocks, or shifts in market sentiment, as they propagate between a network of assets. GNNs are capable of modeling these spillover effects, as they can incorporate a broader set of market dynamics that traditional methods may miss.

In addition, GNNs can handle high-dimensional data efficiently. By leveraging the graph structure, GNNs can learn from a vast array of asset interactions without becoming overwhelmed by the dimensionality of the data. As a result, GNNs can learn complex dependencies from historical data, making them more adept at forecasting future volatility in a multivariate setting. Moreover, GNNs have the ability to adapt to the evolving relationships between assets which allows them to respond to changing market conditions, an especially valuable trait in the fast-moving world of financial markets.

Volatility Forecasting with Text-Based Features LLMs (Large Language Models) facilitate the use of new data sources for generating alpha. They are capable of processing and interpreting vast amounts of text from different sources, including news reports, social media feeds, and earnings call transcripts. As a result, LLMs can capture meaningful insights, subtle sentiment shifts, and nuanced market signals that might elude traditional numeric data analyses. The incorporation of these text-derived features can thus lead to more robust and timely predictions of market volatility, especially in fast-moving or sentiment-driven trading environments.

In the work of Rahimikia, Zohren, and Poon (2021), the authors provide a detailed exploration of how specialized word embeddings can be harnessed to improve realized volatility forecasts. Word embeddings assign numeric vectors to words, ensuring that terms sharing similar meanings or usage patterns lie close together in the vector space. Put differently, these embeddings transform discrete text (strings) into continuous numerical representations, where semantic and contextual affinities are captured by each word's position and proximity. Their methodology emphasizes building domain-specific embeddings tailored to financial terminology and contexts, as opposed to using generic NLP models. By training on a large corpus of financial documents, they are able to detect subtle differences in how words or phrases are used across various market scenarios, such as regulatory changes, earnings surprises, or shifts in investor sentiment.

The paper demonstrates that by integrating these carefully calibrated text-based features with conventional numeric factors in a machine learning framework, one can better capture signals and significantly enhance predictive performance. On typical days, time-series models generally tend to outperform purely news-based models in volatility forecasting. This is because they capture historical price patterns and market dynamics under normal conditions. However, news-based models tend to perform better during volatility shocks, as they can quickly incorporate real-time information from news sources that may drive sudden market fluctuations. Given the strengths of each, the optimal performance is often achieved through models that integrate both text and price data.

Several studies have demonstrated the effectiveness of such hybrid models. For instance, Atkins, Niranjan, and Gerding (2018) show that sentiment analysis from financial news enhances volatility forecasting accuracy. Similarly, Du, Xing, Mao, and Cambria (2024) highlight the benefits of integrating natural language processing with time-series analysis.

6.6.2 Graph-Based Models and LLMs for Portfolio Optimization

Utilizing Graph-Based Models to Improve Portfolio Construction As discussed in Section 3 and Section 6.6.1, GNNs are naturally adept at modeling relationships among different companies. We now introduce the application of graph-based models to construct portfolios. Suppose we have a graph $\mathcal{G} = (V, E)$ where v denotes the nodes which are the companies and E are the edges that represent the relationships between companies. If there are N nodes and each node (asset) has a feature vector $x_i \in \mathbb{R}^d$, we can obtain a node-feature matrix $X \in \mathbb{R}^{N \times d}$ by stacking the individual vectors.

We can build and train a GNN with historical data. To construct a graph, we first need to define the nodes and create the adjacency matrix A. Again, there are many different approaches to obtain the adjacency matrices and the most straightforward way is probably to obtain them from correlation matrices. In Figure 33, we present such an example where we calculate an adjacency matrix by using the correlations of fifty futures contracts. After obtaining the graph, we can then adopt graph layers to model interested outputs. Recapping the derivation of a graph convolutional layer (shown in Equation 69), it processes information as:

$$H^{l+1} = \sigma(\tilde{A} H^{(l)} W^{(l)}), \tag{116}$$

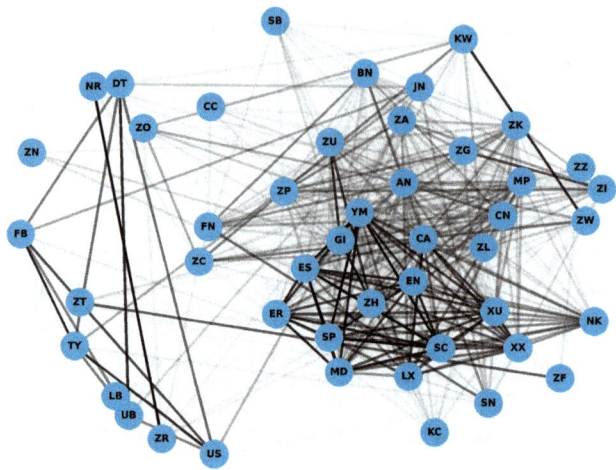

Figure 33 A graph built from adjacency matrix of futures contracts.

where $H^{(l+1)}$ is the matrix of the node embedding at layer l and $H^{(0)} = X$, $W^{(l)}$ is a trainable weight matrix, σ is the nonlinear activation function and $\tilde{A}$ is a normalized version of the adjacency matrix A. Depending on the purpose of the task, the final output embedding can vary.

Ekmekcioğlu & Pınar (2023) extend the framework introduced in Section 6.5 with graph layers to directly learn optimal asset allocations. By treating each asset as a node and connections between assets as edges, they outline a framework to capture intricate relationships that traditional models often overlook. In this approach, GNNs are used as the primary tool for learning these relationships and aggregate signals from each node's neighbors to form more expressive embeddings of each asset. The results indicate that GNN-based models can provide better insights into how assets co-move and how certain market events propagate through a network of financial assets. Moreover, graph-based approaches allow the model to dynamically learn higher-order dependencies among clusters of assets, rather than simply relying upon pairwise correlations or static factor models.

Another interesting work by Korangi, Mues, and Bravo (2024) seeks to capture the evolving relationships among hundreds of assets over extended horizons. They elect to use Graph Attention Networks (GATs) to incorporate dynamic information about how assets co-move and influence one another. In such a framework, each asset is a node in a time-evolving graph, and the adjacency matrix is periodically updated using rolling windows of returns or other market signals. At each network snapshot, the GAT layer uses attention mechanisms to assign weights to edges, so that connections with higher relevance receive proportionally more information flow. The authors demonstrate that the GAT-based model outperforms benchmarks and delivers consistently superior results over the long term.

Additionally, GNNs provide a powerful and flexible framework for integrating alternative datasets that do not consist of purely price or return-based signals. Traditional approaches to portfolio optimization often rely on historical price returns and standard covariance estimates. However, these methods may fail to capture more nuanced or rapidly evolving relationships between assets, particularly when crucial information – such as industry news, social media sentiment, or supply chain linkages – is available. GNNs address this gap by allowing practitioners to construct networks from diverse data sources, where each node represents a company (or other financial entity), and edges capture meaningful relationships derived from any number of alternative datasets.

One concrete example is building a news network, as discussed in Wan et al. (2021). In this setup, a connection (edge) between two companies is formed based on co-mentions in news articles, the frequency of joint coverage, or sentiment correlations extracted from text analytics. Figure 34 shows a graph built from textual data instead of a return correlation matrix. This information might highlight hidden interdependencies. For instance, two companies operating in distant industries may appear uncorrelated based upon their returns but share a major client–supplier relationship. A fact that might be consistently flagged by journalists. By embedding these news-driven relationships into a GNN, the model can learn representations that account not only for price co-movements but also for deeper relational structures present in textual data. As a result, the GNN-based portfolio optimization strategy might spot risks or growth opportunities that purely return-centric models overlook.

Incorporating alternative data sources might also enhance model robustness, as purely price-driven correlations could weaken due to market regime shifts or high volatility. Supplemental links derived from news or other non-price sources may provide more stable signals. This greater diversification of information flows can also help the model identify important patterns – whether it is a sudden strategic alliance, regulatory development, or unforeseen supply chain disruption. Taken together, GNN models help capture a holistic view of how businesses truly connect and interact. Accordingly, they often uncover valuable structural insights that lead to more informed and potentially more profitable portfolio decisions.

Incorporating Text-Based Features and Techniques from LLMs In addition to the application of LLMs for volatility forecasting, we can naturally extend the same concept to portfolio construction. As discussed previously, LLMs

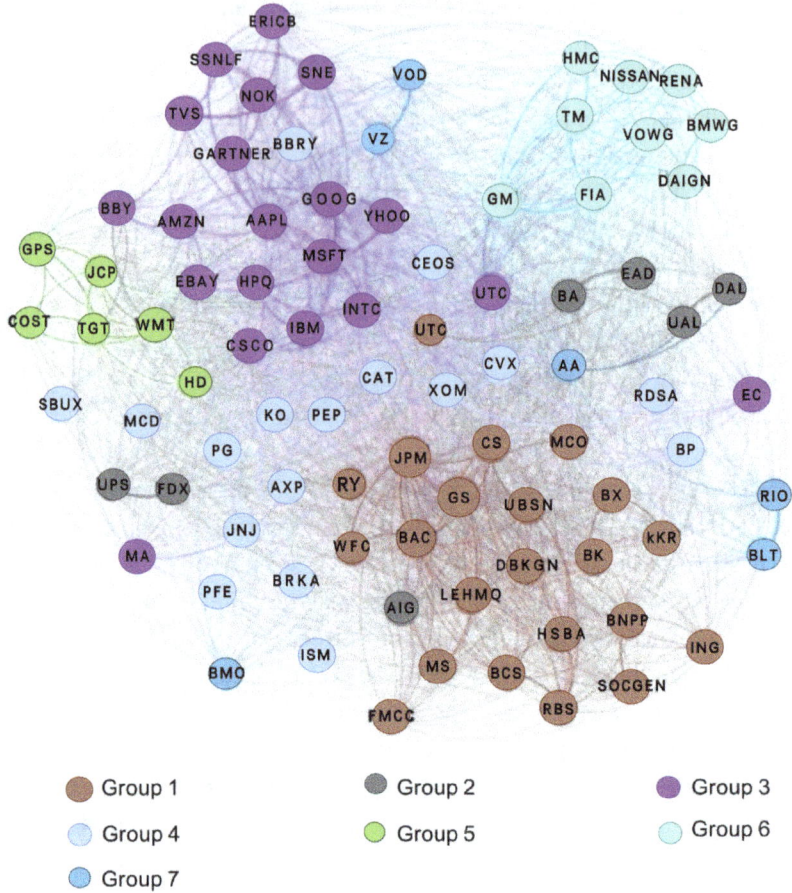

Figure 34 A graph built from a news network. Colors indicate that assets are allocated to the same group.

can be used to extract features from earning call transcripts or macroeconomic reports. This allows them to capture different views on market conditions that are not readily available in price/volume data. By incorporating this information into optimization techniques, we can construct portfolios that are better aligned with the current market environment. Specifically, we look at the work proposed by Hwang, Kong, Lee, and Zohren (2025) where they integrate LLM-derived embeddings directly into the portfolio optimization process. Note that the discussion in this section is rather intuitive, so we omit some details but focus on the ideas underlying the adoption of LLMs for portfolio optimization.

Suppose we have a sequences of asset returns $r_t = \{r_{1,t}, \cdots, r_{N,t}\}$ where $r_{i,t}$ indicates the return of asset i at time t, and $w_t \in \mathcal{R}^N$ is the corresponding portfolio weight at time t. Hwang et al. (2025) constructs a forecasting model f that not only forecasts future returns but also predicts the corresponding portfolio weights:

$$(\boldsymbol{r}_{t+1:t+H}, \boldsymbol{w}_{t+1:t+H}) = f(\boldsymbol{r}_{t-L:t}, \boldsymbol{x}_{t-L:t}), \tag{117}$$

where $\boldsymbol{x}_t$ denotes macroeconomic features, L is the look-back window and H is the predicted horizon. To simultaneously generate predicted returns and portfolio weights, the authors propose a custom loss function:

$$L_{Loss} = \beta L_{MSE} + (1 - \beta) L_{Decision}, \tag{118}$$

where L_{MSE} is the standard MSE loss that measures the discrepancy between actual returns and predicted returns, and $L_{Decision}$ measures how inaccuracies in predicted returns translate into suboptimal portfolio decisions. An input embedding is then used to process data from multiple modalities, specifically time-series decomposition and LLM-enhanced semantic embeddings. After that, several network layers are implemented to detect temporal patterns with LLM-derived semantic embeddings and convert predictions into portfolio weights. Finally, the hybrid loss function (Equation 118) is optimized to derive forecasts and portfolio weights. The field of LLMs in finance is still in its early stage with a limited number of published works. For a broad coverage of how LLMs can be applied to quantitative finance, interested readers can refer to Kong, Nie, et al. (2024).

7 Applications to Market Microstructure and High - Frequency Data

In this section, we delve into the microcosm of the financial world and focus on high-frequency microstructure data. This field is probably the most attractive area for deep learning methods, given the rich and detailed view of market dynamics. High-frequency microstructure data captures every change in market conditions, including price fluctuations, order volumes, and transaction times. This granular view is ideal for training sophisticated algorithms.

Traditionally, in early financial markets, stocks were traded in a format known as pit trading. In this system, traders and brokers gathered in a designated trading floor area, known as the "pit," to conduct transactions via open outcry. This involved shouting and using hand signals to communicate buy and sell orders. The chaotic environment relied heavily on the physical presence and vocal abilities of traders to execute trades quickly and efficiently. Market prices were determined through a process of verbal negotiation and immediate, face-to-face interactions. Despite its seeming disorder, pit trading enabled real-time price discovery and liquidity in an era before electronic trading. However, it had obvious limitations, such as restricted market access for remote participants and slower dissemination of price information. These shortcomings eventually led to the adoption of electronic trading systems.

The transition from traditional pit trading to electronic trading systems, marked a pivotal transformation in financial markets, fundamentally altering the landscape of global finance and paving the way for modern trading practices. This shift began in earnest during the late twentieth century as technological advancements made electronic trading feasible and attractive. One of the earliest and most notable shifts occurred with the establishment of the NASDAQ in the early 1970s. As the first electronic stock market, the NASDAQ used computer and telecommunication technology to facilitate trading without a physical trading floor. Around the same time, the New York Stock Exchange (NYSE) introduced the Designated Order Turnaround (DOT) system, which routed orders electronically to the trading floor, although they were still executed via open outcry.

In the late 1980s and early 1990s, as computers became more powerful and network technology more sophisticated, more exchanges began to explore electronic trading options. The London Stock Exchange (LSE) moved away from face-to-face trading with the "Big Bang" deregulation of 1986, which included the introduction of electronic screen-based trading. This shift was mirrored by exchanges around the world, including the Toronto Stock Exchange (TSE) and the Frankfurt Stock Exchange (FSE).

The development of Globex by the Chicago Mercantile Exchange (CME) in 1992 was another significant advancement. Globex was an electronic trading platform intended for after-hours trading that would eventually become a 24-hour worldwide digital trading environment. Similarly, EUREX, established in 1998 as a result of the merger between the German and Swiss derivatives exchanges, was among the first to go fully electronic, setting a precedent for derivatives trading globally. The adoption of electronic trading and the Limit Order Book (LOB) system revolutionized market dynamics. With the ability to process high volumes of transactions at unprecedented speeds, trading became faster, more efficient, and more accessible. Moreover, electronic trading reduced the costs associated with trading and increased transparency by making market data widely available. It also democratized market access, enabling more participants to engage from remote locations.

Today, nearly all major stock and derivatives exchanges operate electronically. The transition has not only altered how trades are executed but also how markets are monitored and regulated. Advanced algorithms and high-frequency trading strategies that rely on microsecond advantages in electronic trading environments have become prevalent, prompting ongoing discussions about market fairness and stability. In order to digitize trading, every verbal bid and ask needs to be converted into digital orders that can be entered into the LOB. Each trader's shouts and hand signals become electronic messages that specify the quantity, price, and conditions of trades. The electronic LOB system then aggregates these orders, organizing them by price level and quantity. The system then continuously updates as new orders come in, orders are modified, and trades are executed. This shift also enhances transparency by providing all market participants with a detailed real-time view of market activity and depth, something that was not previously possible in the chaotic environment of the trading pit.

Modern exchanges can generate billions of such messages in a day. The high resolution and volume of this data enable deep learning models to discern intricate patterns and dependencies that might be invisible in lower-frequency data. Next, we will give a detailed description of high-frequency microstructure data. This will include an exploration of the inner working mechanism of exchanges and the aggregation of individual order messages into limit order books, which reflect supply and demand at the microstructure level. By leveraging such large datasets, we have numerous opportunities across various financial applications, such as generating predictive signals that drive algorithmic trading decisions, optimizing trade execution strategies, and even creating advanced generative models that can simulate entire exchange markets. Such simulations can be used with reinforcement learning algorithms to design better trading strategies, accounting for market impact, fill rate, and market anomalies. Consequently, high-frequency microstructure data is not just facilitating more informed decisions but is also a key component of many innovations in financial technologies.

7.1 The Inner Working Mechanism of an Exchange

In this section, we detail the order lifecycle and explain how a limit order book is maintained within an exchange. Once a trader places an order, the corresponding message traverses various intermediaries, including exchanges, banks, brokers, and clearing firms. Exchanges typically broadcast these messages in real time through a data feed, enabling the reconstruction of the LOB. In essence, the LOB is simply the organized collection of these order messages.

The comprehensive assembly of these messages, referred to as market by order (MBO) data, is one of the most detailed sources of microstructure information. Specifically, MBO data captures every market participant's order instructions, and activities, such as placing a new order or canceling an existing one. The fundamental elements of MBO data include time stamps, order prices, order volumes (sizes), order directions (sides), order types (a market order, a limit order, etc.), order IDs which serve as a unique and anonymous identifier for each individual order, and actions that describe the specific instruction of a trader (buying, selling, or canceling an order). Table 10 shows a snapshot of sequences of MBO data that contains essential information. For simplicity, we omit some nonessential auxiliary information.

Figure 35 presents a snapshot of the LOB at a given time t which illustrates the collection of all currently active limit orders. When a trader places orders, a market order is matched immediately with an existing, resting order, whereas a limit order enables traders to specify the worst price and quantity they wish to transact. These limit orders stay active. Once an exchange has received a limit order, it will place the order at the appropriate position within the existing LOB. The incoming MBO data continuously alters the LOB and a new snapshot of the LOB is formed whenever it gets updated.

A LOB consists of two primary types of orders: bids and asks. A bid order signifies a willingness to purchase an asset at a specified price or lower, while an ask order indicates an intention to sell an asset at a particular price or higher. As shown in Figure 35, bids or asks have prices $\mathbf{P}(t)$ and sizes (volumes) $\mathbf{V}(t)$. Each rectangle in the graph represents a single order, with its size represented by the square's height. Therefore, each level of a LOB is an ordered queue of all limit orders at that specific price level.

Figure 36 illustrates how a limit order book evolves and demonstrates the impact of an MBO message on the existing LOB. For instance, at the top of Figure 36, a new limit order (ID=46280) is added to the ask side of the order book with a price of 70.04 and a size of 7580. This order addition updates the order book by placing the new order at the corresponding price level. Similarly, the LOB is altered when there is a cancellation (as shown in the middle top figure), a partial cancellation (middle bottom figure), or when a market buy order is executed (bottom figure).

In practice, we can obtain high-frequency microstructure data by subscribing to market exchanges. Exchanges typically offer data across three tiers:

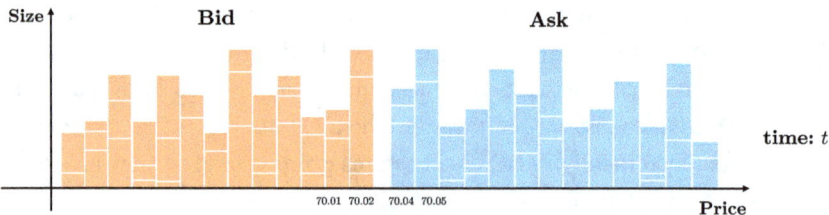

Figure 35 A snapshot of LOB at time t.

Table 10 An example of a sequence of market by order data.

Time stamp	ID	Type	Side	Action	Price	Size
2022-04-06 10:16:15.125873685	5879848654448934894	2	1	1	58.45	1578.0
2022-04-06 10:16:15.875348668	5879848654448937899	1	N/A	2	N/A	N/A
2022-04-06 10:16:16.584863148	5879848654448937899	2	1	0	58.50	4781.0
2022-04-06 10:16:20.871548935	5879848654448931459	1	2	1	58.50	2141.0
2022-04-06 10:16:24.933314896	5879848654448938794	1	N/A	2	N/A	N/A

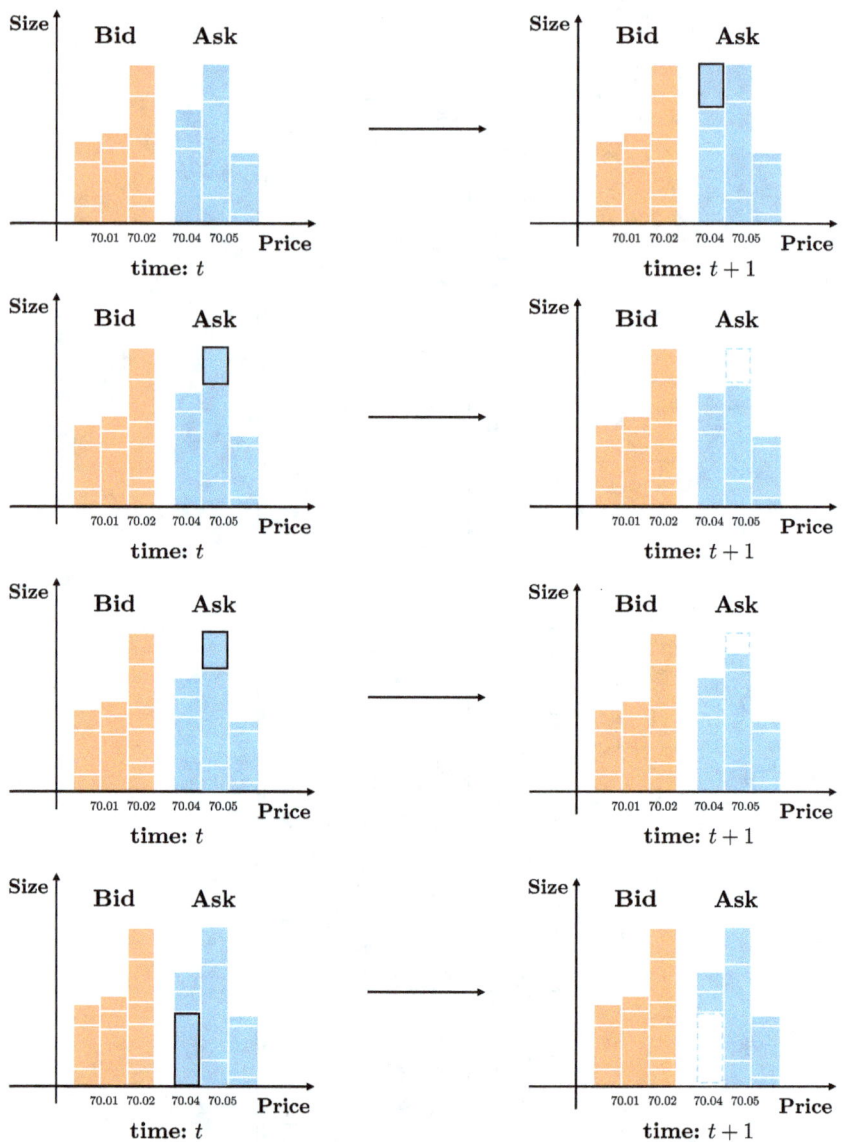

Figure 36 This illustration demonstrates how MBO data modifies a LOB. **Top**: A new limit order is introduced; **Middle top**: An existing order is canceled; **Middle bottom**: An order undergoes a partial cancellation; **Bottom**: A marketable buy limit order crosses the spread.

Level 1, Level 2, and Level 3. Each tier provides progressively more detailed information and capabilities, with corresponding subscription costs:

- Level 1 Data: This tier comprises the price and volume of the latest trade, along with the current best bid and ask prices, which is commonly referred to as quote data.

- Level 2 Data: This tier supplies LOB data, providing more comprehensive information than Level 1 by displaying bid and ask prices along with their respective volumes across multiple deeper levels of the order book.
- Level 3 Data: This tier goes beyond Level 2 by providing unaggregated details of bids and asks placed by individual traders (MBO data), delivering the most granular view of market activity.

The choice of which data source to use depends on the specific application or analysis being conducted. Each tier of market data offers unique advantages and levels of detail suitable for different purposes. LOB data, typically provided at Level 2, aggregates the total available quantities at each price level in the market. This aggregated view gives insight into the overall demand and supply dynamics at a microstructure level, helping analysts assess liquidity, price stability, and potential market impact. However, LOB data lacks information about individual orders, focusing instead on summarized market activity. In contrast, MBO data, available at Level 3, provides granular details about individual market participants' behaviors. It includes unaggregated bids and asks, along with unique order identifiers. This level of detail enables a deeper understanding of queue positions, order prioritization, and the trading strategies employed by participants. MBO data is especially valuable for applications that require precise modeling of order flow dynamics, such as market impact analysis, execution optimization, and algorithmic trading. By combining LOB and MBO data, it is possible to gain both macro and micro views of the market, allowing for more comprehensive analyses tailored to the needs of specific trading strategies or research objectives.

7.2 Deep Learning–Based Predictive Signals

In recent years, the use of deep learning models for analyzing high-frequency microstructure data has gained significant attention. This growing trend is fueled by the immense volume of data generated by modern exchanges, with billions of quotes, orders, and trades produced within a single trading day. High-frequency microstructure data offers a rich source of information for advanced modeling and prediction. Deep learning models are exceptionally effective for analyzing this type of data because they can identify and interpret intricate patterns.(Atsalakis & Valavanis, 2009).

We can take snapshots of limit order books with a look-back window and format them as an "image" that is shown in Figure 37. The topology of LOB shows clear patterns in terms of prices and volumes and can be fed into deep learning algorithms. The work of Tsantekidis et al. (2017a) designs likely the first deep learning model to successfully apply a CNN to predict price movement for

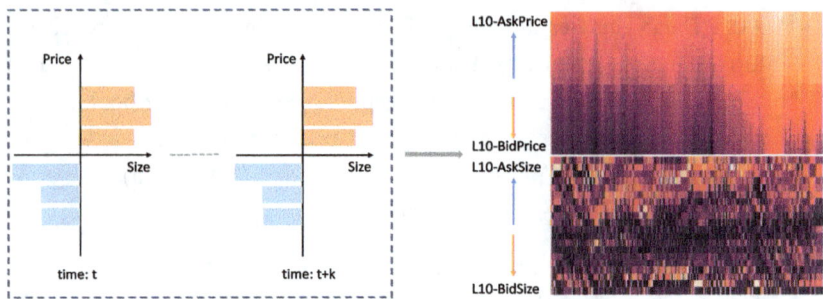

Figure 37 Limit order book data across times.

limit order books. A key advancement in this study is the application of CNNs to directly predict stock prices using LOB data. To do so, the authors adapt CNNs, traditionally successful in image processing, to handle the structured time-series data of LOBs. By treating the LOB as a multidimensional array, CNNs can learn spatial hierarchies and patterns within the order book that are predictive of future price movements. This approach leverages the depth of data available, capturing subtle yet critical shifts in market sentiment that might be indicative of future trends. Other studies (Z. Zhang, Zohren, & Roberts, 2019a) have shown that CNNs can outperform classical statistical models and other machine learning methods in predicting short-term price changes, providing traders with a powerful tool for making more informed decisions.

Interestingly, the work of Sirignano and Cont (2018) has uncovered universal features of price formation in limit order books. By analyzing vast amounts of LOB data across different assets and markets, their models have identified common patterns and dynamics that govern price changes. These insights suggest that despite the apparent complexity and noise within financial markets, there are underlying principles and patterns that can be extracted through deep learning. The ability of deep learning models to distill these features from the data not only enhances predictive accuracy but also provides a deeper understanding of market mechanics.

In a more specialized context, Z. Zhang et al. (2019a) carefully designed a deep network, termed DeepLOB, to predict price movements from LOB data using an architecture that combines convolutional filters and LSTM modules. Convolutional filters are utilized to capture the spatial patterns of the LOB, while LSTM modules are employed to model longer-term temporal dependencies. This proposed network continues to achieve state-of-the-art performance, serving as a benchmark and inspiring a wide range of studies and applications in financial modeling and trading. We implement DeepLOB for a regression problem and attach the code script in Listing 3 in Appendix D.

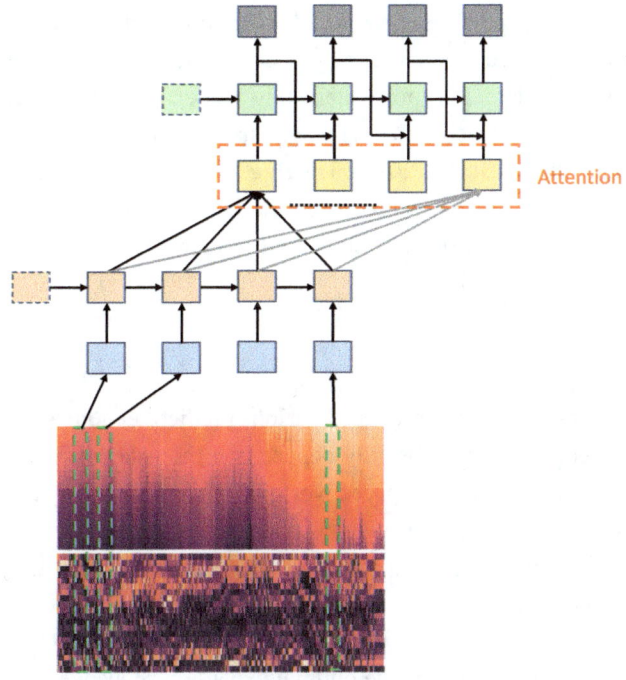

Figure 38 An attention model that utilizes limit order books for multi-horizon forecasting.

However, DeepLOB can only make a single-point estimation. In practice, the predictive horizon remains a hyperparameter that needs be carefully adjusted as it determines holding time, trading frequency, risk, and more. To overcome this, Z. Zhang and Zohren (2021) extends on DeepLOB and implements Seq2Seq and Attention modules for LOB to produce multi-horizon estimates. Instead of obtaining a single-point estimation, they obtain a forecasting path that can be better utilized to generate trading strategies. Figure 38 depicts this Attention structure. It shows that the Attention module places different weights across time, with short-term predictions rolled forward to generate long-term estimates. In addition, the work of Z. Zhang, Lim, and Zohren (2021) utilizes MBO data to predict price movements and demonstrates that predictive signals obtained from MBO data deliver comparable results to models trained on LOB but are less correlated.

For a more complete review of the predictive models for LOB, readers can refer to Briola, Turiel, and Aste (2020), where they have compared and benchmarked several machine learning algorithms and deep networks on the same feature space, dataset, and tasks. The later work Briola, Bartolucci, and Aste (2024) also proposes an innovative operational framework that evaluates predictions' practicality. They studied instruments across various dimensions including tick size, predictive horizon and order book depths. Prata et al. (2024) also carefully compare the predictive power of fifteen cutting-edge DL models based on LOB data. For more interesting works, readers can refer to Bao, Yue, and Rao (2017); Chen, Chen, Huang, Huang, and Chen (2016); Di Persio and Honchar (2016); Dixon (2018); Doering, Fairbank, and Markose (2017); Fischer and Krauss (2017); Nelson, Pereira, and de Oliveira (2017); Selvin, Vinayakumar, Gopalakrishnan, Menon, and Soman (2017); Tsantekidis et al. (2017b, 2017a).

7.3 Deep Learning for Trade Execution

In the previous section, we introduced various predictive models. We now discuss trade execution, which heavily depends on the usage of high-frequency microstructure data. In the fast-paced world of financial markets, the execution of trades with precision and efficiency is paramount. Trade execution focuses on the granular details of executing large orders in financial markets to minimize costs and market impact. This aspect of trade execution delves into the strategies and techniques used to break down large orders into smaller, manageable parts and to determine the optimal execution sequence. The goal is to achieve the best possible execution price while mitigating the adverse effects on the market, such as price slippage and increased volatility.

When executing large orders, the sheer increase in volume can influence the market price, causing unfavorable movements against a trader's interests. By strategically breaking down and timing the execution of these large orders, traders can reduce their market footprint, thus minimizing market impact and realizing more favorable prices. Effective trade execution strategies aim to lower the overall transaction costs. These costs include not only explicit costs like commissions and fees but also implicit costs such as slippage and opportunity costs. By optimizing the execution process, traders can significantly reduce these costs, and increase their net returns.

The execution prices of trades have a direct influence on the success of a trading strategy. Effective trade execution ensures transactions are carried out at the most favorable prices possible, thereby reducing slippage – the gap between the anticipated trade price and the price at which the trade is actually executed. This is particularly important in fast-moving markets where prices can change rapidly. The quality of trade execution is critical for large orders. Poor execution can result in significant deviations from the expected trade price, adversely affecting the overall trading strategy. Implementing sophisticated execution algorithms and techniques can improve execution quality, ensuring that transactions are executed at or close to the target price levels.

One of the foundational works in trade execution is the study of Bertsimas and Lo (1998). They introduce a framework for minimizing the cost of executing large orders by considering the trade-off between market impact and price risk. They use dynamic programming approaches to determine the optimal trade execution path and highlight the importance of considering both temporary and permanent market impact when executing large trades. This work lays the foundation for modern trade execution strategies by formalizing the optimization problem faced by traders.

Another important work is Almgren and Chriss (2001). They develop a model to optimize trade execution by balancing market impact costs against the variance of the execution price. This work introduces the concept of an efficient frontier in trade execution, where different strategies can be evaluated based on their cost-risk profiles, providing a quantitative basis for the development of execution algorithms that are used in practice. Their framework has become a cornerstone in the field, influencing both academic research and practical implementations of execution algorithms.

In Gatheral (2010), the authors extend previous models by incorporating more realistic assumptions about market impact and price dynamics. Their work provides deeper insights into the temporal evolution of market impact, helping traders to develop more effective execution strategies over longer time horizons. The work of Obizhaeva and Wang (2013) presents a model that incorporates supply and demand dynamics in determining optimal trading strategies. They also suggest optimal execution paths that adapt to changing market conditions and liquidity.

The integration of deep learning models into trade execution leverages high-frequency data and sophisticated algorithms to optimize execution strategies further. This has led to the concept of Deep Reinforcement Learning (DRL), a branch of machine learning that merges reinforcement learning (RL) (Sutton & Barto, 2018) with deep learning. DRL takes advantage of deep neural networks to understand complex representations and to make decisions based on these representations in environments where the results of actions are both uncertain and delayed. This framework fits the problem of trade execution, which is essentially a classical sequential decision-making process. Our goal is therefore to find an optimal order placement strategy that aims to optimize some evaluation metrics, such as minimizing transaction costs without causing adverse market impact.

We now briefly introduce RL and discuss several works that apply DRL to trade execution. RL provides a framework in which agents are trained to make a series of decisions by interacting with their environment (shown in Figure 39). Specifically, at any time t, an agent receives some representations (S_t) of current

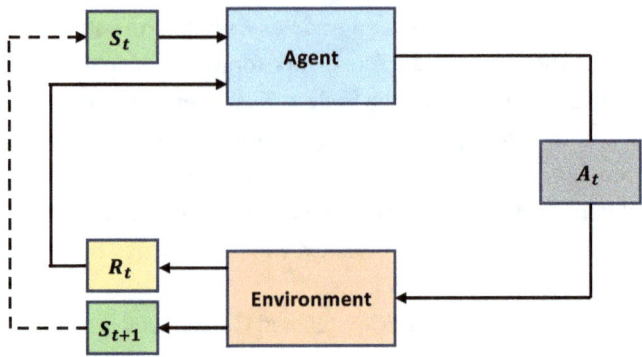

Figure 39 A schematic description of RL.

environments and takes an action (A_t) based on the observed information. This action either leads to a reward (R_t) or a penalty that indicates the goodness of the chosen action. The agent then moves to the next state (S_{t+1}), and this procedure continues until the environment concludes. Throughout, the agent's objective is to maximize the expected total rewards ($E(\sum R_t)$).

DRL combines the components of RL with deep neural networks to learn complex state spaces and effective policies from high-dimensional inputs. There are a range of DRL algorithms. Deep Q-Networks (DQNs) mark a major advancement in reinforcement learning by integrating Q-learning principles with the robust function approximation abilities of deep neural networks. Traditional Q-learning, which is a model-free reinforcement learning method, depends on a Q-table to record and update Q-values for every state-action combination. A Q-value represents the network's estimate of the expected discounted sum of future rewards when taking a specific action in a given state according to the current optimal policy. However, in its traditional form, this technique becomes unmanageable in environments with extensive or continuous state spaces because the memory and computational demands grow exponentially.

DQNs address this challenge by using deep neural networks to approximate the Q-value function, enabling them to process high-dimensional inputs such as images or intricate market data. A key advancement in DQNs is the implementation of experience replay. This method involves retaining past interactions in a replay buffer and randomly re-selecting mini-batches of these experiences during training. By disrupting the temporal sequences in the data, experience replay helps to stabilize the learning process and enhance the algorithm's overall performance. Furthermore, DQNs incorporate a target network, which is an intermittently updated replica of the Q-network. This target network provides consistent target values for training, thereby improving the stability and convergence of the learning process. By incorporating these techniques, DQNs have achieved remarkable success across various domains, such as playing Atari games at superhuman levels. Their capabilities also hold great promise for applications in fields like finance, robotics, and beyond.

Policy Gradient methods constitute another category of reinforcement learning algorithms that directly optimize the policy by modifying the policy function's parameters to maximize the expected reward. Value-based approaches create policies by estimating value functions. In contrast, policy gradient techniques parameterize the policy itself – commonly with a neural network – and then adjust these parameters in a manner that increases the expected reward. This straightforward method of policy optimization provides several benefits, including more efficient management of high-dimensional and continuous action spaces.

One key method within policy gradient techniques is the REINFORCE algorithm. This algorithm utilizes Monte Carlo sampling to approximate the gradient of the expected reward relative to the policy parameters and then updates these parameters through gradient ascent. More sophisticated strategies, like Actor-Critic algorithms, integrate policy gradient methods with value function approximation. This combination helps to lower the variance in gradient estimates, resulting in more stable and efficient learning processes. Policy gradient methods are widely applied to complex tasks like robotic control, game playing, and financial trading, where the ability to directly optimize the policy offers significant advantages in terms of flexibility and performance.

DQNs and policy gradient methods form the basis of DRL. More advanced algorithms tend to be extensions of these two approaches. Some well-known techniques, such as Deep Deterministic Policy Gradient (DDPO) and Proximal Policy Optimization (PPO), offer unique advantages and address different challenges in DRL. DDPG is built to handle environments with continuous action spaces and utilizes an actor-critic architecture. In this framework, the actor network is responsible for selecting actions, while the critic network evaluates their performance. To stabilize learning, DDPG uses experience replay and target networks, which help reduce correlations in the training data and smoothen the update process. PPO, on the other hand, aims to simplify the policy optimization process while ensuring stability. It strikes a balance between exploration and exploitation by clipping the probability ratios between the new and old policies during updates. This prevents excessively large updates that can destabilize learning, making PPO robust and widely applicable to various problems.

In the study by Nagy, Calliess, and Zohren (2023), DRL combined with experience replay is utilized to train a trading agent with the objective of

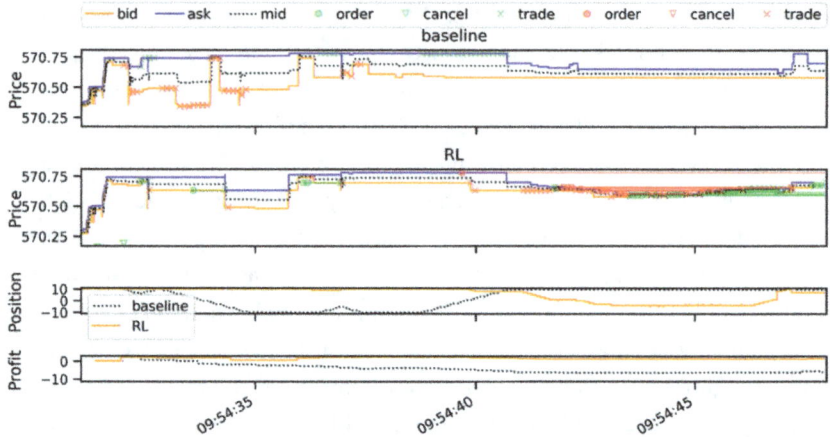

Figure 40 A brief comparison between the baseline strategy and RL policy for AAPL on 2012-06-14. New limit orders that are not immediately executed are represented by circles, executed trades by crosses, and order cancellations by triangles. Lines connect open orders to their corresponding cancellations or executions.

maximizing trading returns. The findings reveal that the RL agent formulates an effective strategy for inventory management and order placement, surpassing a heuristic benchmark trading strategy that employs the same signals. Figure 40 illustrates a 17-second segment from the testing period, comparing the baseline strategy with the RL approach. The first two panels show the highest bid, lowest ask, and mid-prices, alongside trading activities for buy orders (highlighted in green) and sell orders (highlighted in red). Since the simulation encompasses the entire LOB, the influence of trading actions on bid and ask prices is observable. The third panel depicts the progression of inventory positions for both strategies, and the final panel displays the trading profits in USD over the duration of the period.

The findings indicate that both strategies impact the prices within the LOB by introducing new order flows into the market. These new orders interact with existing ones, thereby influencing liquidity at the top bid and ask levels. Throughout the examined timeframe, the baseline strategy experiences minor losses attributed to frequent changes in its signals which alternate between anticipating declining and rising future prices. This behavior results in aggressive trading, causing the strategy to incur the spread cost with each transaction. On the other hand, the RL strategy outperforms by employing a more subdued approach. This minimizes the effects of market volatility while allowing the RL strategy to effectively manage its positions. It trades prudently when exiting long positions and makes strategic decisions when establishing new ones. In

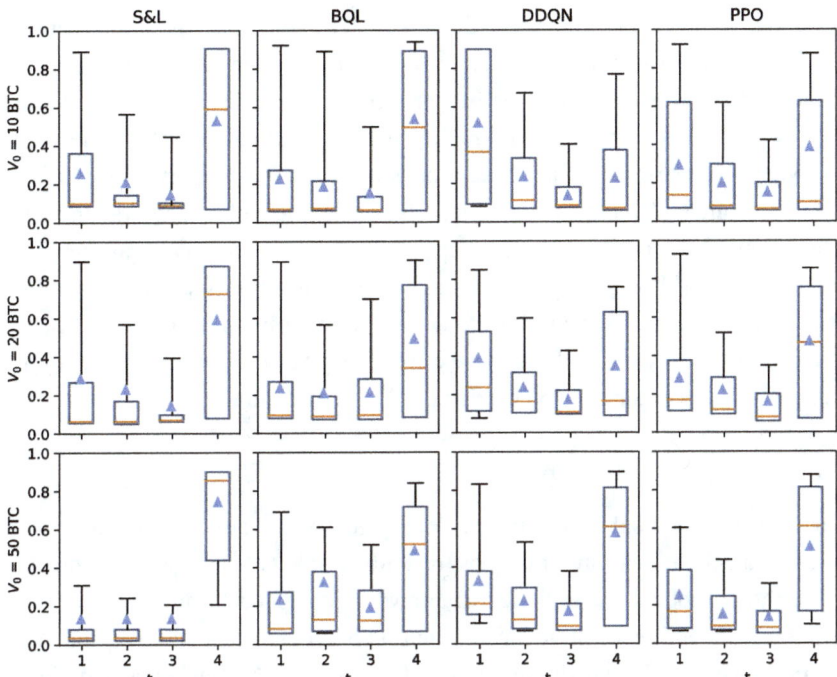

Figure 41 The distribution of executed volume per time step, with the horizontal axis representing the time step, vertical axis indicating the volume, and columns corresponding to different execution strategies. The box plots show the interquartile ranges, medians (marked by orange lines), means (indicated by blue triangles), and the 10th and 90th percentiles (represented by whiskers).

the latter part of the observed period, the RL strategy notably increases its passive buy orders (depicted as green circles in the second panel of Figure 40). These orders are connected by green lines to their respective executions or cancellations, with some actions occurring beyond the timeframe shown in the figure.

To further present how different DRL algorithms affect execution paths, we take an example from Schnaubelt (2022) that optimizes order placements on cryptocurrency exchanges. Figure 41 illustrates the executed volume across various time steps for four different strategies: submit-and-leave (S&L), backwards-induction Q-learning (BQL), deep double Q-networks (DDQN), and proximal policy optimization (PPO). Several consistent patterns are observed in the average executed volume fractions. Firstly, a substantial portion of the volume is typically executed in the final time step, which usually involves completing any remaining volume through a market order. Secondly, when analyzing the volume fractions within the first three time steps, the majority of the execution generally occurs in the initial step. Thirdly, as the initial volume v_0 increases, the volume executed in the final time step also rises, while the volume fraction executed in the earlier steps tends to decrease. These trends can be attributed to the limited liquidity available during the initial time steps.

When comparing various execution strategies, it becomes apparent that the S&L method handles a smaller portion of the volume within the first three time steps compared to the deep reinforcement learning approaches PPO and DDQN. Although the S&L strategy maintains a positive average volume fraction, its median fraction is zero across all three initial time steps. In contrast, both DDQN and PPO agents exhibit similar execution patterns, with the majority of the volume being carried out in the first time step.

7.4 Generative Models for Limit Order Books

In the section's final part, we look at generative models, an expanding area within machine learning that has recently attracted considerable interest. Generative models are statistical frameworks designed to produce new data instances that closely mimic the distribution of an existing dataset. Unlike discriminative models, which aim to classify or predict outcomes based on input data, generative models focus on learning the joint probability distribution of the data. This capability allows them to generate realistic and innovative data samples that align with the inherent patterns and structures present in the training dataset.

Generative models encompass a broad range of applications and are beneficial for enhancing data availability and quality across multiple fields. In numerous disciplines, acquiring extensive, high-quality datasets for training machine learning models is often challenging due to factors such as privacy issues, substantial costs, and data access restrictions. Generative models address these obstacles by producing realistic synthetic data that accurately reflects the statistical properties of the original datasets. This synthetic data can supplement existing datasets, resulting in the development of more robust and precise machine learning models. For instance, in the healthcare sector, generative models can generate synthetic patient records that preserve the critical patterns found in real data while ensuring patient privacy is maintained.

In the creative arts, generative models can produce innovative images, music, and artwork, expanding the possibilities of digital creativity. In scientific research, such models can simulate experiments, predict molecular structures, and generate new hypotheses, helping to accelerate discovery and innovation. Furthermore, generative models enable the creation of personalized experiences across various applications. In recommendation systems, they can simulate user preferences and generate tailored content suggestions, improving user satisfaction and engagement. In gaming, generative models can craft personalized environments and narratives suited to each player's preferences. By utilizing the power of generative models, developers can create more customized and engaging experiences, boosting user satisfaction and retention.

For high-frequency microstructure data, we can use generative models to enhance simulations by generating realistic, high-fidelity data that is accurately representative of complex financial markets. This is particularly useful for modeling market impact as such interactions are difficult to simulate with static historical data. Furthermore, we can use high-quality synthetic data to study the problem of regime shift, a notorious problem for financial time-series that often leads to overfitting and poor generalization. By improving the modeling of market dynamics, generative models enhance decision-making processes and improve risk management.

The roots of generative modeling lie in traditional statistical methods, which focus on modeling the underlying distributions of data. Some of the foundational approaches include Gaussian Mixture Models (GMMs) and Hidden Market Models (HMMs). GMMs represent data as a mixture of multiple Gaussian distributions, each capturing a different aspect of the data distribution. GMMs are effective for clustering and density estimation but struggle with high-dimensional data. HMMs are used to model sequential data, where the data-generating process is assumed to follow a Markov process with hidden states. They are frequently applied in speech recognition and time-series analysis, but they struggle to capture complex dependencies.

Advancements in deep learning algorithms have profoundly transformed the generative modeling landscape over the past several years, shifting it from conventional statistical approaches to advanced deep learning frameworks. This progression has been fueled by the demand for models that are more precise, efficient, and capable of generating complex data. Neural networks, with their proficiency in learning intricate representations, have been instrumental in developing more robust and adaptable generative models.

There are several remarkable works that leverage the power of deep networks to provide a new paradigm for generative modeling. Variational Autoencoders (VAEs) introduced by Kingma and Welling (2013) combine principles from Bayesian inference and neural networks. They use an encoder-decoder architecture to learn a probabilistic representation of data, enabling efficient generation of new samples. VAEs marked a significant step forward in generating realistic data while providing a solid theoretical foundation.

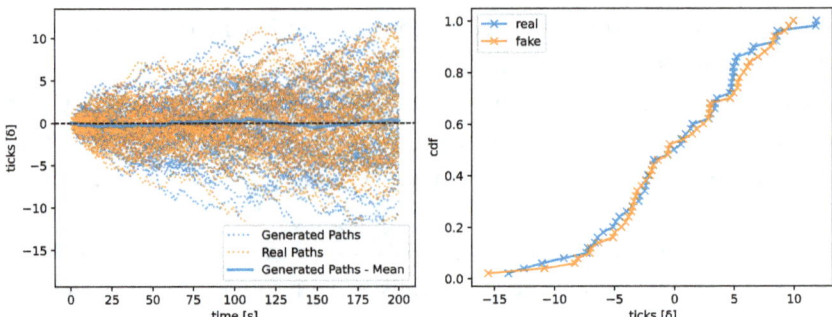

Figure 42 Price trajectories and the associated percentiles of terminal prices for both real and generated data.

Generative Adversarial Networks (GANs) are a pivotal development that has significantly advanced the field of generative modeling (Goodfellow et al., 2014). A GAN is composed of two distinct neural networks: the generator and the discriminator. These networks engage in a competitive minimax game, in which the generator creates synthetic data samples and the discriminator evaluates their authenticity. Through this adversarial training process, GANs are capable of producing highly realistic and convincing data.

One of the most significant applications of generative models has been to study LOB market dynamics, a task that is generally assumed to be very difficult. Understanding and modeling market dynamics is important for studying market impact and avoiding adverse price movements. In Cont, Cucuringu, Kochems, and Prenzel (2023), the authors introduce a nonparametric method for modeling the dynamics of a limit order book by utilizing a GAN. Given time-series data obtained from the order book, this GAN is trained to learn the conditional distribution of the LOB's future state based on its current state.

Figure 42 presents an example of simulated LOBs. In it, we can see that both distributions of generated and real price paths align closely. The right side of the figure illustrates the percentiles of the terminal prices, where the distribution of price changes over 200 transitions is generally well-matched, especially for the middle percentiles (from 5% to 95%). However, noticeable discrepancies appear at the extreme points, corresponding to the 1% and 99% quantiles, representing the minimum and maximum values. This suggests that the generated paths do not capture the same tail characteristics as the real data. Although the 0% and 100% quantiles are often noisy, this deviation remains a consistent observation.

Nagy, Frey, et al. (2023) introduces an alternative approach to simulate LOB with an end-to-end auto-regressive generative model that directly generates tokenized LOB messages. Figure 43 juxtaposes the return distributions

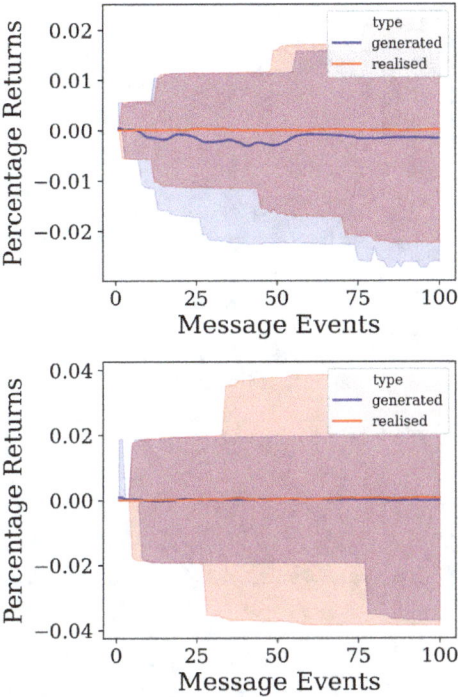

Figure 43 The distributions of mid-price returns for generated (blue) and realized (red) data with the mean (solid lines) and 95% confidence intervals (shaded regions). **Left**: Google; **Right**: Intel.

of the generated data with those of the actual realized data over the span of 100 future messages. The findings demonstrate that the model effectively mirrors the mid-price return distributions, even though these were not directly included in the training loss function. The average returns exhibit no significant drift or trend, and the shaded areas, representing the 95% confidence intervals of the distributions, align closely.

To further test the authenticity of the generated data, returns are sampled from the generative model, and correlation is calculated between the generated returns r_{t+s}^g and the realized returns r_{t+s}^r for 100 future messages ($s \in [1, \cdots, 100]$). As shown in the top of Figure 44, there exists a consistently positive correlation for both Google ($\rho \approx 0.1$) and Intel ($\rho \approx 0.2$). The lower panel displays the corresponding p-values from t-tests evaluating the alternative hypothesis $H_1 : \rho > 0$ against the null hypothesis $H_0 : \rho = 0$. The dotted line represents the 5% significance level. For the Google model, the p-values remain at or near the 5% threshold for up to 80 future messages, whereas for Intel, the correlations stay statistically significant for at least 100 messages. The sustained positive correlation indicates directional forecasting power which suggests new possibilities for alpha.

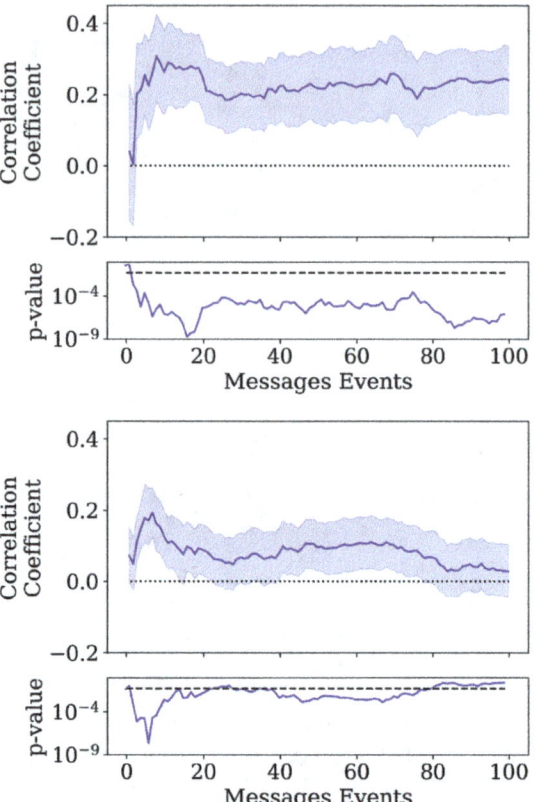

Figure 44 Top: Pearson correlation coefficient ρ between the generated and actual returns, reflecting the performance of directional forecasting; **Bottom**: the corresponding p-values. **Left**: Google; **Right**: Intel.

By generating realistic LOB data, researchers and industry professionals can obtain meaningful insights into the behaviors of market participants and the dynamics of order flow. In turn, this helps them study the execution of large orders and analyze their impact on the market. In addition, we can use generative models as environments for DRL algorithms. Historical data is static whereas the real market is dynamic and reacts to actions. Generative models create realistic synthetic data, allowing DRL agents to train in a simulated environment that mirrors real market conditions. This approach not only accelerates the development and testing of DRL-based trading algorithms but also ensures that these algorithms are robust and adaptable to a wide range of market scenarios.

The prospects for generative models in the financial sector are bright, with promising avenues for future research and implementation. One other key area of interest is utilizing generative models for stress testing and scenario analysis.

This application enables financial institutions to better evaluate their ability to withstand extreme market conditions and build more resilient risk management systems. Additionally, improving the interpretability of generative models and developing standardized evaluation metrics will enhance their practical utility and facilitate their adoption in the financial industry. As these models advance and become increasingly refined, they are certain to facilitate cutting-edge research initiatives and play a crucial role in shaping the future of trading and market analysis.

8 Conclusions

This final section concludes our exploration of the applications of deep learning to quantitative finance. It aims to summarize key insights from the Element and discuss future opportunities and challenges in integrating these fields, providing a foundation for future work.

8.1 Summary and Key Takeaways

Deep learning is revolutionizing contemporary quantitative trading and reshaping the world of financial markets. This Element provides an in-depth analysis of the methods and models underpinning this development. It also highlights the capacity of deep learning models to automatically extract complex features, uncover hidden patterns within extensive financial datasets, and facilitate the development of more precise and effective trading strategies.

This Element is aimed at quantitative researchers in academia and industry, as well as data scientists and developers interested in the field. It blends foundational concepts with real-world applications and practical use cases to demonstrate how these models can be used to automate decision-making, enhance predictive accuracy, and improve trading performance in dynamic and high-stakes market environments. We provide a dedicated GitHub repository[9] to demonstrate examples included in the Element.

This Element is divided into two main sections: Foundations and Applications. The first part focuses on the fundamental aspects of financial time-series, covering topics such as statistical analysis, hypothesis testing, and related concepts. Financial datasets possess unique characteristics, and a solid understanding of their statistical properties is important for conducting meaningful financial analysis. Following this, we introduce the concept of supervised learning, along with an overview of deep learning models. The covered concepts

---

[9] See DeepLearningQuant.com or https://github.com/zcakhaa/Deep-Learning-in-Quantitative-Trading.

range from simple fully connected layers to the more advanced attention mechanism, which is particularly effective in capturing long-range dependencies within structured datasets.

Although deep learning has achieved significant advancements, deep networks frequently face issues such as overfitting, where models perform exceptionally well on training data but have difficulty generalizing to new, unseen datasets. To mitigate this issue, this Element outlines a complete workflow for implementing deep learning algorithms in quantitative trading. The workflow covers crucial stages, including data collection, exploratory data analysis, and cross-validation methods specifically adapted for financial datasets. These stages address key aspects like data distribution, stationarity, and the distinctive characteristics of financial time-series. These considerations are critical for creating models that achieve not only high accuracy but also robustness and reliability for implementation in real-world trading environments.

The second part of the Element is dedicated to the application of deep learning algorithms to various financial contexts. It places a key focus on one of the core tasks in quantitative trading: generating predictive signals. We explore a range of deep learning architectures designed for this purpose, demonstrating how these models can effectively forecast market movements. On top of this, we delve into advanced applications, such as improving momentum trading and cross-sectional momentum strategies. Additionally, we address portfolio optimization by introducing methods that enable the direct optimization of portfolio weights from market data. This end-to-end approach eliminates the need for intermediate steps, such as estimating returns and working with covariance matrices of returns, which are often difficult to implement in practical scenarios.

We provide an in-depth examination of the operational dynamics of modern securities exchanges, illustrating the processes behind financial transactions and the generation of high-frequency microstructure data, including order book updates and trade executions. Furthermore, we analyze the unique attributes of different asset classes, such as equities, bonds, commodities, and cryptocurrencies, highlighting the specific challenges and opportunities for applying deep learning techniques effectively to each.

8.2 Future Possibilities and Challenges

As the convergence of deep learning and quantitative trading progresses, the field presents immense opportunities alongside significant challenges. Next, we discuss some areas that are worth future exploration.

In this Element, our primary focus is on time-series data, including prices and trading volumes. However, we also explore the inclusion of alternative data, such as text, and techniques specific to those data types as potential sources of additional alpha. In Section 3, we look at how recent advances in NLP, such as transformer-based models like BERT and GPT, have made it feasible to extract nuanced information from unstructured textual data. Such methods could be used to evaluate data from news articles, social media, and earnings call transcripts to inform sentiment analysis and event prediction. Similarly, computer vision models can be used to analyze visual patterns in images. Practitioners could thus use satellite data, product shelves, or even weather imagery to provide insights into supply chain activity or predict market trends.

Another interesting area of further research is the explainability of deep networks. As deep learning models become increasingly sophisticated, the lack of interpretability poses challenges to understanding why a model makes specific decisions. In quantitative trading, where financial stakes and regulatory scrutiny are high, explainable algorithms are essential for building trust in model outputs and avoiding unintended biases. For trading strategies, explainability should encompass not only technical factors but also ethical considerations. It is important to ensure that algorithms do not exploit market inefficiencies in ways that harm retail investors or contribute to systemic risks. For instance, on May 6, 2010, the U.S. stock market underwent the Flash Crash, during which the Dow Jones Industrial Average plummeted by nearly 1,000 points within minutes before swiftly rebounding. This sudden decline was initiated by a substantial sell order executed by a mutual fund employing a trading algorithm intended to reduce market impact. The algorithm indiscriminately offloaded a large volume of E-mini S&P 500 futures contracts, ignoring prevailing prices and market conditions. HFT algorithms quickly picked up on this activity, starting a cascade of rapid-fire selling that spread across markets.

Interpretability has already been studied in academia, and methods like SHAP (Shapley Additive Explanations), Integrated Gradients (IG), and LIME (Local Interpretable Model-Agnostic Explanations) can be used to provide insights into model behavior. SHAP assigns each feature a contribution score for each prediction that indicates that feature's importance. Differently, IG is an attribution-based method and assesses the impact of each input feature on the predicted output by summing the gradients along a path from a baseline to the input. Similarly, LIME takes an approximation method that adopts a simpler model to explain individual predictions. Despite their utility, these methods still face significant challenges that limit their effectiveness in certain contexts. For example, SHAP can be computationally expensive and LIME relies on local approximations that may not accurately capture global model behavior. Additionally, these methods can struggle with capturing interactions among features in time-series or nonlinear domains, leading to incomplete interpretations.

Accordingly, the interpretability of models still remains a promising research direction, offering opportunities to develop more robust, efficient, and domain-specific tools that bridge the gap between complex predictions and actionable insights.

Quantum computing is poised to revolutionize many fields, and quantitative trading is no exception. In theory, quantum computers can address specific types of problems exponentially faster than classical machines, offering efficient parallel processing and the ability to solve high-dimensional challenges. This can be particularly valuable for tasks such as optimizing portfolio allocations or identifying high-dimensional nonlinear relationships in market data. By leveraging quantum-enhanced deep learning algorithms, we have the potential to optimize model training and explore complex patterns that classical systems can not handle. However, quantum computing technology is still in its infancy and access to scalable, fault-tolerant quantum systems is limited. Moreover, a wide gap between quantum algorithms and deep learning frameworks still remains. This research area will require interdisciplinary expertise to address the open questions regarding the practical applicability and cost-efficiency of quantum systems in trading.

Deep learning's potential for quantitative trading is vast, offering transformative possibilities for the financial industry. To harness the full power of these advanced techniques, sustained and focused research is essential. This commitment to ongoing research will allow financial institutions to refine trading strategies, enhance performance, and adopt these innovations responsibly. It is equally important that the use of such technologies upholds market integrity and operates within an ethical framework. It is our hope that this Element serves as a foundational resource in advancing this shared vision, fostering progress while contributing to market stability and fairness.

Acronyms

ACF Auto Correlation Function.
AR Autoregressive Model.
ARMA Autoregressive Moving Average Model.
BERT Bidirectional Encoder Representations from Transformers.
BTC Bitcoin.
CAPM Capital Asset Pricing Model.
CBOE Chicago Board Options Exchange.
CDS Credit Default Swaps.
CME Chicago Mercantile Exchange.
CNNs Convolutional Neural Networks.
DDPO Deep Deterministic Policy Gradient.
DeFi Decentralized Finance.
DMNs Deep Momentum Networks.
DOT Designated Order Turnaround.
DQNs Deep Q-Networks.
DRL Deep Reinforcement Learning.
ETF Exchange-Traded Fund.
ETH Ethereum.
FCNs Fully Connected Networks.
FPR False Positive Rates.
FSE Frankfurt Stock Exchange.
FX Foreign Exchange Market.
GANs Generative Adversarial Networks.
GBM Geometric Brownian Motion.
GCNs Graph Convolutional Neural Networks.
GED Generalized Error Distribution.
GMMs Gaussian Mixture Models.
GNNs Graph Neural Networks.
GP Gaussian Process.
GRUs Gated Recurrent Units.
HAR Heterogeneous Autoregressive.
HEAVY High-Frequency Based Auto-regressive and Volatility.
HL Huber Loss.
HMMs Hidden Market Models.
IG Integrated Gradients.
IPOs Initial Public Offerings.

IRD Interest Rate Differential.
Leaky-ReLU Leaky Rectified Linear Units.
LIME Local Interpretable Model-Agnostic Explanations.
LLMs Large Language Models.
LOBSTER Limit Order Book System.
LSE London Stock Exchange.
LSTM Long Short-Term Memory.
MA Moving Average Model.
MACD Moving Average Crossover Divergence.
MAE Mean Absolute Error.
MedAE Median Absolute Error.
MSE Mean Squared Error.
NBBO National Best Bid and Offer.
NYSE New York Stock Exchange.
OTC Over-the-Counter.
PACF Partial Autocorrelation Function.
PDF Probability Density Function.
PMF Probability Mass Function.
PPO Proximal Policy Optimization.
REITs Real Estate Investment Trusts.
ReLU Rectified Linear Units.
RL Reinforcement Learning.
RNNs Recurrent Neural Networks.
ROC Receiver Operating Characteristics.
Seq2Seq Sequence to Sequence Learning.
SHAP Shapley Additive Explanations.
SMA Simple Moving-Average Crossover.
SMBO Sequential Model-Based Optimization.
S&P500 Standard & Poor's 500.
TPR True Positive Rates.
TSE Toronto Stock Exchange.
VAEs Variational Autoencoders.
VaR Value at Risk.
WRDS Wharton Research Data Services.

Appendix A
Different Asset Classes

We here introduce several key asset classes that are particularly relevant to the topics discussed in this Element and are widely traded in financial markets. These asset classes include equities, bonds, foreign exchange (FX), futures, options, exchange-traded funds (ETFs), and cryptocurrencies, each of which presents unique characteristics and potential applications of deep learning. While our focus is on these prominent categories, it is important to note that this list is by no means exhaustive. Financial markets encompass a broad range of additional asset classes, such as real estate investment trusts (REITs) and derivatives like spread-betting, each offering distinct challenges and applications. Our goal is to establish a basic comprehension of these key asset classes, allowing readers to better understand the deep learning methods presented in the Element. Future exploration of other asset classes can further enrich the contextual knowledge base and expand the practical scope of these methodologies.

A.1 Equity Markets

Equities are among the most well-known financial securities, representing ownership stakes in companies. As of December 2024, global equity markets have reached a total market capitalization exceeding 123 trillion USD, surpassing the previous record set in October 2021. When companies decide to go public through Initial Public Offerings (IPOs), their shares are traded on major exchanges, such as the New York Stock Exchange (NYSE) or NASDAQ, making them available to a wide spectrum of investors. While equities are exchange-traded, equity markets are highly fragmented, consisting of primary exchanges, secondary exchanges, and alternative trading venues like dark pools. This fragmentation can lead to complexities in price discovery and execution. Liquidity in these markets is typically facilitated by market makers, who play the crucial role of ensuring that there is always a counterparty to trades. A key feature of equity trading in the United States is the National Best Bid and Offer (NBBO), which requires brokers to execute trades at the best available bid and offer prices across all venues. This regulation aims to protect investors, but its implementation can create challenges, particularly in high-frequency trading environments or during volatile market conditions.

Investors need to be mindful of several issues unique to equities. Delistings, for example, can significantly impact a portfolio and often lead to survivorship bias in historical datasets. This bias arises because delisted or failed companies are removed from indices and databases, skewing performance analyses. Additionally, corporate actions such as dividends, stock splits, and mergers must be properly accounted for in price series to avoid misinterpreting historical data. Adjusting prices for these actions ensures that analyses and back-tests accurately reflect the financial realities of investing in equities. Beyond single stocks, indices such as the S&P 500 and Dow Jones Industrial Average aggregate the prices of multiple equities to monitor the performance of specific areas within equity markets. These indices are constructed and weighted in various ways, for example price-weighted, equal-weighted, or market-cap-weighted, depending upon the index-specific methodology. Indices serve multiple purposes: They provide benchmarks for fund performance, offer insights into market trends, and serve as tradable instruments themselves.

A.2 Bonds

Bonds are fixed-income instruments that represent loans provided by lenders to borrowers, typically corporations or government entities. They offer predictable income and a range of maturities to suit diverse investment goals. Companies issue corporate bonds to obtain capital for purposes such as expansion, operational needs, or refinancing existing debts. Corporate bonds typically provide higher yields compared to government bonds to compensate for the increased credit risk taken on by lenders. The risks of these bonds are evaluated and classified by agencies like Moody's and Standard & Poor's. Conversely, government bonds are issued by national, state, or municipal authorities to finance public expenditures and infrastructure projects. Bonds from stable governments, such as U.S. Treasuries, are considered some of the safest investments, while sovereign debt from emerging markets may carry higher yields but also greater risk due to economic and political volatility.

The bond market operates primarily in an over-the-counter (OTC) format, where trades are negotiated directly between buyers and sellers rather than on centralized exchanges. This OTC structure allows for flexibility in terms of transactions but often results in lower transparency compared to equity markets. Despite this, the bond market is enormous, with an estimated global market size exceeding 130 trillion USD. This valuation underscores its importance alongside equities as a cornerstone of financial systems worldwide. Instead of trading OTC, investors can gain exposure to bonds in several other ways. ETFs provide a simple and efficient method for individuals to access a diversified basket of bonds. These ETFs track indices composed of corporate, government, or municipal bonds and allow investors to trade bond exposure on stock exchanges with ease. Bond futures provide an alternative means for investors to protect against interest rate fluctuations or to engage in speculative trading based on price changes. These instruments are widely used by institutional investors because of their liquidity and leverage. Mutual funds and index funds focused on bonds also provide a way to access professionally managed portfolios, offering diversification and, in the case of index funds, cost efficiency.

When investing in bonds, several factors must be considered. Interest rate sensitivity is a crucial aspect, as bond prices have an inverse relationship with interest rates. Rising rates can thus lead to capital losses, especially for bonds with longer maturities. Credit risk is another key consideration, as the probability of an issuer failing to meet its obligations changes significantly between corporate and government bonds. Liquidity can also be a concern, while government bonds are generally liquid, corporate bonds might encounter liquidity issues, especially during times of market turmoil. Overall, bonds are essential components of a well-diversified portfolio, especially given their relatively low correlation. Bonds are generally favored by investors seeking stable income, capital preservation, and reduced portfolio volatility. Whether accessed through OTC trading, ETFs, futures, or mutual funds, bonds provide versatile tools to meet a range of investment objectives. Their importance in financial markets cannot be overstated, as they continue to serve as a foundation of income and stability for both individual and institutional investors.

A.3 Foreign Exchange Market

The foreign exchange market, often referred to as Forex or FX, is the largest and most liquid financial market globally, with over 7 trillion USD in daily trades. Forex market participants trade currencies for purposes of international trade, investment flows, and speculative interests. Unlike equities and bonds, Forex does not trade on centralized exchanges. Instead, trading occurs OTC, with participants ranging from large institutions and governments to retail traders. This structure ensures the market is active 24 hours a day, spanning key financial centers including London, New York, Tokyo, and Sydney.

Forex trading entails simultaneously purchasing one currency while selling another, forming currency pairs such as EUR/USD or GBP/JPY. These pairs are divided into multiple categories, notably including majors, minors, and exotics. Majors include the most traded currencies globally, such as the U.S. Dollar (USD), Euro (EUR), and Japanese Yen (JPY). Minors exclude the USD but include other major currencies. Lastly, exotics consist of less liquid and more volatile currencies from emerging markets.

Market participants engage in Forex for different reasons. Corporations and governments trade currencies to manage and hedge their exposure to currency price fluctuations that might affect international trade or the value of their reserves. Financial institutions, hedge funds, and retail traders often engage in Forex for speculative purposes, seeking to profit from changes in exchange rates. Exchange rate movements are influenced by multiple elements such as interest rate disparities, geopolitical incidents, economic indicators, and central bank strategies. Leverage plays an important role in Forex trading by allowing traders to hold positions substantially larger than the amount of capital they commit as collateral. This magnifies both possible gains and associated risks. Accordingly, the high levels of leverage available in Forex can lead to significant losses, particularly for inexperienced traders. Moreover, the decentralized and largely unregulated nature of the market means participants should choose brokers carefully to ensure transparency and fair dealing.

Access to the Forex market has been democratized significantly through technology, allowing retail traders to participate via online platforms. These platforms provide traders with exposure to Forex markets through spot trading, forward contracts, and options. Beyond direct trading, investors can also gain exposure to currency movements through ETFs that track the performance of currency indices or specific currency pairs. Futures contracts on major currencies offer yet another way to speculate or hedge currency exposure, providing a regulated alternative to OTC Forex trading.

A.4 Futures

Futures are standardized financial agreements that require a buyer to purchase, or a seller to sell, an underlying asset at a set price on a designated future date. Futures are essential instruments in global financial markets, used both for speculation and hedging against price movements. The total market for futures is vast, spanning financial instruments, commodities, and more. The Chicago Mercantile Exchange (CME) is the most prominent and liquid futures exchange globally. Futures contracts are intrinsically tied to "future deliverables," meaning a contract specifies the terms for the delivery of the respective underlying asset at expiry. However, in practice, most futures contracts are either cash-settled or closed out prior to delivery, particularly for financial futures where physical delivery is less common. The ability to settle contracts in cash adds flexibility for traders and investors, reducing the logistical challenges associated with taking physical delivery of assets, such as oil or agricultural products.

Each futures contract has a specific expiry date, and traders often need to "roll" contracts if they wish to maintain their position beyond that expiration date. Rolling consists of closing the position in the nearing expiration contract and simultaneously establishing a position in a future-dated contract. This process is subject to price differences between contracts, particularly in markets with contango or backwardation. Contango and backwardation refer to how current futures prices compare to the spot (current) price of an underlying asset. Contango means that the futures price is higher than the current spot price, and backwardation is the opposite. Thus, to maintain a consistent price series for analysis, adjustments are often required. Backward adjustments, as discussed in Section 5, modify historical prices to account for differences between successive contracts, ensuring continuity in time-series data. However, these adjustments distort historical price levels. Consequently, traders and investors must carefully manage their positions, particularly around contract expiry, and be aware of the implications of rolling contracts and adjusting historical prices.

Futures are particularly popular due to their high liquidity, low trading fees, and the leverage that can be exercised through margin accounts. Using margin, traders can manage large positions with only a small portion of their capital, thereby increasing both potential profits and risks. This leverage, combined with the standardized nature of contracts, makes futures a preferred choice for both retail and institutional traders. Among the most traded futures contracts globally are the S&P 500 futures on the CME, which allow investors to gain or hedge exposure to the performance of the broader U.S. equity market. Additionally, futures are not limited to financial instruments and they are widely used in commodities markets, covering assets such as crude oil, gold, agricultural products, and natural gas. These contracts enable producers, consumers, and traders to hedge against price volatility and secure future prices. However, the popularity of certain commodity futures can decline over time and lead to their delisting, as similarly occurs in equity markets.

A.5 Options

Options are financial derivatives that provide the holder with the right, but not the obligation, to buy or sell an underlying asset at a predetermined price, known as the strike price, on or before a specific expiration date. Similar to futures, options are extensively utilized for hedging, speculative activities, and income generation. They are traded on centralized exchanges such as the Chicago Board Options Exchange (CBOE) and OTC markets. The options traded on these exchanges are standardized to ensure greater liquidity and transparency. There are two primary types of options: call options and put options. A call option grants the holder the right to purchase the underlying asset, while a put option allows the holder to sell it. Each option contract requires the payment of a premium, which is the cost the buyer pays to the seller for the rights the option provides. The value of an option is influenced by various factors, including the price and expected volatility of the underlying asset, the time remaining until expiration, and prevailing interest rates.

Unlike futures, which impose mandatory obligations, options offer greater flexibility. The purchaser of an option has the discretion to decide whether to exercise the contract, whereas the seller (or writer) must adhere to the contract terms if the buyer chooses to exercise it. Options are available on a wide range of underlying assets, such as stocks, indices, commodities, currencies, and even interest rates. For example, an investor with a stock portfolio might buy put options to protect against a potential drop in stock prices. Similarly, a business exposed to fluctuating commodity prices might purchase call options to guarantee maximum costs for raw materials. Speculators use options to profit from anticipated price movements, benefiting from the contracts' relatively low upfront cost compared to that of the underlying asset to gain leverage to price movements.

However, the flexibility of options comes with complexity. A key characteristic of options is their expiration date, after which a contract expires worthless if not exercised. This creates the need for strategic decision-making around whether and when to exercise an option. Rolling options or closing a position in a near expiry option and simultaneously opening a new position in a longer-dated contract is a common practice to maintain exposure beyond an approaching expiration date. Another key feature of options is the leverage they offer. A slight fluctuation in the price of the underlying asset can cause large percentage changes in an option's value. This leverage can amplify both profits and losses, requiring careful position sizing and risk management.

Options trading has grown significantly in popularity, driven by technological advancements and the rise of retail trading platforms. Exchange-traded options, such as those on major indices like the S&P 500, are among the most actively traded due to their high liquidity and broad appeal. Meanwhile, OTC options allow for customized contracts tailored to specific needs, but they come with less transparency and higher counterparty risk.

A.6 Exchange-Traded Funds

Exchange-traded funds (ETFs) are investment instruments that blend the diversification benefits of mutual funds with the trading flexibility of individual stocks. They are structured to mirror the performance of a specific index, sector, commodity, or asset class, providing investors with an easy and cost-efficient method to access a broad array of markets. Over the years, ETFs have revolutionized the world of passive investing, contributing to a significant shift in how capital is allocated across global markets. The rise of passive investing through ETFs has been remarkable. From their inception in the early 1990s, ETFs have grown exponentially, with global assets under management now exceeding 10 trillion USD. This increase highlights the trend that investors are increasingly favoring investment strategies that are cost-effective, transparent, and efficient, rather than traditional active management. ETFs make it possible for investors to gain exposure to broad market indices like the S&P 500 or MSCI World Index without the need for individual stock selection, making them ideal for those seeking diversification with minimal effort.

Similar to individual stocks, ETFs are traded on exchanges, providing investors with the benefits of liquidity and flexibility. Unlike mutual funds which are priced solely at the end of the trading day, ETFs can be purchased and sold throughout the trading session. Market makers critically ensure liquidity and facilitate smooth intraday trading in ETF markets. They do so by buying and selling both ETF shares and the underlying securities that an ETF tracks. These market makers are also responsible for delivering the underlying "basket" of securities at the end of each trading day. The arbitrage mechanism maintains a tight alignment between ETF prices and their net asset value (NAV). Beyond traditional market-cap-weighted ETFs, the industry has seen significant innovation, particularly in the realm of smart beta (a better risk-adjusted beta). Smart beta ETFs deviate from conventional indices by weighting their components based on alternative criteria such as value, momentum, or volatility. These methods are designed to take advantage of certain risk premiums or enhance returns while retaining the benefits of transparency and cost-effectiveness.

The ETF market has transformed the investment landscape, making it easier than ever for individuals to access a wide array of assets and strategies. Whether used for passive exposure to global markets or tactical allocations through smart beta, ETFs continue to shape modern portfolio management. Their combination of simplicity, efficiency, and adaptability suggests that they will remain a cornerstone of investment portfolios worldwide.

A.7 Cryptocurrency

Cryptocurrencies are digital or virtual currencies that are built upon decentralized blockchain technologies and leverage cryptography to ensure their security. They possess several features that distinguish them significantly from traditional major asset classes. Primarily, cryptocurrencies are usually not governed by any central authority, making them resistant to government interference or manipulation. Most decentralized digital assets do not provide ownership in any underlying entity or physical asset, whereas stocks, for example, represent fractional ownership in a company that provides shareholders with a portion of the company's profits along with voting privileges. Additionally, the transactions of cryptocurrencies are generally recorded on a public ledger that is accessible to anyone. Thus, while many equity transactions are not public and corporations only intermittently disclose information, blockchain-based currencies offer much greater, real-time transparency

Cryptocurrency markets operate 24/7 on both centralized and decentralized exchanges. Centralized exchanges such as Binance, Coinbase, and Kraken offer spot, derivative, and staking markets. However, centralized exchanges come with inherent counterparty risks as the collapse of FTX (one of the largest cryptocurrency exchanges). The fraud and mismanagement at FTX led to catastrophic losses for its users. Such incidents underscore the importance of due diligence and risk management when dealing with centralized platforms. Compounding these challenges is the fragmentation of cryptocurrency markets across thousands of cryptocurrencies and a multitude of exchanges. This dispersion can lead to liquidity issues, pricing discrepancies, and security concerns, making the cryptocurrency ecosystem both vibrant and complex.

Decentralized Finance (DeFi) offers an alternative to centralized exchanges by using blockchain-based smart contracts to enable financial transactions without intermediaries. Platforms like Uniswap and Aave demonstrate how DeFi can facilitate peer-to-peer trading and lending with enhanced transparency and reduced reliance on centralized entities. This approach mitigates counterparty risk while expanding access to financial services, though it introduces new considerations such as smart contract vulnerabilities.

Spot trading forms the backbone of cryptocurrency markets, where digital assets like Bitcoin (BTC) and Ethereum (ETH) are bought and sold directly at current market prices, with immediate settlement. Beyond spot trading, the market offers a range of derivative instruments, including futures contracts and perpetual futures. Perpetual futures, in particular, have gained widespread popularity due to their unique design, allowing traders to maintain leveraged positions indefinitely without an expiration date, as long as margin requirements are met. These products are heavily traded on platforms like Binance and Bybit, offering significant liquidity and trading opportunities.

For investors who prefer not to directly hold cryptocurrencies, there are several other ways to gain exposure to their price movements. Spot ETFs provide a regulated avenue for tracking the value of assets like BTC and ETH without the need for direct ownership. Futures-based products, which track Bitcoin or Ethereum, also offer a way to participate in the market, though they carry risks associated with rolling contracts. These financial products bridge the gap between traditional investment frameworks and the digital asset space, making it easier for institutional and retail investors to enter the market.

A.8 Others

Besides the major asset classes, there are numerous other products that provide investors with diverse opportunities to achieve their financial goals. We list a few here. Commodities, although often traded via futures, also exist as a standalone asset class. This category encompasses physical goods such as gold, silver, crude oil, natural gas, and agricultural items like wheat and corn. Investors can participate in the commodities market by owning these assets directly, engaging in futures contracts, or investing in ETFs that track commodities. Commodities are particularly valued for their role as inflation hedges and their historically low correlation with traditional financial assets, making them useful for portfolio diversification.

While futures and options are the most frequently traded derivatives, other types of derivatives also hold significant importance in financial markets. For instance, swaps are extensively utilized in the interest rate and currency sectors. Interest rate swaps enable parties to exchange fixed-rate payments for floating-rate payments, or the other way around, allowing them to manage their exposure to interest rate variability. Currency swaps involve the exchange of principal and interest payments in different currencies, serving as essential tools for multinational corporations and governments to manage foreign exchange risks. Additionally, credit default swaps (CDS) function as a type of insurance against a borrower's default, playing a crucial role in credit markets and risk management strategies.

The real estate market is another prominent market. Often, the cost of buying or selling a property is high and the process is time-consuming. However, real estate investment trusts (REITs) offer investors a way to access the real estate market without directly owning physical properties. By pooling funds from multiple investors, these investment entities can purchase, oversee, and finance income-producing real estate assets such as office buildings, retail centers, apartment complexes, and industrial facilities. Publicly traded REITs are listed on stock exchanges, with liquidity and ease of access similar to that of equities. Private non-traded REITs are also available to accredited investors and often focus on niche markets. REITs attract income-oriented investors due to legal requirements that compel them to pay out a significant share of their earnings as dividends, typically offering higher returns than conventional equities. Nonetheless, their success can be impacted by factors like interest rate changes, trends in the property market, and economic cycles, rendering them sensitive to macroeconomic shifts. Note that some dividends from REITs are qualified as capital gains rather than income which can get more favorable taxation.

Private equity and venture capital represent another distinct asset class, providing opportunities to invest in companies that do not trade on public markets. Venture capital targets early-stage, high-growth startups, while private equity focuses on mature companies, often involving buyouts or growth investments. These investments usually involve committing capital over an extended period and bearing higher risks, but they also provide the potential for considerable returns.

Appendix B
Access to Market Data

B.1 Professional

For professionals, there are a variety of established third-party providers that deliver high-quality market data, tailored to the needs of institutional investors, traders, and financial analysts. Providers such as Bloomberg, Refinitiv, and S&P Global offer comprehensive datasets spanning multiple asset classes, along with advanced analytical tools and integration options. These platforms have become industry staples, ensuring reliable and timely access to financial information critical for decision-making. In addition to third-party providers, many professional market participants access direct market feeds from exchanges. These feeds deliver raw, real-time data, including order book details, trade executions, and price updates, providing the low-latency access required for high-frequency trading and algorithmic strategies. Beyond traditional market data, there is also a growing demand for alternative data, non-conventional datasets that provide unique insights into market trends and behavior. This can include information from annual reports, social media sentiment, credit card transactions, and forum discussions. Alternative data has become a critical tool for gaining a competitive edge, offering perspectives not available from standard financial datasets. Together, these resources constitute the standard data sources accessed by professionals.

B.2 Academic

Academics often have access to subsidized data sources formatted specifically for research and academic use. These resources can be tailored to meet the requests of universities and researchers. Such data is often used to study financial markets, corporate behavior, and economic trends.

One of the primary resources for academics is Wharton Research Data Services (WRDS), a global data platform that hosts a huge amount of data (more than 350 TB) aggregated from global data vendors. WRDS encompasses a range of databases including Compustat, CRSP, TFN (THOMSON), TAQ and many others. WRDS not only covers historical financial time-series data but also provides access to corporate fundamentals, macroeconomic indicators and more. Most academics can gain access to the WRDS platform through a subscription provided by their universities. As a result, WRDS is widely used in academic research.

Another notable resource is LOBSTER (Limit Order Book System), which was established in 2013 and offers high-frequency limit order book data. Since its inception, the focus of LOBSTER has shifted to serving the academic community by providing reconstructed limit order book data for all the stocks traded on NASDAQ. Accordingly, the LOBSTER dataset is derived from NASDAQ's Historical Total View ITCH files and encompasses the complete depth of the order books. Each historical snapshot includes the bid and ask data for up to 200 price levels, with the number of price levels varying based on the specific security. This data source is particularly suited to researchers who are interested in market microstructure, trading dynamics, order flow and market efficiency.

In addition to these platforms, academics may also access resources like Quandl for economic and financial data, S&P Capital IQ for corporate insights, and DataStream for macroeconomic and time-series data. Many universities partner with these providers to offer discounted or free access to their students and faculty. For niche research needs, open-source data repositories, government databases, and exchange-specific resources can also provide valuable datasets.

B.3 Personal Enthusiast

For personal enthusiasts, accessing market data is easier than ever, with a variety of platforms and tools offering low-cost or even free data solutions. These resources cater to hobbyists, retail investors, and independent developers who want to explore financial markets, test strategies, or simply stay informed. Cryptocurrency market data is likely a good starting point for enthusiasts since it is easy to obtain high-quality market data from cryptocurrency exchanges like Binance that deliver real-time data directly to users through REST, WebSocket, and FIX APIs. Additionally, other platforms like CoinGecko and CoinMarketCap offer extensive information on prices, trading volumes, and blockchain statistics at no cost. This easily accessible high-quality market data places retail investors on a more level playing field with professionals.

For other asset classes, such as equities, fixed-income securities, and ETFs, other popular free platforms like Yahoo Finance, Google Finance, and TradingView provide access to live prices, historical charts, and basic financial metrics. These platforms are user-friendly, making them ideal for beginners who want to track markets and learn about investing without significant upfront costs. For enthusiasts looking for more advanced data, platforms like Alpha Vantage, Polygon.io, and Finnhub offer affordable APIs that deliver market data in customizable formats, including live prices and fundamental information. These tools are especially popular among developers and quantitative enthusiasts who want to integrate financial data into their own projects or build custom trading algorithms.

Finally, for those interested in more niche or alternative datasets, open-source repositories and public APIs from organizations like AlphaQuery and Kaggle can offer unique insights and opportunities for experimentation. The wide availability of these tools ensures that personal enthusiasts have plenty of options to explore financial markets, regardless of their respective experience levels or budgets.

Appendix C
Investment Performance Metrics

Here, we introduce various metrics that are used to gauge the performance of a portfolio or a trading strategy. We denote the daily trade returns from a strategy as R_t:

$$R_t = w_{t-1} r_t - C|w_t - w_{t-1}|,$$
$$r_t = \frac{p_t - p_{t-1}}{p_{t-1}}, \qquad (C.1)$$

where p_t denotes daily price series and w_t is our trading positions. We here use a fixed commission cost C. Note that this is a linear cost model and we do not consider market impact. In practice, trading a large volume could lead to higher costs as there might be not enough volume on the opposite side and we have to accept worse prices to liquidate our positions.

Annualized Expected Return:

$$E(R_{Annual}) = E(R_t) \times AF, \qquad (C.2)$$

where AF is the annualization factor. If we do not consider the compounding factor, we can set AF equal to 252 to get a quick view of the annualized expected return.

Annualized Standard Deviation:

$$Std(R_{Annual}) = Std(R_t) \times \sqrt{AF}. \qquad (C.3)$$

Annualized Sharpe Ratio:

$$Sharpe = \frac{E(R_{Annual} - R_f)}{Std(R_{Annual})}, \qquad (C.4)$$

where R_f is the risk-free rate and we can set it as the treasury yields or LIBOR. In this Element, we set it to 0 for simplicity. Sharpe ratio and Sortino ratio are risk-adjusted returns that measure the return per unit risk.

Annualized Downside Deviation:

$$DD(R_{Annual}) = Std(R_t < 0) \times \sqrt{AF}. \qquad (C.5)$$

Annualized Sortino Ratio:

$$Sortino = \frac{E(R_{Annual} - R_f)}{DD(R_{Annual})}, \qquad (C.6)$$

where R_f is again the risk-free rate.

Appendix C

Maximum Drawdown refers to the largest decline from an investment's peak value to its lowest point over a specific timeframe. We can calculate the maximum drawdown (MD) as:

$$MD = \frac{p_t^{High} - p_t^{Low}}{p_t^{High}}, \qquad (C.7)$$

where p_t^{High} is the peak value before the largest price drop and p_t^{Low} is the subsequent lowest price before new high is established.

Percentage between Positive and Negative Returns:

$$\% + Ret = \frac{E(R_t > 0)}{E(R_t < 0)}. \qquad (C.8)$$

Appendix D
Code Scripts

```python
def rolling_forward_cv(X_torch, y_torch, train_end_fractions =
    [0.7, 0.8, 0.9], val_fraction = 0.1):
    """Perform 3-fold rolling forward CV. Each validation is 10%
    of data"""
    N = len(X_torch)
    all_data []
    for frac in train_end_fractions:
        train_end = int(frac * N)
        val_end   = int((frac + val_fraction) * N)
        # Safety check if val_end exceeds dataset size
        if val_end > N:
            break  # no more folds possible if we run off the end
        # Create train/val splits
        X_train, y_train = X_torch[:train_end], y_torch[:train_end]
        X_val,   y_val   = X_torch[train_end:val_end], y_torch[train_end:val_end]
        all_data.append((X_train, y_train, X_Val, y_val))
    return all_data
```

Listing 1: A rolling forward cross-validation approach.

```python
import torch.nn as nn

class MLP(nn.Module):
    def __init__(self, seq_length, n_features, y_dim):
        super().__init__()

        self.fc = nn.Sequential(
            nn.Flatten(),
            nn.Linear(seq_length*n_features, 4),
            nn.Tanh(),
            nn.Linear(4, y_dim))

    def forward(self, x):
        x = torch.flatten(x, start_dim=1)
        x = self.fc(x)
        y = torch.softmax(x, dim=1)
        return y
```

Listing 2: A MLP network for deep portfolio optimization with a long-only constraint.

```python
import torch.nn as nn

class deeplob(nn.Module):
    def __init__(self, device):
        super().__init__()
```

```python
        self.device = device

        self.conv1 = nn.Sequential(
            nn.Conv2d(in_channels=1, out_channels=32, kernel_size=(1,2), stride=(1,2)),
            nn.LeakyReLU(negative_slope=0.01),
            nn.BatchNorm2d(32),
            nn.Conv2d(in_channels=32, out_channels=32, kernel_size=(4,1)),
            nn.LeakyReLU(negative_slope=0.01),
            nn.BatchNorm2d(32),
            nn.Conv2d(in_channels=32, out_channels=32, kernel_size=(4,1)),
            nn.LeakyReLU(negative_slope=0.01),
            nn.BatchNorm2d(32),
        )
        self.conv2 = nn.Sequential(
            nn.Conv2d(in_channels=32, out_channels=32, kernel_size=(1,2), stride=(1,2)),
            nn.Tanh(),
            nn.BatchNorm2d(32),
            nn.Conv2d(in_channels=32, out_channels=32, kernel_size=(4,1)),
            nn.Tanh(),
            nn.BatchNorm2d(32),
            nn.Conv2d(in_channels=32, out_channels=32, kernel_size=(4,1)),
            nn.Tanh(),
            nn.BatchNorm2d(32),
        )
        self.conv3 = nn.Sequential(
            nn.Conv2d(in_channels=32, out_channels=32, kernel_size=(1,10)),
            nn.LeakyReLU(negative_slope=0.01),
            nn.BatchNorm2d(32),
            nn.Conv2d(in_channels=32, out_channels=32, kernel_size=(4,1)),
            nn.LeakyReLU(negative_slope=0.01),
            nn.BatchNorm2d(32),
            nn.Conv2d(in_channels=32, out_channels=32, kernel_size=(4,1)),
            nn.LeakyReLU(negative_slope=0.01),
            nn.BatchNorm2d(32),
        )

        self.inp1 = nn.Sequential(
            nn.Conv2d(in_channels=32, out_channels=64, kernel_size=(1,1), padding='same'),
            nn.LeakyReLU(negative_slope=0.01),
            nn.BatchNorm2d(64),
            nn.Conv2d(in_channels=64, out_channels=64, kernel_size=(3,1), padding='same'),
            nn.LeakyReLU(negative_slope=0.01),
            nn.BatchNorm2d(64),
        )
```

```python
        self.inp2 = nn.Sequential(
            nn.Conv2d(in_channels=32, out_channels=64,
    kernel_size=(1,1), padding='same'),
            nn.LeakyReLU(negative_slope=0.01),
            nn.BatchNorm2d(64),
            nn.Conv2d(in_channels=64, out_channels=64,
    kernel_size=(5,1), padding='same'),
            nn.LeakyReLU(negative_slope=0.01),
            nn.BatchNorm2d(64),
        )
        self.inp3 = nn.Sequential(
            nn.MaxPool2d((3, 1), stride=(1, 1), padding=(1, 0)),
            nn.Conv2d(in_channels=32, out_channels=64,
    kernel_size=(1,1), padding='same'),
            nn.LeakyReLU(negative_slope=0.01),
            nn.BatchNorm2d(64),
        )

        # lstm layers
        self.lstm = nn.LSTM(input_size=192, hidden_size=64,
    num_layers=1, batch_first=True)
        self.fc1 = nn.Linear(64, 1)

    def forward(self, x):
        # h0: (number of hidden layers, batch size, hidden size)
        h0 = torch.zeros(1, x.size(0), 64).to(self.device)
        c0 = torch.zeros(1, x.size(0), 64).to(self.device)
        x = x.unsqueeze(1)
        x = self.conv1(x)
        x = self.conv2(x)
        x = self.conv3(x)
        x_inp1 = self.inp1(x)
        x_inp2 = self.inp2(x)
        x_inp3 = self.inp3(x)
        x = torch.cat((x_inp1, x_inp2, x_inp3), dim=1)
        x = x.permute(0, 2, 1, 3)
        x = torch.reshape(x, (-1, x.shape[1], x.shape[2]))
        x, _ = self.lstm(x, (h0, c0))
        x = x[:, -1, :]
        x = self.fc1(x)[:,0]
        return x
```

Listing 3: The network architecture for DeepLOB for a regression problem.

References

Akiba, T., Sano, S., Yanase, T., Ohta, T., & Koyama, M. (2019). Optuna: A next-generation hyperparameter optimization framework. In *Proceedings of the 25th acm sigkdd international conference on knowledge discovery & data mining* (pp. 2623–2631).

Almgren, R., & Chriss, N. (2001). Optimal execution of portfolio transactions. *Journal of Risk, 3*, 5–40.

Atkins, A., Niranjan, M., & Gerding, E. (2018). Financial news predicts stock market volatility better than close price. *The Journal of Finance and Data Science, 4*(2), 120–137.

Atsalakis, G. S., & Valavanis, K. P. (2009). Surveying stock market forecasting techniques–Part II: Soft computing methods. *Expert Systems with Applications, 36*(3), 5932–5941.

Bachelier, L. (1900). Théorie de la spéculation. In *Annales scientifiques de l'école normale supérieure* (Vol. 17, pp. 21–86). Elsevier

Bahdanau, D., Cho, K., & Bengio, Y. (2014). Neural machine translation by jointly learning to align and translate. *arXiv preprint arXiv:1409.0473*.

Bao, W., Yue, J., & Rao, Y. (2017). A deep learning framework for financial time series using stacked autoencoders and long-short term memory. *PloS one, 12*(7), e0180944.

Beck, M., Pöppel, K., Spanring, M., et al. (2024). xlstm: Extended long short-term memory. *arXiv preprint arXiv:2405.04517*.

Bengio, Y., Simard, P., & Frasconi, P. (1994). Learning long-term dependencies with gradient descent is difficult. *IEEE transactions on neural networks, 5*(2), 157–166.

Bertsimas, D., & Lo, A. W. (1998). Optimal control of execution costs. *Journal of financial markets, 1*(1), 1–50.

Blondel, M., Teboul, O., Berthet, Q., & Djolonga, J. (2020). Fast differentiable sorting and ranking. In Hal Daumé & Singh, Aarti (eds), *International conference on machine learning* (pp. 950–959). PMLR

Borovykh, A., Bohte, S., & Oosterlee, C. W. (2017). Conditional time series forecasting with convolutional neural networks. *arXiv preprint arXiv:1703.04691*.

Boureau, Y., Ponce, J., & LeCun, Y. (2010). A theoretical analysis of feature pooling in vision algorithms. In *Proceedings of international conference on machine learning (icml'10)* (Vol. 28, p. 3).

Briola, A., Bartolucci, S., & Aste, T. (2024). Deep limit order book forecasting. *arXiv preprint arXiv:2403.09267*.

Briola, A., Turiel, J., & Aste, T. (2020). Deep learning modeling of limit order book: A comparative perspective. *arXiv preprint arXiv:2007.07319*.

Cesa, M. (2017). A brief history of quantitative finance. *Probability, Uncertainty and Quantitative Risk, 2*(1), 1–16.

Chen, J.- F., Chen, W.- L., Huang, C.- P., Huang, S.- H., & Chen, A.- P. (2016). Financial time-series data analysis using deep convolutional neural networks. In *Cloud computing and big data (ccbd), 2016 7th international conference on* (pp. 87–92).

Cho, K., Van Merriënboer, B., Gulcehre, C., et al. (2014). Learning phrase representations using rnn encoder-decoder for statistical machine translation. *arXiv preprint arXiv:1406.1078*.

Cont, R., Cucuringu, M., Kochems, J., & Prenzel, F. (2023). Limit order book simulation with generative adversarial networks. *SSRN 4512356*.

Cuturi, M., Teboul, O., & Vert, J.- P. (2019). Differentiable ranking and sorting using optimal transport. *Advances in Neural Information Processing Systems, 32*.

Devlin, J., Chang, M.- W., Lee, K., & Toutanova, K. (2018). Bert: Pre-training of deep bidirectional transformers for language understanding. *arXiv preprint arXiv:1810.04805*.

Di Persio, L., & Honchar, O. (2016). Artificial neural networks architectures for stock price prediction: Comparisons and applications. *International Journal of Circuits, Systems and Signal Processing, 10*, 403–413.

Dixon, M. (2018). Sequence classification of the limit order book using recurrent neural networks. *Journal of Computational Science, 24*, 277–286.

Doering, J., Fairbank, M., & Markose, S. (2017). Convolutional neural networks applied to high-frequency market microstructure forecasting. In *Computer science and electronic engineering (ceec), 2017* (pp. 31–36).

Du, K., Xing, F., Mao, R., & Cambria, E. (2024). Financial sentiment analysis: Techniques and applications. *ACM Computing Surveys, 56*(9), 1–42.

Ekmekcioğlu, Ö., & Pınar, M. Ç. (2023). Graph neural networks for deep portfolio optimization. *Neural Computing and Applications, 35*(28), 20663–20674.

Fischer, T., & Krauss, C. (2017). Deep learning with long short-term memory networks for financial market predictions. *European Journal of Operational Research, 270*(2), 654–669.

Frazier, P. I. (2018). Bayesian optimization. In *Recent advances in optimization and modeling of contemporary problems* (pp. 255–278). Informs.

Gatheral, J. (2010). No-dynamic-arbitrage and market impact. *Quantitative finance, 10*(7), 749–759.

Goodfellow, I., Bengio, Y., & Courville, A. (2016). *Deep learning.* MIT Press. (www.deeplearningbook.org)

Goodfellow, I., Pouget-Abadie, J., Mirza, M., et al. (2014). Generative adversarial nets. *Advances in neural information processing systems, 27.*

Grover, A., Wang, E., Zweig, A., & Ermon, S. (2018). Stochastic optimization of sorting networks via continuous relaxations. In *International conference on learning representations.*

Gu, A., & Dao, T. (2023). Mamba: Linear-time sequence modeling with selective state spaces. *arXiv preprint arXiv:2312.00752.*

He, K., Zhang, X., Ren, S., & Sun, J. (2016). Deep residual learning for image recognition. In *Proceedings of the ieee conference on computer vision and pattern recognition* (pp. 770–778).

Hochreiter, S., & Schmidhuber, J. (1997). Long short-term memory. *Neural computation, 9*(8), 1735–1780.

Hornik, K., Stinchcombe, M., & White, H. (1989). Multilayer feedforward networks are universal approximators. *Neural networks, 2*(5), 359–366.

Hwang, Y., Kong, Y., Lee, Y., & Zohren, S. (2025). Decision-informed neural networks with large language model integration for portfolio optimization.

Jin, M., Wang, S., Ma, L., et al. (2023). Time-LLM: Time series forecasting by reprogramming large language models. *arXiv preprint arXiv:2310.01728.*

Kalman, R. E. (1960). A new approach to linear filtering and prediction problems. *Journal of Basic Engineering, Transactions of the ASME, 82*(1), 35–45.

Kingma, D. P., & Welling, M. (2013). Auto-encoding variational Bayes. *arXiv preprint arXiv:1312.6114.*

Kipf, T. N., & Welling, M. (2016). Semi-supervised classification with graph convolutional networks. *arXiv preprint arXiv:1609.02907.*

Kong, Y., Nie, Y., Dong, X., et al. (2024). Large language models for financial and investment management: Applications and benchmarks. *Journal of Portfolio Management, 51*(2) 162–210.

Kong, Y., Wang, Z., Nie, Y., et al. (2024). Unlocking the power of lstm for long term time series forecasting. *arXiv preprint arXiv:2408.10006.*

Korangi, K., Mues, C., & Bravo, C. (2024). Large-scale time-varying portfolio optimisation using graph attention networks. *arXiv preprint arXiv:2407.15532.*

Krizhevsky, A., Sutskever, I., & Hinton, G. E. (2012). Imagenet classification with deep convolutional neural networks. *Advances in neural information processing systems, 25.*

Krizhevsky, A., Sutskever, I., & Hinton, G. E. (2017). Imagenet classification with deep convolutional neural networks. *Communications of the ACM, 60*(6), 84–90.

Lim, B., Arık, S. Ö., Loeff, N., & Pfister, T. (2021). Temporal fusion transformers for interpretable multi-horizon time series forecasting. *International Journal of Forecasting, 37*(4), 1748–1764.

Lim, B., & Zohren, S. (2021). Time-series forecasting with deep learning: A survey. *Philosophical Transactions of the Royal Society A, 379*(2194), 20200209.

Lim, B., Zohren, S., & Roberts, S. (2019). Enhancing time-series momentum strategies using deep neural networks. *The Journal of Financial Data Science, 1*(4), 19–38.

Liu, T.- Y. (2009). Learning to rank for information retrieval. *Foundations and Trends® in Information Retrieval, 3*(3), 225–331.

Liu, Y., Hu, T., Zhang, H., et al. (2023). itransformer: Inverted transformers are effective for time series forecasting. *arXiv preprint arXiv:2310.06625*.

Luong, M.- T., Pham, H., & Manning, C. D. (2015). Effective approaches to attention-based neural machine translation. *arXiv preprint arXiv:1508.04025*.

Maas, A. L., Hannun, A. Y., Ng, A. Y., et al. (2013). Rectifier nonlinearities improve neural network acoustic models. In *Proc. icml* (Vol. 30, p. 3).

Markowitz, H. (1952). Portfolio selection. *The Journal of Finance, 7*(1), 77–91.

Mhaskar, H. N., & Micchelli, C. A. (1993). How to choose an activation function. *Advances in neural information processing systems, 6*.

Moreno-Pino, F., & Zohren, S. (2024). Deepvol: Volatility forecasting from high-frequency data with dilated causal convolutions. *Quantitative Finance, 24*(8), 1105–1127.

Moskowitz, T. J., Ooi, Y. H., & Pedersen, L. H. (2012). Time series momentum. *Journal of Financial Economics, 104*(2), 228–250.

Nagy, P., Calliess, J.- P., & Zohren, S. (2023). Asynchronous deep double dueling q-learning for trading-signal execution in limit order book markets. *Frontiers in Artificial Intelligence, 6* 1151003.

Nagy, P., Frey, S., Sapora, S., et al. (2023). Generative AI for end-to-end limit order book modelling: A token-level autoregressive generative model of message flow using a deep state space network. In *Proceedings of the fourth ACM international conference on AI in finance* (pp. 91–99).

Nair, V., & Hinton, G. E. (2010). Rectified linear units improve restricted Boltzmann machines. In *Icml* (pp. 807–814).

Nelson, D. M., Pereira, A. C., & de Oliveira, R. A. (2017). Stock market's price movement prediction with LSTM neural networks. In *Neural networks (ijcnn), 2017 international joint conference on* (pp. 1419–1426).

Nie, Y., Nguyen, N. H., Sinthong, P., & Kalagnanam, J. (2022). A time series is worth 64 words: Long-term forecasting with transformers. *arXiv preprint arXiv:2211.14730*.

Obizhaeva, A. A., & Wang, J. (2013). Optimal trading strategy and supply/demand dynamics. *Journal of Financial markets, 16*(1), 1–32.

Ogryczak, W., & Tamir, A. (2003). Minimizing the sum of the k largest functions in linear time. *Information Processing Letters, 85*(3), 117–122.

Poh, D., Lim, B., Zohren, S., & Roberts, S. (2021a). Building cross-sectional systematic strategies by learning to rank. *The Journal of Financial Data Science, 3*(2), 70–86.

Poh, D., Lim, B., Zohren, S., & Roberts, S. (2021b). Enhancing cross-sectional currency strategies by context-aware learning to rank with self-attention. *arXiv preprint arXiv:2105.10019*.

Poh, D., Lim, B., Zohren, S., & Roberts, S. (2021c). Enhancing cross-sectional currency strategies by ranking refinement with transformer-based architectures. *arXiv preprint arXiv:2105.10019*.

Poh, D., Roberts, S., & Zohren, S. (2022). Transfer ranking in finance: applications to cross-sectional momentum with data scarcity. *arXiv preprint arXiv:2208.09968*.

Prata, M., Masi, G., Berti, L., et al. (2024). Lob-based deep learning models for stock price trend prediction: A benchmark study. *Artificial Intelligence Review, 57*(5), 1–45.

Pu, X. S., Roberts, S., Dong, X., & Zohren, S. (2023). Network momentum across asset classes. *Stephen and Dong, Xiaowen and Zohren, Stefan, Network Momentum across Asset Classes (August 7, 2023)*.

Rahimikia, E., Zohren, S., & Poon, S.- H. (2021). Realised volatility forecasting: Machine learning via financial word embedding. *arXiv preprint arXiv:2108.00480*.

Reisenhofer, R., Bayer, X., & Hautsch, N. (2022). Harnet: A convolutional neural network for realized volatility forecasting. *arXiv preprint arXiv:2205.07719*.

Schnaubelt, M. (2022). Deep reinforcement learning for the optimal placement of cryptocurrency limit orders. *European Journal of Operational Research, 296*(3), 993–1006.

Selvin, S., Vinayakumar, R., Gopalakrishnan, E., Menon, V. K., & Soman, K. (2017). Stock price prediction using LSTM, RNN and CNN-sliding window model. In *Advances in computing, communications and informatics (icacci), 2017 international conference on* (pp. 1643–1647).

Simonyan, K., & Zisserman, A. (2014). Very deep convolutional networks for large-scale image recognition. *arXiv preprint arXiv:1409.1556*.

Sirignano, J., & Cont, R. (2018). Universal features of price formation in financial markets: Perspectives from deep learning. *arXiv preprint arXiv:1803.06917*.

Soleymani, F., & Paquet, E. (2021). Deep graph convolutional reinforcement learning for financial portfolio management–deeppocket. *Expert Systems with Applications, 182*, 115127.

Sun, Q., Wei, X., & Yang, X. (2024). Graphsage with deep reinforcement learning for financial portfolio optimization. *Expert Systems with Applications, 238*, 122027.

Sutskever, I., Vinyals, O., & Le, Q. V. (2014). Sequence to sequence learning with neural networks. In *Advances in neural information processing systems* (pp. 3104–3112).

Sutton, R. S., & Barto, A. G. (2018). *Reinforcement learning: An introduction*. MIT press.

Theron, L., & Van Vuuren, G. (2018). The maximum diversification investment strategy: A portfolio performance comparison. *Cogent Economics & Finance, 6*(1), 1427533.

Tsantekidis, A., Passalis, N., Tefas, A., et al. (2017a). Forecasting stock prices from the limit order book using convolutional neural networks. In *Business informatics (cbi), 2017 ieee 19th conference on* (Vol. 1, pp. 7–12). IEEE.

Tsantekidis, A., Passalis, N., Tefas, A., et al. (2017b). Using deep learning to detect price change indications in financial markets. In *Signal processing conference (eusipco), 2017 25th european* (pp. 2511–2515).

Van Den Oord, A., Dieleman, S., Zen, H., et al. (2016). Wavenet: A generative model for raw audio. *arXiv preprint arXiv:1609.03499, 12*.

Vaswani, A., Shazeer, N., Parmar, N., et al. (2017). Attention is all you need. *Advances in neural information processing systems, 30*.

Vergara, J. R., & Estévez, P. A. (2014). A review of feature selection methods based on mutual information. *Neural Computing and Applications, 24*, 175–186.

Wan, X., Yang, J., Marinov, S., et al. (2021). Sentiment correlation in financial news networks and associated market movements. *Scientific Reports, 11*(1), 3062.

Wang, J., Zhang, S., Xiao, Y., & Song, R. (2021). A review on graph neural network methods in financial applications. *arXiv preprint arXiv:2111.15367*.

Wang, Y., Wu, H., Dong, J., et al. (2024). Deep time series models: A comprehensive survey and benchmark. *arXiv preprint arXiv:2407.13278*.

Wood, K., Giegerich, S., Roberts, S., & Zohren, S. (2021). Trading with the momentum transformer: An intelligent and interpretable architecture. *arXiv preprint arXiv:2112.08534*.

Wood, K., Kessler, S., Roberts, S. J., & Zohren, S. (2023). Few-shot learning patterns in financial time-series for trend-following strategies. *arXiv preprint arXiv:2310.10500*.

Wood, K., Roberts, S., & Zohren, S. (2021). Slow momentum with fast reversion: A trading strategy using deep learning and changepoint detection. *arXiv preprint arXiv:2105.13727*.

Wu, H., Xu, J., Wang, J., & Long, M. (2021). Autoformer: Decomposition transformers with auto-correlation for long-term series forecasting. *Advances in Neural Information Processing Systems, 34*, 22419–22430.

Wu, Z., Pan, S., Chen, F., et al. (2020). A comprehensive survey on graph neural networks. *IEEE transactions on neural networks and learning systems, 32*(1), 4–24.

Zhang, C., Pu, X., Cucuringu, M., & Dong, X. (2023). Graph neural networks for forecasting multivariate realized volatility with spillover effects. *arXiv preprint arXiv:2308.01419*.

Zhang, C., Pu, X., Cucuringu, M., & Dong, X. (2024). Graph-based methods for forecasting realized covariances. *Journal of Financial Econometrics*, nbae026.

Zhang, C., Zhang, Z., Cucuringu, M., & Zohren, S. (2021). A universal end-to-end approach to portfolio optimization via deep learning. *arXiv preprint arXiv:2111.09170*.

Zhang, X., Chowdhury, R. R., Gupta, R. K., & Shang, J. (2024). Large language models for time series: A survey. *arXiv preprint arXiv:2402.01801*.

Zhang, Y., & Yan, J. (2023). Crossformer: Transformer utilizing cross-dimension dependency for multivariate time series forecasting. In *The Eleventh International Conference on Learning Representations*.

Zhang, Z., Lim, B., & Zohren, S. (2021). Deep learning for market by order data. *Applied Mathematical Finance, 28*(1), 79–95.

Zhang, Z., & Zohren, S. (2021). Multi-horizon forecasting for limit order books: Novel deep learning approaches and hardware acceleration using intelligent processing units. *arXiv preprint arXiv:2105.10430*.

Zhang, Z., Zohren, S., & Roberts, S. (2019). Deep convolutional neural networks for limit order books. IEEE Transactions on Signal Processing, *67*(11), 3001–3012.

Zhang, Z., Zohren, S., & Roberts, S. (2019a). Deeplob: Deep convolutional neural networks for limit order books. *IEEE Transactions on Signal Processing, 67*(11), 3001–3012.

Zhang, Z., Zohren, S., & Roberts, S. (2019b). Extending deep learning models for limit order books to quantile regression. *Proceedings of Time Series Workshop of the 36 th International Conference on Machine Learning, Long Beach, California, PMLR 97, 2019*.

Zhang, Z., Zohren, S., & Roberts, S. (2020). Deep learning for portfolio optimization. *The Journal of Financial Data Science*, *2*(4), 8–20.

Zhou, H., Zhang, S., Peng, J., et al. (2021). Informer: Beyond efficient transformer for long sequence time-series forecasting. In *Proceedings of aaai* (pp. 11106–11115).

Zhou, Y.- T., & Chellappa, R. (1988). Computation of optical flow using a neural network. In *Icnn* (pp. 71–78).

Acknowledgments

We owe our profound gratitude to everyone who contributed to the successful completion of this book. To begin with, we wish to acknowledge our families for their unfailing support. We also want to recognize the assistance of our colleagues and friends, whose insightful conversations, constructive criticism, and fresh perspectives helped us to shape the content of this book. In particular, we would like to thank our senior colleagues, Steve Roberts, Xiaowen Dong, Jan Calliess, Mihai Cucuringu, Alex Shestopaloff, Janet Pierrehumbert, Jakob Foerster, Ani Calinescu, Nick Firoozye, Chao Ye, Xiaoqing Wu, and Yongjae Lee, as well as research students and postdocs whose work was featured here, Bryan Lim, Kieran Wood, Daniel Pho, Will Tan, Fernando Moreno-Pino, Chao Zhang, Vincent Tan, Xingyue Pu, Yaxuan Kong, Yoontae Hwang, Felix Drinkall, Dragos Gorduza, Peer Nagy, Xingchen Wan, Binxin Ru, and Sasha Frey. Special thanks also to Samson Donick for proofreading the entire manuscript, as well as several of the above students for proofreading individual sections. Additional thanks goes to George Nigmatulin, Yaxuan Kong and Yonntae Hwang for helping with didactic materials around the book. Moreover, we would like to thank Bank of America for hosting a short lecture series based on the book attended by 200 quants. In particular, special thanks go to Robert De Witt, Ilya Sheynzon and Shih-Hau Tan for organising the event, as well as to Leif Andersen for carefully reading the manuscript and providing additional comments.

Our thanks extend as well to the editorial and publishing team, in particular our editor Riccardo Rebonato for his insightful feedback and patience along the process. We are deeply thankful to the Machine Learning Research Group and the Oxford-Man Institute, at the University of Oxford for providing us with a supportive research environment. We would also like to thank Man Group for sponsoring the institute and their engagement through their academic liaisons Anthony Ledford and Slavi Marinov. Without all your support, this book would never have come to fruition.

To our families

Cambridge Elements

Quantitative Finance

Riccardo Rebonato
EDHEC Business School

Editor Riccardo Rebonato is Professor of Finance at EDHEC Business School and holds the PIMCO Research Chair for the EDHEC Risk Institute. He has previously held academic positions at Imperial College, London, and Oxford University and has been Global Head of Fixed Income and FX Analytics at PIMCO, and Head of Research, Risk Management and Derivatives Trading at several major international banks. He has previously been on the Board of Directors for ISDA and GARP, and he is currently on the Board of the Nine Dot Prize. He is the author of several books and articles in finance and risk management, including *Bond Pricing and Yield Curve Modelling* (2017, Cambridge University Press).

About the Series

Cambridge *Elements in Quantitative Finance* aims for broad coverage of all major topics within the field. Written at a level appropriate for advanced undergraduate or graduate students and practitioners, *Elements* combines reports on original research covering an author's personal area of expertise, tutorials and masterclasses on emerging methodologies, and reviews of the most important literature.

Cambridge Elements

Quantitative Finance

Elements in the Series

Machine Learning for Asset Managers
Marcos M. López de Prado

Advances in Retirement Investing
Lionel Martellini and Vincent Milhau

A Practitioner's Guide to Discrete-Time Yield Curve Modelling: With Empirical Illustrations and MATLAB Examples
Ken Nyholm

Girsanov, Numeraires, and All That
Patrick S. Hagan and Andrew Lesniewski

Causal Factor Investing: Can Factor Investing Become Scientific?
Marcos M. López de Prado

The Behavioral Economics and Politics of Global Warming: Unsettling Behaviors
Hersh Shefrin

Hydrodynamics of Markets: Hidden Links Between Physics and Finance
Alexander Lipton

Deep Learning in Quantitative Trading
Zihao Zhang and Stefan Zohren

A full series listing is available at: www.cambridge.org/EQF

For EU product safety concerns, contact us at Calle de José Abascal, 56–1º,
28003 Madrid, Spain or eugpsr@cambridge.org.

www.ingramcontent.com/pod-product-compliance
Lightning Source LLC
LaVergne TN
LVHW021947060526
838200LV00043B/1951